writing from experience

writing
from
experience

EDITED BY

William Nichols

DENISON UNIVERSITY

HARCOURT BRACE JOVANOVICH, INC.

New York   Chicago   San Francisco   Atlanta

ISBN: 0-15-597861-6

Library of Congress Catalog Card Number: 74-17745

Printed in the United States of America

ILLUSTRATION CREDITS

Cover photo by Richard Watherwax of a painting by Benedict Umy. P. 1, HBJ collection; p. 31, "October Piece," detail of an etching by Peter Milton, from the collection of Mr. and Mrs. Gordon R. Fairburn, New York; p. 79, Arthur Tress; p. 119, Harvey Stein; p. 161, Harvey Stein; p. 205, Lynda Gordon; p. 247, Hiroji Kubota from Magnum.

preface

This text is meant especially for those students who have little confidence in their own writing ability and not much faith in writing as an effective way of communicating. As a teacher during the past seven years, I have observed a strange paradox: my students seem increasingly able to handle language with considerable mechanical skill, and yet many of them approach the writing process as reluctantly as a nonswimmer might dive into deep water.

Writing, such students have told me, is a process that denies authentic feeling, for the writer must turn within and search for ways to frame ideas and emotions. Not only is this a tedious process, but, having completed it, one often finds that one is misunderstood: the reader—who perhaps too often is a flinty, fusty English teacher—still misses the point. The writer's frustration in such instances has been aggravated in recent years by the growing emphasis placed on nonverbal means of communication—inflection, facial expression, body movement, touch. Much more than in the past, people are aware of how often they use these actions to modify or even contradict their spoken words.

Moreover, my students have suggested, the most important kinds of experience may be beyond the scope of language, written or spoken. There may be perceptions that simply cannot be shared, private experiences that must be felt because they cannot be described.

The gloomiest view of writing I have yet heard is that each of us is trapped in an essentially self-centered world, where the best that writing can do is help us to see the trap clearly. I recall a discussion of Hermann Hesse's *Demian,* a book my literature class picked to read by an overwhelming vote. I was bothered, I admitted to the students, by their enthusiasm for a novel in which human love and community exist only as abstractions. And I described the main character, Emil Sinclair, as a man who sees the external world and the people who inhabit it as nothing more than mirrors reflecting his own inner self. For the most part the class agreed with my description of the *Demian* world but resisted my inclination to be critical of the novel because of it. "What kind of world did Hesse see to commune with?" asked one student; and several others argued that the kind of self-conscious alienation that Hesse dramatized was precisely what they experienced every day. In such a world, where genuine communication usually fails, writing becomes little more than an empty ritual; and that is how many students seem to view it.

But writing at its best is really a communal experience. To be an effective writer you must be deeply conscious of your readers. For them your words may be all that is known of you; no vocal inflection, smile, or shaking fist will amend your written statements. Perhaps one reason professional writers often seem to be very private people is that writing can become a very public act. Anyone who has had an intercepted note read aloud by the teacher or a diary discovered by a friend knows that even the most private kinds of writing can become public. The commonplace act of writing words on paper can render the self vulnerable to other people as few other acts can.

Let me admit that, as a teacher, I have not always respected that vulnerability as fully as I might have: it is much easier to note simple errors in the margins of an essay than to help a student discover his or her writing strengths. One of the premises of this text is that most students have undiscovered strengths as writers and that many of those strengths can be revealed if students are encouraged to value and to write about their own experience. It is my belief that no amount of preaching on the wonders of good writing—the subtlety and precision it makes possible, the way it can be a means of discovery for the writer—will answer the gloomy views I have summarized above. Instead, a student must experience the sense of achievement that comes with having written well about a subject that seems genuinely important.

Consider this analogy: you attend a dance concert and are invited onstage to participate. Skillful dancers move about you, responding to music with intricate, joyous movements; they beckon you to join them. Unless you are a most unusual and fortunate person, you are likely to believe that your own body and its ways of moving would look graceless and ugly in such a context. But imagine a much less formal situation in which you are invited to join a group of people with varied expertise in dance who are trying to share what they know about the art. If the group's purpose is honestly to learn together about the movements and skills involved in dance, you might feel much less inhibited about participating. You might use such an experience, in fact, to learn not only about dance but about yourself as well.

This text is meant to resemble the second invitation. The selections in it represent a wide spectrum of skills; they range from James Baldwin's "Notes of a Native Son," a masterpiece of autobiographical writing, to a sampling of some rough and tentative entries from my own journal. I have also included essays by three students from the college at which I teach, as well as an essay of my own, which will allow the reader an opportunity to decide whether I practice what I preach about writing.

The seven chapters of the text represent a set of writing assignments that I have developed for my freshman classes. With the exception of the journal assignment in Chapter One, which carries through the whole term, the assignments at the end of each chapter involve short and medium-length essays. Happily, these essays often fit together in interesting ways so that by the end of the term the student can produce a sustained piece of autobiographical writing.

Since it seems to me that one cannot be expected to write effectively about complex issues or ideas until one has first turned within oneself and learned to describe with precision some of the simple and important experiences that make up one's own past, the assignments tend to be increasingly difficult. Students are asked to describe an early memory or a place of some importance, for example, before they are asked to discuss the relationship between an individual and history. This progression of assignments is by no means inviolable, however; I can imagine writing courses that might alter it considerably. Another characteristic of the sequence of assignments—the most important one, in my view—is a movement from a rather self-enclosed world to a more inclusive world of shared experience. The increasing importance of others' experience in the writing assignments is responsible, it seems to me, for their increasing difficulty. An understanding of this correlation may be the most important lesson the student of writing can learn.

My approach to the teaching of writing has been influenced by many people; the following names only a few. Willoughby Johnson at the University of Missouri first showed me that when students are helped to write confidently about subjects that honestly engage them, many mechanical errors simply disappear. Among my colleagues at Denison University, Tony Stoneburner suggested many of the ideas implicit in this text, and he has guided my study of autobiography; Richard Kraus has generously influenced my approach to literature; John Miller, a fine poet, has taught me a good deal about the process of revision; and Jack Kirby, a historian, has helped me to look at literature and teaching in new ways. It will be obvious, I hope, that my students have taught me a great deal about the writing process. I am especially grateful to them.

WILLIAM NICHOLS

contents

four: selfhood and event

five: the self and others

six: art as experience

seven: the self and history

one: the journal

from
the diary of
Anaïs Nin

ANAÏS NIN (1903 –   ) has recently published five volumes of a diary she has kept for many years, and, though these volumes represent only a small portion of the total work, many critics have already proclaimed it a masterpiece. Nin is also the author of several novels and works of literary criticism, including: *D. H. Lawrence: An Unprofessional Study* (1932), *Under a Glass Bell* (1944), *The Four-Chambered Heart* (1950), and *Collages* (1964).

[1940]. Dinner at Dorothy Norman's. The same subdued, formal, arctic climate. But after dinner Luise Rainer arrived in a long, white, floating dress, her hair floating, her gestures light and graceful, flowing too, a mobile, fluid quality and radiance. Her face expressive, animated, showing as it did in her films a greater sadness than the role called for. She has a childlike impulsiveness, swinging between gentleness and sudden quick decisions.

Her face is small, her eyes dark and mischievous, her neck so slender one feels immediately protective. Her voice has a whispering quality, her laughter is tentative and subdued. Muted tones, yet eloquent, arresting.

She can reach extremes of feminine coquetry as in *Frou-Frou*, or extremes of self-sacrifice as in *The Great Waltz*. Even in this formal room she remained as exposed as she did in her acting, revealing tenderness, vulnerability, feminine provocativeness, devotion. In her acting she gives herself while remaining true to herself, and she was doing the same that evening. She wears no make-up, she repudiates the outer signs of her stardom as an actress. I always thought her one of the most moving figures in film acting. And here she was, soft, yielding, imperious, pliant, seeming deeper than anyone around her emotionally, making them all appear suddenly wooden, trapped in their clothes, unable to move. Her tragic face makes every role seem deeper, and now when she lifts her eyelids, the story is lost and there appears a woman with a sadness older than the world.

Her authoritarianism is that of a child, and I respond to it and loved her instantly.

* * *

Dorothy Norman invited me to her summer house in Woods Hole for the weekend. A beautiful large house by the sea. I met Luise Rainer there. Nothing fascinates me more than the actress who makes visible, expressive, every mood and feeling, whose every gesture reveals, communicates, fascinates one. Luise's walk, with her swinging hair, her voice, her impetuous gestures, a constantly varied spectacle. Her voice ranges from a whisper to a shout, her face changes every moment, quicker than the lights and shadows of the day, sun, shade, evening or morning light. Even when she reaches for the jam, or leaps up to go for a swim, there is something to watch. I was in my room combing my hair when she shouted imperiously under my window. "Anaïs! COME DOWN!"

She was waiting in her red open sports car. She wanted to drive to the ocean. There was a fine mist, and the wind blew through our hair. We stopped at the edge of the ocean. Luise said, "Across this vast ocean is Europe."

Europe!

What was she remembering? She was born in Düsseldorf. Her father was a banker. She had a comfortable childhood. She wanted to be an actress. She had the whims of a child, the sudden impulses, the leaping quality, and a wistfulness so deep that one did not dare question the cause of it.

We stood on the beach, looking out to sea, yearning for Europe. Then suddenly we laughed at ourselves. I told her how among ourselves we had sworn never to mention the past again and each time one of us did it we would say: "White Russians!" Paris was full of White Russians who had once lived luxurious lives. It became a cliché, like the hard-luck stories of prostitutes. One knew that every taxi driver was in the past a Russian prince who had lived in a palace and had chauffeurs of his own. They ran all the night clubs, they wore their sumptuous uniforms while performing doormen's duties. They wept and told such stories so frequently that one ceased to believe them.

I had met an authentic White Russian. She was a quiet, well-bred woman who sewed for a living. When she came to get work from me, she asked if instead of taking it home she might stay and sew in my home, just to breathe again some beauty and grace she had once known in her own home.

[September, 1941]. Evening with Luise. A fragile Luise lying in her ivory-white satin bed, among mirrors and rows of outsize bottles of perfume. Her body and face so expressive that they do not seem made of flesh but of trembling antennae, a breath, a nerve, a vibration. She, the exhausted one, runs downstairs to spare her servant a trip. She lies back like a tired child in a sophisticated white fluffy nightgown which does not seem made for her. Her voice vanishes to a whisper as if she herself were going to vanish, and I hold my breath to hear her. Her head seems completely free of her body, like the Balinese dancers. Her hands are separately eloquent, as if they were puppets pulled by wise and accurate strings, two small puppets depicting a drama of their own.

She was destroyed by her marriage to Clifford Odets. It seemed at first such a romantic marriage. She had just won a top acting prize, and he a prize for the best playwright on Broadway. He was a Brooklyn boy, who had never traveled, and was harsh and narrow.

*   *   *

Went to see Luise act in Barrie's A Kiss for Cinderella.

How to describe the transfiguration of Luise in her acting? Her voice has a wide range, and many shadings. Her expression is so intense it is like a mystic's trance. Her eyes shine almost unbearably. She dissolves and becomes ecstatic. It is more than the role calls for. Artaud would have loved her. She could become a flame and burn before your eyes. Her vulnerability is completely exposed. It is a shock to see a soul so naked. She makes the play appear inadequate and puny. She would make a fantastic Joan of Arc.

Acting throws her into an exalted state. I was amazed when she joined me that she expressed doubts, that she was unsure, unaware of what she had done. She felt empty and filled with doubts. She does not know her own power. In her, acting fuses with feeling and she consumes herself as she does it. It produces a miracle. I felt that she was not acting but dreaming out her own life. If she feels anxiety afterwards it must be to have revealed so much of her own emotions.

In the car, riding home, she kept her hand in mine and I kept telling her what I felt about her acting. I had brought her an appropriate gift, my Cinderella gold slippers, the last poetic gift I bought in Paris, the first transparent plastic, with gold heels.

She used the word exhibitionism in connection with acting. I contradicted her. "You want to make acting a magic ceremony. The public seemed terrifyingly opaque, heavy, inert. They do not think of acting in this way, as a ritual in which you must participate. It is because they did not participate that you felt exhibited. You had dreamt of being one with the public."

I brushed away from her small nose one of the artificial snowflakes which had stayed there all through the performance. When she left the car for a moment there remained on the seat a very tiny pocketbook like a child's, a bag of plums which she had been munching avidly as children do when they are eager to join the games. She is unconscious of her tangled hair, likes her face washed of make-up, has no desire to present to the world off stage the mask of the actress, the false eyelashes, the redesigned mouth. She will not be an actress in life.

"Write a play for me, Anaïs. Odets always promised that he would write a play for me, and he never did."

I do see a drama in Luise's life, but it is not one which would make a play. I see a conflict between the woman and the actress. She wants to act out projections of herself, to be herself on stage, and not become other women. She seeks extensions of herself. On the other hand, she repudiates the actress which brings an enhanced, heightened vision of life and character. She denies what the actress might bring into her life. It is a quest for her personal integration rather than the quest of an actress. As if acting would free her of her confused and uncertain self, help her find her core through the roles.

*   *   *

Luise drove me to Cold Springs, to have lunch in a restaurant overlooking the water, a gentle peaceful place. Later, we sat on the edge of the water, took our dresses off and sunbathed in our panties and bras. We talked about our lives, confided.

I had thought she and Siegfried might love each other. But her impression of him was shallow. She only noted the singer's self-confidence, the on-stage charms. I was trying to tell her what lay hidden behind this appearance. When people think he is superficial, then he acts superficially. It offends his pride and he refuses then to reveal himself. But Luise thinks I am inventing Siegfried.

Luise said, "I feel in you the woman who can give herself, lose herself, but also a power of understanding beyond that. You can analyze and rescue yourself. I don't have this. I get confused. I am trapped and shattered. My first love died tragically. His plane crashed into a mountain in Tanganyika."

When she drives she seems to be scarcely touching the wheel.

A miraculous airiness. She makes me so aware of her imponderability that I find it more and more difficult to describe her tangibly. Her eyes are dark and glowing, almost as though there were tears in them. Her skin is slightly tanned. Her hair is long and dark. While she was talking of her life with Odets, I realized we can never understand why people love each other, because to the lover they show a side we do not know. It is the lover who operates a transformation and it is to this lover we give our fullest self, our fullest gifts. We outsiders never see the enlarged human being who appears in the spotlight of an intense love.

I cannot see the Odets Luise loved. We give to our friends only a small part of ourselves. In the climate of love another being emerges. Possibly Odets never existed except in the light of Luise's love, invisible to me because I do not love him. I could see why Odets might love Luise. The actor allows us such intimate glimpses of human beings in a state of love and openness. An actress's way of making love on the stage or on film, we feel, is derived from her way of making love in life. The actress shares this moment with us. I could see from having seen her act, how her voice would sound in a moment of love. I could see how her smile would offer such open tenderness. On the stage you are taken into the secret being of another and witness the exposure of a human being usually only uncovered in moments of love. That may be why we fall in love with actors. They offer us those very special gestures, special tonalities of the voice by which we are enchanted and drawn to the one we love. This openness is the miraculous openness which takes place in love and it creates a current of love between audience and actor as between lover and beloved. The greater the richness of an actor, the more loved he is by many.

But in life, we cannot always obtain from the lover a full image or revelation of what he sees in his loved one. It remains hidden from our eyes. Because love not only can detect a potential, an unborn personality, a buried one, a disguised one, but also bring it into reality. So that all reality appears to me each day more and more subjective, dependent on the eyes of the lover, the eye of the camera, the eye of the painter, even as a room can appear one day glowing with color and the next day grey, according to our mood.

Luise is always saying that the Luise on the screen is not she. It is an image born of lighting, or artifice, enhanced by acting. She did not recognize or love the actress. Luise's image of herself and the image on the screen do not match. The woman on the screen is a stranger to her. She repudiated the worship, the flowers, the love letters addressed to her, as if the person on the screen were a fraud. She could not understand how I related them, how they fed each other, how together they did represent a complete Luise, one freed by acting, the other bound, one confident, the other filled with doubt.

It was strange, when I watched her dress once, opening closets full of movie-star clothes, movie-star hats on stands, movie-star shoes, movie-star furs and bags, she reached for a tiny skull cap with two inches of veil over the eyes, for the simplest beige dress, the simplest shoes, the ones least likely to appear glamorous.

In her very large, very spacious movie-star bed she did not sleep well, except when she covered her head as she did when she was a child and was frightened by a nightmare. The nightmare here seemed to be what this apartment, these clothes, these people, these film scripts and plays demanded and expected of her.

[*Summer, 1947*]. Texas, the Panhandle country, flatlands, cattle. The men get taller, and have a grand style of entering a coffee shop, ordering, sitting. They have a style as definite as that of the bullfighter in Spain, the Gaucho in South America, the style of a vocation which has an individual character.

Just before Santa Fe, there was a ranch we visited, in Pecos. It was built by the river. Mountains, river, and trees were stark, all in shades of ash and sand and spring-pea green. I do not know why I suddenly wanted to stay here. The city drains your strength. This place gave strength.

A total break with everything I had known. A bare simplicity. A Lawrencian simplicity. A wooden ranch house, trees, a river. That was all. I felt drawn to it.

But the Ford Model A was leaving in the morning. On to Albuquerque, New Mexico. On to Santa Fe and Taos, to visit Mrs. D. H. Lawrence.

And now we are in Indian country. The bright-colored clothes, predominantly red, the necklaces of coral and turquoise, the long black braided hair. Indians living in hogans made of small timbers, thatchwork, and mud. They weave, they farm. Native corn and grain are still milled on primitive grindstones, as in Mexico.

We climbed toward Taos. I could feel the rarified air, the height, the cold air of the mountains. It seemed sand-colored and half-deserted at twilight, when we arrived. A few Indians in rather tattered costumes sold tourist items. Necklaces, semi-precious stones, woven textiles, blankets. The architecture was of adobe brick, and the white walls and dark wood gave a Spanish air. It was late, and we had to have dinner and sleep first. We could not call on Mrs. D. H. Lawrence until the next day. I had written to her because she had once said that my book on Lawrence was the best. She replied that she would be glad to see us.

The next morning we drove to her house. I expected a tall, imposing woman from Lawrence's descriptions. I found a tiny old lady, all smiles and liveliness. As she led us into the living room, I wondered if it was Lawrence who had seen her as so imposing, like all men who never escape the child's idea of the mother as big and powerful. Age could not have shrunk her so.

The room was immense enough to hold on each wall one of Lawrence's very large paintings, and sometimes more than one. I recognized the fleshy figures, the fleshy tones, trees and figures similar in feeling to Gauguin's nature worship. But these figures were not sun-tanned. They were English. They were in grayer tones, the flesh not rosy as in Renoir or Boucher, but sunless, as if long covered by winter. There was no sun or gold in his paintings, as I remembered from reproductions. They seemed slightly faded. Was it the paint he used? Was it that I expected Mediterranean colors of joy?

Meanwhile, Mrs. Lawrence showed us scores on the piano and we talked about music. She sings German lieder. She would have sung for us if we had stayed longer.

The light was sharp and clear. The light of mountaintops. A modest, quiet man had opened the door for us and then disappeared. He knew people came to talk about Lawrence, and perhaps he felt in the way. In the back of the house, he had his pottery kiln. We went to visit and talk with him.

Mrs. Lawrence was cheerful, talked easily about Lawrence, but admitted she was tired of visitors and monotonous questions. "They ask things they would know if they had read him carefully," she said. She would write her own book.

We did not stay long. As we left, on the way out, the modest man came and with signs led us to the bathroom and the kitchen. He pointed to his paintings on the wall, all very small, as if he did not want to take up too much space, not as much space as D. H. Lawrence. We admired them, and he smiled. Then he led us out. We could have stayed in the cottage up the mountain, where D. H. Lawrence first lived when he came. But I was as reluctant to go into the past of my literary loves as of my human ones. I was curious about tomorrow, about what new places we were going to discover.

North to Denver, Colorado, to Boulder, to the Rocky Mountain National Park, over the top of the Rockies, the Continental Divide, to Fraser, Colorado, Central City, and west through Royal

Gorge to Grand Junction, Colorado, the Colorado National Monument. There I began to find things I had never seen, the beginning
of those red rocks, like rocks taken out of an intense fire. *Colorado*
in Spanish means "red." The Colorado River carries this red sand or
red earth two thousand miles to the Pacific Ocean.

West to Utah, south to Moab, driving along the Colorado
River. The Arches National Monument, the strange lunar aspect
of Utah. The Mormon land. The white salt lakes, the deserts, and
the small canyons of gray sandstone, tipped with pale-yellow
crowns. Something so subtle, such as one expects of other planets.
Here the severity and sparseness was beautiful, like the paintings
of Tanguy. The canyons, with their mythical shapes, crenelated
towers, castle turrets, like the stalagmites designed under the
earth by water. Here it is the wind which is the most skillful and
intricate sculptor. The layered geological strata in all shades from
gray to gold at dawn, fan-shaped furrows, the feet of birds, fish and
shells implanted on the sandstone. The sea has been here. The sandy
textures give to all the colors of earth, canyons, hills, rocks, a
soft focus, like that of a shredded crayon.

The Indians match the landscape. Other people seem like trans-
plants, and go about their work like visitors, guides, transients.
Indifferent, anonymous, not connected to the land. Closed faces,
anonymous faces. I cannot remember their faces. I remember the Indians, sharp-faced, proud, haughty bearings. When they are about,
then I can link the canyons with the pyramids of Egypt, the
Great Wall of China. The land of America, so beautiful, offering
snow-capped mountains, African deserts, rivers, caves, mines, treasure, coal, silver, oil, petrified trees, strange flowers, strange birds.

Now traveling through the Navajo Indian reservation. Slept
at a ranch in the middle of the fantastic sculptured canyons, in
the middle of a soft, sepia-colored sand.

In Utah no sign of the severe and rigid Mormons. But their
choice of Utah, with its severe and often bare landscape, its white
salt fields, its bare mountains, seemed appropriate to their discipline.

I saw, around the bend of a mountain road, at dusk, a covered
wagon. I thought it was a movie prop, could not believe it was
real.

I saw the Indian homes carved in the rocks, the highest floors
reached by ladders. I wanted more Indians around. They looked
sparse, decimated. Weaving rugs, and making jewelry for the tourist.

Blanding and Bluff, Mexican Hat, through Monument Valley

to Tuba City, to Lee's Ferry, where the boat starts down the Colorado, to Bright Angel Point and then the north rim of the Grand Canyon.

The earth-red canyons, layered in geological strata, rising to a height of awesome proportions, peak after peak. The work of a myth, a force beyond our grasp, silencing human beings, evoking religions and gods unknown. Temples, pyramids, tombs, palaces. The colors in a wide range of sepias, reds, maroons, silvered at the top by light.

Standing there stunned by the mass of colors changing in the light, we heard a subtle vibration, a faint symphony of sounds. It was the wind, traveling through changing depths and heights, affected by curves, towers, heights, abysses, issuing prolonged musical whispers.

If one has lost in the city the sense of nature, its greatness and vastness, if one has lost awe, wonder, or faith, the Grand Canyon reinstates this vision of immensity and beauty.

On the way to Las Vegas, the real vast desert, burning and arid. Saguaro forests standing up like fingers of giant hands from the parched sand. The Joshua tree with its strange hairy arms flowering in green, pine-like tips. The cactus in bloom, the violent contrast between the prickly branch and the soft vivid petals of the flower in many colors.

The ocotillo. The fire-red blossoms resemble tassels, or feathery birds at times. There is a desert cactus which is all claws and thorns, and bears no flowers. The desert yucca in bloom appears like a dazzling white Christmas tree, straight and tall, bearing a rich ivory-white flower. All were blooming like spring, and by contrast with the sandy soil, the burnt, lava-like rock, the parched, thirsty earth, they seem miraculous, almost heroic. Compared with the flowers tended by gardeners, watered, protected, set in their appropriate soil and climate, these are defiant and strong, a vivid garden.

I do not describe the places I disliked, such as Las Vegas. Approaching Los Angeles, I smelled in the night the sweet smell of orange groves, exuding a rich perfume.

In Los Angeles I visited Lloyd and Helen Wright. He is the son of the famous architect Frank Lloyd Wright.

I saw first of all a high wall, like the wall of a medieval castle. And a giant tree, which seemed to extend its ancient branches to keep the house from prying eyes. The door on the left led to the architectural offices of Lloyd Wright. On the right, a winding staircase led to the door of his home.

For the first time in many years in America I entered a home where beauty reigned, in a world created entirely by an artist.

Loyd Wright stood up. Over six feet tall, gray hair, a full round head with a very high forehead, laughing eyes, and an emotional mouth. He has a powerful voice, gracious manners, a hearty laugh. Next to him a tiny woman with a very sweet voice, sea-blue eyes, large and melting with softness. This is Helen, his wife, who was an actress and now gives dramatic readings of plays.

There was so much to see in the room that one could not become aware of it all at once. It took me all evening to absorb the pre-Columbian sculptures, the exceptionally beautiful Japanese screen, the heavy furniture designed by Lloyd. The room was full of mystery. The uneven shape, the trellised wall made of patterned blocks, the long, horizontally-shaped window, overlooking the patio below, and the old tree that, like a great umbrella, sheltered the whole house; patio and balcony filled with plants and the wondrous cereus, that passionate and exquisite white flower which only blooms once, at night.

The fireplace of soft-green patterned stone was throwing its colors and shadows on the room. The lighting was diffused, indirect, softened by the latticed-stone screened walls.

The colors were soft and blended together. The shelves held books, Japanese dishes of gray and blue with the rare fish pattern, crystal glasses, silver. Helen served a dinner lovingly and carefully prepared to blend with the place and the talk. Everything gave a feeling of luxury created by aesthetics, not by money. By work of the hands and imagination. The atmosphere was rich and deep and civilized.

Lloyd's presence gave a feeling of power. The sensitivity I saw later, when he took me to his office and showed me his drawings and projects, and models for future buildings. His drawings were very beautiful in themselves, the concepts absolutely original and poetic. That was the first word which came to my mind; he is a poet. He is the poet of architecture. For him a building, a home, a stone, a roof, every inch of architecture has meaning, was formed from an inner concept. It was also a triumph over the monotony and homeliness which I had seen from New York throughout the Middle West, in every city.

I saw the model of the Wayfarer's Chapel he was planning for the Swedenborg Society. It was all glass, a perfect symbol for the spirit's transparency, a perfect expression of transcendent acceptance of infinite space. Man's religious spirit on an altar open to the universe through the transparency of glass—candlelight, starlight, moonlight, and golden ornaments shining through, opening

out through the sanctuary to the sea, the sky, the trees, and to
infinity beyond. He had planted a forest of redwood trees which
would form arches over the chapel, like those in Gothic cathedrals,
only Lloyd Wright had returned to the natural arches formed by
the trees themselves.

I saw his plans for Los Angeles. It could have been the most
beautiful city in the world, for everyone to come to see, as people
went to see Venice. But architecture had been taken over by businessmen, and Lloyd the artist was not allowed to carry out his
incredibly rich, fecund concepts. The room was full of them. When
he took a rolled-up drawing from the shelves and spread it over the
table, I saw buildings which equaled the wonders of the past. All
the images of famous architecture I had read of came to my mind:
from India, Japan, Mexico, Peru, the Middle Ages in Europe, Cambodia, Thailand.

Strength was obvious in him, but sensitivity and imagination
were in his drawings. Homes, churches, plans for entire cities. A
universe of lyrical beauty in total opposition to the sterile, monotonous, unimaginative "box"-buildings now seen all over the world.

He was not only continuing the first poetic and organic concepts his father had developed on the West Coast, where as a
young architect he supervised and participated in the construction
of many buildings. He was also creating in his own style. He designed and built the first Hollywood Bowl, and many private
homes.

I expected Los Angeles to be filled with his buildings. This was
not the case. Fame highlighted his father's work, but not Lloyd's—
not as he deserved. If his plans had been carried out, the world
would have been dazzled by them. His work was on a scale which
should have appealed to the spirit of grandeur in the American
character, a dramatic and striking expression of a new land. But instead, American architects chose to take the path of imitating
Europe, of uniformity, monotony, dullness. In Lloyd's work there
was space, invention, poetry, a restrained and effective use of the
romantic, surprises always in the forms, new and imaginative use of
structural parts, rooms, windows, and materials.

He has a gift for involvement in many-leveled lives, for the
variations, caprices, and nuances necessary to the human spirit. Every stone, every roof-tile, every window, every texture or material
was designed for the consistent development of his building, its
environment, and designed to elevate the quality of people's lives.

Uniformity and monotony kill individuality, dull the senses.
Lloyd designed his work to reinforce individuality with poetry,

beauty, and integrity. It was planned to create a more beautiful and satisfying human environment. Architecture as poetry.

It was my initiation into architecture as an art. Lloyd is a complete and uncompromising artist. He talks about the organic home, built of materials natural and available at the site; of his respect for trees and the form of a hill; his sense of nature, of the continuity of the natural environment, and of how architecture must contribute to it, not destroy it. To hear him talk about color, materials, textures, forms, was like listening to a painter talk of painting, a musician of composition. In his art he synthesized them all. He drew like a painter, he used words with a biblical simplicity, but his ideas were subtle and complex.

By contrast, the commonplace, shoddy, temporary movie-set houses around him were painful to see. He called them "cracker boxes," shabby, thin, motel-type homes for robots.

Some of his houses, which I visited the next day, have the stronghold quality of a castle, a castle for unique individuals, to stem the rising tide of ugliness. Pride. Why did the millionaire father of Kendall not have Lloyd build him an American castle, instead of importing a European one, stone by stone, and rebuilding it in Dallas? What kind of people prefer to live inside of an imitation which has no relation to their personality? The story of Hearst, repeated again and again. And all the other imitations of Italian, Spanish, French, Swiss, and German architecture I had seen on my trip.

The Wright pride. Yes, the pride in quality. He supervises his buildings, takes care of every detail: searches for masons who care about stonework, painters who can paint, metalworkers who are skillful. Today, in an age of amateurs, this is a most difficult achievement.

At times his mouth grows bitter; he vituperates, he berates commercialism, he curses greed and land manipulators. He is a crusader for quality. His work suffers indignities. His houses pass into other hands and are mangled, damaged, altered. The acoustically perfect Hollywood Bowl was torn down, rebuilt, and ruined. It is now monstrously ugly.

Lloyd's work belongs to the great moments of architecture, but today's America has no sense of eternity or history. The transient, the meretricious, the imitation, the pseudo rule the day.

We looked over more plans. Projects. Dreams. Dream of a beautiful campus, with individual units to house the students, shaped like a sea shell. A marina with buildings also inspired by sea shells.

Certain plans lie gathering dust. They were made for some capricious rich man or woman who was not aware of their beauty. And then, now and then, a fervent, a devoted person, who understands his work and works with him, co-operating to carry out his plans. Out of this came a gay and whimsical nursery school.

His struggle is against uniformity and wholesale design. He speaks out boldly, as Varèse did. If he sounds like a moralist, it is because beauty, quality, and ethics are inseparable. Beauty and integrity. And for them one has to be willing to make sacrifices.

Another visit. The flowers in the room are arranged by Lloyd's big hands with an art equal to that of a Japanese flower arrangement. Friends call him and his two sons the giants of the West. He has gruff ways at times. Helen is there like a diffused light, to create warmth, harmony, refinement, like the cushion and the velvet against the wounds dealt to the artist.

We talk about his bohemian life in New York, with friends such as Djuna Barnes, Theodore Dreiser, Helen Wesley, Eugene O'-Neill.

Ibsen would have written about this Master Builder, with one great difference. This architect never falls off the high standards, the heights he established for himself. The mediocre and the deformed sprout around him, like weeds, ugly buildings which do not endure and which look shabby after a few months. He is offended, but he does not surrender. He finds it "futile, offensive, and all-persuasive, but not inevitable."

Among Lloyd Wright's notes and comments on architecture I found the following:

> I am concerned with our natural environment, how we can discover and utilize form, and perfect the endlessly varied, stimulating and beautiful services it provides for mankind. It is the architect's opportunity and responsibility to understand and practice the *art* of creating with and out of them a suitable environment for mankind—advancing the art with every conceivable means, including, among others, poetic license and poetic prescience. And now, after billions of years of experience and preconditioning on this earth (from the development of the first one-celled amoeba to our present human complex) we have no valid excuse for not performing superbly.

from
the journal of
Henry David Thoreau

HENRY DAVID THOREAU (1817–1862) is best known for
Walden (1854), a book based on the two years in which he
lived alone at Walden Pond, outside his home city of Con-
cord, Massachusetts. As a result he is sometimes viewed as
a hermit or misanthrope. Such characterizations are inaccurate, however; for Thoreau led a rich and varied life. Attesting
to this fact is his journal, which played an important part in
his development as a writer. Thoreau usually revised passages with great care before including them in the journal,
and even a casual reading of its contents reveals the seeds
of ideas developed more fully in his later writings.

July 14 [1845]. What sweet and tender, the most innocent and
divinely encouraging society there is in every natural object, and so
in universal nature, even for the poor misanthrope and most melan-
choly man! There can be no really black melan-choly to him who
lives in the midst of nature and has still his senses. There never
was yet such a storm but it was Aeolian music to the innocent
ear. Nothing can compel to a vulgar sadness a simple and brave man.
While I enjoy the sweet friendship of the seasons I trust that
nothing can make life a burden to me. This rain which is now wa-
tering my beans and keeping me in the house waters me too. I
needed it as much. And what if most are not hoed! Those who
send the rain, whom I chiefly respect, will pardon me.

Sometimes, when I compare myself with other men, methinks
I am favored by the gods. They seem to whisper joy to me beyond
my deserts, and that I do have a solid warrant and surety at their
hands, which my fellows do not. I do not flatter myself, but if it
were possible *they* flatter me. I am especially guided and guarded.

What was seen true once, and sanctioned by the flash of Jove,
will always be true, and nothing can hinder it. I have the warrant
that no fair dream I have had need fail of its fulfillment.

Here I know I am in good company; here is the world, its
centre and metropolis, and all the palms of Asia and the laurels of
Greece and the first of the Arctic Zone incline thither. Here I can
read Homer, if I would have books, as well as in Ionia, and not wish
myself in Boston, or New York, or London, or Rome, or Greece. In
such place as this he wrote or sang. Who should come to my lodge
just now but a true Homeric boor, one of those Paphlagonian men?
Alek Therien, he called himself; a Canadian now, a woodchopper, a
post-maker; makes fifty posts—holes them, *i.e.*—in a day; and who
made his last supper on a woodchuck which his dog caught. And he
too has heard of Homer, and *if it were not for books, would not know
what to do* rainy days. Some priest once, who could read glibly from
the Greek itself, taught him reading in a measure—his verse, at
least, in his turn—away by the Trois Rivières, at Nicolet. And
now I must read to him, while he holds the book, Achilles' reproof
of Patroclus on his sad countenance.

"Why are you in tears, Patroclus, like a young child (girl)?"
etc., etc.

> Or have you only heard some news from Phthia?
> They say that Menoetius lives yet, son of Actor,
> And Peleus lives, son of Aeacus, among the Myrmidons,
> Both of whom having died, we should greatly grieve.

He has a neat bundle of white oak bark under his arm for a
sick man, gathered this Sunday morning. "I suppose there's no harm
in going after such a thing to-day." The simple man. May the
gods send him many woodchucks.

And earlier to-day came five Lestrigones, railroad men who take
care of the road, some of them at least. They still represent the
bodies of men, transmitting arms and legs and bowels downward
from those remote days to more remote. They have some got a rude
wisdom withal, thanks to their dear experience. And one with
them, a handsome younger man, a sailor-like, Greek-like man, says:
"Sir, I like your notions. I think I shall live so myself. Only I should
like a wilder country, where there is more game. I have been among
the Indians near Appalachicola. I have lived with them. I like your
kind of life. Good day. I wish you success and happiness."

Therien said this morning (July 16th, Wednesday), "If those
beans were mine, I shouldn't like to hoe them till the dew was
off." He was going to his woodchopping. "Ah!" said I, "that is one
of the notions the farmers have got, but I don't believe it." "How
thick the pigeons are!" said he. "If working every day were not my
trade, I could get all the meat I should want for a week in one
day."

I imagine it to be some advantage to live a primitive and frontier life, though in the midst of an outward civilization. Of course all the improvements of the ages do not carry a man backward nor forward in relation to the great facts of his existence.

Our furniture should be as simple as the Arab's or the Indian's. At first the thoughtful, wondering man plucked in haste the fruits which the boughs extended to him, and found in the sticks and stones around him his implements ready to crack the nut, to wound the beast, and build his house with. And he still remembered that he was a sojourner in nature. When he was refreshed with food and sleep he contemplated his journey again. He dwelt in a tent in this world. He was either threading the valleys, or crossing the plains, or climbing the mountain-tops.

* * *

Dec. 29 [1853]. We survive, in one sense, in our posterity and in the continuance of our race, but when a race of men, of Indians for instance, becomes extinct, is not that the end of the world for them? Is not the world forever beginning and coming to an end, both to men and races? Suppose we were to foresee that the Saxon race to which we belong would become extinct the present winter—disappear from the face of the earth—would it not look to us like the end, the dissolution of the world? Such is the prospect of the Indians.

All day a driving snow-storm, imprisoning most, stopping the cars, blocking up the roads. No school to-day. I cannot see a house fifty rods off from my window through [it]; yet in midst of all I see a bird, probably a tree sparrow, partly blown, partly flying, over the house to alight in a field. The snow penetrates through the smallest crevices under doors and sides of windows.

P.M.—Tried my snow-shoes. They sink deeper than I expected, and I throw the snow upon my back. When I returned, twenty minutes after, my great tracks were not to be seen. It is the worst snow-storm to bear that I remember. The strong wind from the north blows the snow almost horizontally, and, beside freezing you, almost takes your breath away. The driving snow blinds you, and where you are protected, you can see but little way, it is so thick. Yet in spite, or on account, of all, I see the first flock of arctic snowbirds (*Emberiza nivalis*) near the depot, white and black, with a sharp, whistle-like note. An hour after I discovered half a pint of snow in each pocket of my greatcoat.

What a contrast between the village street now and last summer! The leafy elms then resounding with the warbling vireo, robins, bluebirds, and the fiery hangbird, etc., to which the villagers, kept indoors by the heat, listen through open lattices. Now it is like a street in Nova Zembla,—if they were to have any there. I wade to the post-office as solitary a traveller as ordinarily in a wood-path in winter. The snow is mid-leg deep, while drifts as high as one's head are heaped against the houses and fences, and here and there range across the street like snowy mountains. You descend from this, relieved, into capacious valleys with a harder bottom, or more fordable. The track of one large sleigh alone is visible, nearly snowed up. There is not a track leading from any door to indicate that the inhabitants have been forth to-day, any more than there is track of any quadruped by the wood-paths. It is all pure untrodden snow, banked up against the houses now at 4 P.M., and no evidence that a villager has been abroad to-day. In one place the drift covers the frontyard fence and stretches thence upward to the top of the front door, shutting all in, and frequently the snow lies banked up three or four feet high against the front doors, and the windows are all snowed up, and there is a drift over each window, and the clapboards are all hoary with it. It is as if the inhabitants were all frozen to death, and now you threaded the desolate streets weeks after that calamity. There is not a sleigh or vehicle of any kind on the Mill-Dam, but one saddled horse on which a farmer has come into town. The cars are nowhere. Yet they are warmer, merrier than ever there within. At the post-office they ask each traveller news of the cars,—"Is there any train up or down?"—or how deep the snow is on a level.

Of the snow bunting, Wilson says that they appear in the northern parts of the United States "early in December, or with the first heavy snow, particularly if drifted by high winds." This day answers to that description exactly. The wind is northerly. He adds that "they are . . . universally considered as the harbingers of severe cold weather." They come down from the extreme north and are common to the two continents; quotes Pennant as saying that they "inhabit not only Greenland but even the dreadful climate of Spitzbergen, where vegetation is nearly extinct, and scarcely any but *cryptogamous* plants are found. It therefore excites wonder, how birds, which are graminivorous in every other than those frost-bound regions, subsist: yet are there found in great flocks both on the land and ice of Spitzbergen." P. also says that they inhabit in summer "the most naked Lapland Alps," and "descend in rigorous seasons into Sweden, and fill the roads and fields; on which account" the Uplanders call them *"hardwarsfogel,"* hard-weather birds. Also P. says "they overflow [in winter] the more southern countries in amazing multitudes." W. says their colors are very variable, "and the whiteness of their plumage is observed to

be greatest towards the depth of winter." Also W. says truly that
they seldom sit long, "being a roving restless bird." Peabody says
that in summer they are "pure white and black," but are not seen
of that color here. Those I saw to-day were of that color, behind
A. Wheeler's. He says they are white and rusty-brown here.

These are the true winter birds for you, these winged snow-
balls. I could hardly see them, the air was so full of driving snow.
What hardy creatures! Where do they spend the night?

The woodchopper goes not to the wood to-day. His axe and
beetle and wedges and whetstone he will find buried deep under a
drift, perchance, and his fire all extinguished.

As you go down the street, you see on either hand, where erst
were front yards with their parterres, rolling pastures of snow, un-
spotted blankness swelling into drifts. All along the path lies a
huge barrow of snow raised by the arctic mound-builder. It is like
a pass through the Wind River Mountains or the Sierra Nevada,—a
spotless expanse of drifted snow, sloping upward over fences to the
houses, deep banks all along their fronts closing the doors. It lies
in and before Holbrook's piazza, dwarfing its columns, like the sand
about Egyptian temples.

The windows are all sealed up, so that the traveller sees no
face of inhabitant looking out upon him. The housekeeper thinks
with pleasure or pain of what he has in his larder. No shovel is put
to the snow this day. To-morrow we shall see them digging out.
The farmer considers how much pork he has in his barrel, how much
meal in his bin, how much wood in his shed. Each family, perchance,
sends forth one representative before night, who makes his way
with difficulty to the grocery or post-office to learn the news; _i.e._,
to hear what others say to it, who can give the best account of
it, best can name it, has waded farthest in it, has been farthest
out and can tell the biggest and most adequate story; and hastens
back with the news.

I asked Therien yesterday if he was satisfied with himself. I was
trying to get a _point d'appui_ within him, a shelf to spring an arch
from, to suggest some employment and aim for life. "Satisfied!" said
he; "some men are satisfied with one thing, and some with
another, by George. One man, perhaps, if he has got enough, will
be satisfied to sit all day with his back to the fire and his belly
to the table; that will satisfy him, by gorry." When I met him
the other day, he asked me if I had made any improvement. Yet
I could never by any manoeuvring get him to take what is called
a spiritual view of things, of life. He allowed that study and education was a good thing, but for him it was too late. He only
thought of its expediency; nothing answering to what many call

their aspirations. He was humble, if he can be called humble who never aspires.

He cut his trees very low, close to the ground, because the sprouts that came from such stumps were better. Perhaps he distinguished between the red and scarlet oak; one had a pale inner bark, the other a darker or more reddish one. Without the least effort he could defend prevailing institutions which affected him, better than any philosopher, because he implicitly accepted them and knew their whole value. He gave the true reason for their prevalence, because speculation had never suggested to him any other. Looking round among the trees, he said he could enjoy himself in the woods chopping alone in a winter day; he wanted no better sport. The trees were frozen,—had been sometimes,—but would frequently thaw again during the day. Split easier for it, but did not chop better.

The woodchopper to-day is the same man that Homer refers to, and his work the same. He, no doubt, had his beetle and wedge and whetstone then, carried his dinner in a pail or basket, and his liquor in a bottle, and caught his woodchucks, and cut and corded, the same.

The thoughts and associations of summer and autumn are now as completely departed from our minds as the leaves are blown from the trees. Some withered deciduous ones are left to rustle, and our cold immortal evergreens. Some lichenous thoughts still adhere to us.

from
William Nichols'
journal

WILLIAM NICHOLS (1938 –   ) . The following excerpts from my own journal are offered as examples of journal-keeping by the nonprofessional writer. They also give some idea of how this anthology developed.

Thursday, Feb. 10, 1972. An editor with a major publishing house has an idea for a freshman English text that would make use of autobiographical writing and would help students who were doing autobiographical writing themselves. He says he will write to encourage me to think about the idea. Might make use of some of our discoveries in the January term project.

* * *

Monday, February 14. It would be important to have a section on the limitations of autobiography, the danger of solipsism. Here I could use some discussion of the search for other autobiographies, the attempt to get in touch with lives other than one's own. It might be interesting to do something with *Demian* here: maybe a section from the book or a discussion of that impulse (solipsism) in *Demian.*

Might have a section on the *experimental* view of the self's experience. This might include something from Thoreau, "Where I Lived, and What I Lived For," or an excerpt from Gandhi's *An Autobiography; or the Story of My Experiments with Truth.*

* * *

Thursday, Feb. 17. A couple of possible titles: *Writing Toward Community* or *Beyond the Self* or *Writing as Public Performance* or *Beyond Loneliness: Writing Toward Community.*

* * *

21

Sunday, March 5.   How do you make use of first-rate insights in papers written by students? I suspect that reading them aloud doesn't do them justice. Maybe I should take notes on two or three of them and then talk informally about their insights.

* * *

Saturday, June 24.   Sharon Curtin, "Aging in the Land of the Young," *Atlantic* (July 1972), pp. 68–78. This is a very sensitive, dark statement, largely narrative, about the aged in America. It makes use of some autobiographical information, which gives it a special credibility; but interestingly, it does not refer at all to the parents or grandparents of the author. Might be a useful essay as background for people in the autobiography course who wish to write about the life of an older person.

What about using one or two of Norman Mailer's autobiographical essays? And it might be good to balance one of Baldwin's older ones (maybe "Notes of a Native Son") against something from his latest book.

* * *

Wednesday, July 12.   Reading the essay titled simply "Names" in Mary McCarthy's *Memories of a Catholic Girlhood,* I wonder if there might be a category of autobiographical writing, "Symbols and Selfhood." Maybe some of Loren Eiseley's essays in *The Immense Journey* would fit into such a category. In this sort of essay the writer looks back at an event or an artifact not so much for its significance in itself but for what it came to symbolize in his later life.

* * *

Thursday, July 13.   In a character sketch in *Memories,* Mary McCarthy makes a statement that might sum up one underlying theme in this kind of writing: "It did not, of course, occur to me that there was also 'another' me, behind the Catilinarian pose—that my discovery of Miss Gowerie was disclosing, unbeknownst to me, certain strange landscapes in myself (153–54)." This might be a good essay to use in *Beyond Loneliness.*

* * *

Friday, July 14.   This morning sometime after 3:30—we stayed up to hear McGovern's acceptance speech—I heard the preface to *Writ-*

ing Beyond Loneliness bouncing around in my mind: Our society seems to breed loneliness. Sensitivity and encounter groups, communes, and collectives are all, in part, attempts to get beyond loneliness. But what does that have to do with writing? Writing, first of all, can be a profoundly lonely experience. The writer must rely on his own inner resources to transform unstructured ideas, observations, and feelings into organized written language. And when the writer's intentions are misunderstood, as often happens with young people learning to deal with increasingly complex issues, then writing becomes especially frustrating and lonely.

Among college students in the past few years I have seen something that might be called a rebellion against the writing process. Students seem to be saying that, for all but the best writers, writing is a form of communication that inevitably carries with it a distortion and artificiality. Better to communicate face to face, hear the inflection, see the facial expressions, and perhaps feel the grip of the person with whom you are talking. Writing, in comparison, seems inevitably corrupt, a form of communication to be used only when more immediate, more satisfactory, ones are impractical. Writing, to put it baldly, *produces* loneliness.

Moreover, educators are vulnerable to the charge that we have overestimated or at least overemphasized the significance of the *written* word as a measure of intelligence. As a result, we have rejected, ignored, and otherwise discouraged students with extraordinary gifts and even verbal skill because they could not write in ways that seemed acceptable to us. We have, in short, often defined intelligence in terms of a very formal and rather limited concept of language.

* * *

Saturday, July 15. The problem, then (see above), is to find a way to write that is not phoney or self-violating. An analogy: I have known people whose personalities seem to change radically when they are thrust into formal, uncomfortable social situations. When something like that happens, I tend to ask, "Why can't Sam just be *himself?*" The transformation is similar to what happens when most of us write. We develop either a reticence comparable to a stutter, or we assume a style that we know is not our own.

* * *

Wednesday, July 26. Each student should find by the end of the semester one example of "life-writing"—autobiography, journal, perhaps collected letters, biography—and we can spend a day or so in class introducing each other to some new works.

* * *

Tuesday, August 1.   Margaret Bottrall, *Every Man a Phoenix: Studies in Seventeenth-Century Autobiography* (London, John Murray, 1958): "The autobiographical impulse is favoured by disturbed social conditions. When traditional structures are breaking down, when men are no longer conscious of a clear pattern by which to order their moral existence, when the sense of belonging to a community is lost, then the value of individual personality has the chance to be keenly apprehended and asserted (p. 11)."

* * *

Wednesday, Aug. 2.   In considering some of the hurdles in the way of good autobiographical writing, it might be good to try something like a sensitivity technique. If people in the class were to try to talk about, say, their fathers with as much candor as they can muster in such a situation, and if other members of the class tried to react very honestly to the descriptions, I think we would find how difficult it is to describe fully, honestly, and imaginatively the personhood of someone whose life has impinged on our own. Might try this with other subjects—early memory and place, for example.

* * *

Friday, Sept. 8.   Today was the second meeting of my Freshman English course. We read the introduction ("To the Reader") to Mary McCarthy's *Memories of a Catholic Girlhood.* I asked if any of them had the same sense of their family's past that McCarthy has. About half the class said they had heard lots of stories about their grandparents and parents. (Maybe if I pursued the question with them individually, I'd find that they remember less than they think; but their impressions surely are important.) About half the class felt, as I do, essentially unfamiliar with their parents' and grandparents' lives. In any event, a number of people seemed eager to talk in class about such questions. I really felt that people were talking not because they believed they should talk in class but because they could hardly resist saying something about their own experience when it was clear that others found it significant. It makes me think that the autobiographical focus gets at something that students find genuinely interesting.

* * *

Wednesday, Oct. 11. In Volume 17, No. 7, of *Contemporary Psychology*, Sidney Jourard reviews Amedeo Giorgi's *Psychology as a Human Science: A Phenomenologically Based Approach.* In the review Jourard says: "Exemplary biography, autobiography, and fiction, it seems to me, are human science at its best. When a man shows and tells his action, and then tells us why he did what he did, and *how* he did it, he is letting others know *their* possibilities." And he adds: "I am willing to guess, and to try to make my guess a self-fulfilling prophecy, that the advances in humanistic psychology, or a human science of psychology, will consist in perfecting the art of biography and autobiography, so that men will be able to share their experience at taming facticity, but not at taming their fellow men."

* * *

Friday, Oct. 13. Might add an assignment that asks a student to respond to a work of art—a painting, poem, movie, concert, novel—as he might respond to a person or an event. What was the impact of the work on his own life?

* * *

Saturday, Dec. 2. I need to do something with the essay on the self and history. The assignment just doesn't make enough sense to students. And the actual essays were, by and large, not as good as others written by the same students. Maybe it's the word *history* that does it. Somehow the word seems unrelated to anything that can be taken personally. Another indication of the problem with the assignment is the fact that a number of the essays on "the self and art" were much stronger. With *art* as the external focus students were able to develop specific, sustained examples. Somehow the history assignment needs to be made more specific, more manageable.

* * *

Wednesday, Dec. 6. Just thinking about the search for life stories, I'm struck by the relationship between the successful interviewer and the effective teacher. Roy Pascal points out (*Design and Truth in Autobiography,* p. 50) that the early autobiographers at the end of the eighteenth century and the beginning of the nineteenth shared a "kind of wonder and awe with regard to themselves." It seems to me that the successful interviewer will often need to encourage and instill that wonder in a subject who may never have considered his/her life story worthy of attention.

* * *

Saturday, December 9. A student suggested to me yesterday that he would have welcomed the opportunity to indulge in some fantasy in both his reading and his writing. He suggested this assignment: tell the biggest lie you can imagine. Would this be a good way to move into the world of fiction? It might produce some good writing, but I worry about connecting fiction with dishonesty.

* * *

Friday, January 19, 1973. William Gibson, *A Mass for the Dead* (Atheneum Publishers, 1968). There is some beautiful writing in this book. Might want to include a selection in *Beyond Loneliness.* Gibson tells of a time when his sister broke a doll and moaned half the night, "Daddy, I broke my dollie." Gibson's comment is moving: "my parents in their bed listened in that grief for a child's grief which a child cannot suspect; love like water tumbles downhill between generations." I don't accept Gibson's judgment on love, however.

* * *

Friday, January 26. When you are away from home and lonely, a good letter can help. In fact, writing a good letter can help, probably because the writing of a good letter is an act of reaching out that carries with it the belief in shared experience.

* * *

Thursday, March 8. Today we divided the small groups in half, and we all wrote description. Half of each group described a child's confrontation with authority from inside, half from outside—that is, relying on external description and dialogue rather than explicit statements about thoughts and feelings. That, in any event, was the way we set it up; and I had the feeling that everyone understood pretty well. What happened was that each writer, including me, found it impossible to abide by the limitations. Mine was to be an internal description, but I found it necessary to give some external description as well.

* * *

Tuesday, May 15. I talked with Karen Nagle today about her essay on a Jethro Tull concert. It was her best essay of the semester and one of the best written in the course. Her method of writing it might be worth mentioning in *Beyond Loneliness.* She went back to her dorm and put on the album "Thick as a Brick," which she had heard first in a concert at Ohio University. Then she sat on her bed, put on headphones, and wrote notes as the music touched off specific memories of the concert. As the essay testifies, she remembered colors, shapes, actions in the crowd, the appearance of the group, and the range of thought and feeling that had moved her as she listened to the concert.

* * *

Saturday, June 23. Talking with Dick Kraus about his two-hour automatic writing exercises, I was reminded of three things that should be implicit in the commentary for *Beyond Loneliness:* (1) When the two-hour spontaneous writing assignment was given at Stanford, it was pointed out that, typically, writing teachers can deal only with the planned, rational structural part of writing. The automatic writing assignment tries to deal with another part of the writing process. (2) Dick reminded me that this kind of assignment can be a way of bringing thought and feeling together— which may be one key to learning to write well. (3) It seems to me that much of the suspicion of language I find among McLuhanesque young people results from their fear that language cannot include the most important kinds of feeling. It isn't just that they doubt the value of their experience, then, but that they often believe their experience cannot be rendered in language. Perhaps automatic writing speaks to that attitude toward language: the student-writer can *discover* the possibilities of language.

AFTERWORD

Writers keep journals for a variety of reasons. Anaïs Nin's diary focuses primarily on the author's relationships with an array of unusually interesting and talented people; Henry Thoreau generally used his journal to record his observations on nature and human society, sometimes copying into it extended passages from his reading. Two journals may have methodological differences as well. For some writers a journal is a private workbook in which they can experiment with ideas and styles that may prove worthy of fuller and more formal development elsewhere; for others a journal is a more finished product. Thoreau, for instance, revised many of his entries with care, and similarly, Anaïs Nin seems to have assumed from the beginning of her journal that it would someday be made public.

In the context of a writing course, the best journals usually fall somewhere between the private workbook and the polished public statement. They are workbooks in that the writer experiments freely with subjects and styles and feels no obligation to develop each entry into a finished essay; yet they resemble public statements in that they anticipate a reader who is not necessarily familiar with all the subjects discussed. Such a reader might be the instructor in a writing course, or he might be simply the writer himself at a time in the future, when he has forgotten many of the details associated with a particular journal entry. Informative details are crucial to an effective, interesting journal if the writer hopes to capture the complexity of his own experience and make it accessible to another reader or to an older version of himself.

If a journal is written in a manner that does not assume a reader other than the writer, it is likely to include an entry like this one:

> *Thursday, March 17.* Made the 9:30 Soc. course this morning and got the usual enigmatic smile from Sharon. What the hell does it mean? Gave up on that and ignored the razzle-dazzle jargon of Prof. Stone. Spent the rest of the morning sitting in the Union putting in face time.

There are at least three interesting literary possibilities in that entry. First, the enigmatic smile from Sharon warrants at least some physical description, and the speculation on the meaning of that smile suggests that Sharon and the writer share a relationship worthy of some further discussion. Second, the reference to the sociology professor's "razzle-dazzle jargon" hints that the writer is bored by the teacher's approach to sociology and, more importantly, that he or she knows the source of that boredom to be language. An entry that included examples of Professor Stone's use of language and attempted some analysis of its failure to interest the writer would be a valuable piece of reflection. Perhaps the most interesting possibility of all is the reference to "putting in face time." It is difficult to understand, but it may mean that the writer is aware of participating in a student ritual ("face time") as a response to a general boredom and dissatisfaction with college life. Such an interpretation of the sentence implies that the writer has a good deal of self-awareness and an ironic view of student behavior. Some discussion of what the "face time" ritual means to the writer might provide a fascinating picture of college life. As it stands, however, the entry is private and nearly inaccessible. Its cryptic sentences were undoubtedly rather easy to write, but after a little time has passed, even the writer will probably find it difficult to determine what they were supposed to mean.

There are a number of ways to use a journal for experimentation. For example, when you discover a writer whose style has a special appeal, you can use a journal entry to attempt an imitation of that style. Or you can devote an entry to a new kind of writing, something you would hesitate to attempt in a formal essay—perhaps a wild fantasy or a description of a dream. A journal is also a good place to try out a subject in which you have an interest but less than sufficient material for a full-length essay. Assume, for example, that you have often thought of yourself in some exotic occupation. By writing about it occasionally in your journal, you may find you have enough ideas and memories connected with it to attempt a rich, vivid essay.

One more use of the journal may be worth mentioning here, even though it is much broader than those suggested above: a journal can provide a way of integrating the complexities of college experience. One of the most interesting things that can happen in college is to discover relationships among the various parts of your intellectual and social life. To notice, for instance, that a movie you saw on Friday night involves a problem that was discussed on Wednesday in your sociology course can enrich both experiences. A journal can be both the occasion and the incentive for making such connections.

Suggested writing assignment

Keep a journal for two or three months, making entries at least every other day. Use the journal as a reservoir of writing ideas and a place for literary experimentation. You may find your journal so useful that you will choose to continue it through, and perhaps beyond, your college career.

two: early memory

from
the education
of an American

MARK SULLIVAN (1874–1952) was a well-known journalist
and the author of a six-volume history of the United States.
The Education of an American (1938), from which the following excerpt is taken, is his autobiography, which, most re-
viewers agree, reaches its heights through Sullivan's memories of farm life during his early childhood.

My earliest memory, that I can identify, is of a scent. It was late
on a sunny September afternoon, "potato-digging time." My father
was plowing up the long furrows of fresh earth in the potato field,
which sloped southward from the house. Following behind him, my
mother gathered the potatoes into pails which, when full, she
emptied into bags set at intervals along the rows. She rarely
worked in the fields—with a family of growing boys she did not
need to, but potato digging coincided with the opening of school.
In order that the children should go the first day, and every day,
she took on herself the potato picking. Because there was no one
in the house to look after me she took me to the field with her.
I was not more than two or three years old; I suppose I spent the
afternoon playing in the fresh earth. Here and there among the
uprooted potato vines grew two herbs, pennyroyal and St-John's-
wort. Both were strong-scented and were prized in our neighborhood as having medicinal value. Some wisps of these my mother
gathered into a small bundle which she laid aside. In the evening,
walking back to the house, she carried me, the fragrant pennyroyal
and St-John's-wort in her hand brushing my face.

There this memory ends. But other memories recall the herbs
tied into bundles and hung from hooks in the kitchen ceiling,

against the winter weather when the children would have colds, for which "pennyrile tea" was believed to be a remedy.

All the more vivid of my early memories are of smells, farm smells: the acrid scent of burning weeds in the fall, at the end of a day of clearing the field for planting wheat; the faint fragrance of blossoms wafted down from the orchard in May, followed in midsummer by the strong, mellow odor of ripening apples, and in fall by the cidery scent of apples pared and sliced and spread in wooden racks in the sun, to provide our winter store of dried apples; the harvest smell of mown grass and of threshed straw; the barn smell of dried hay; the dank scent of the woods after a rain; the odor of bloodroot, the first spring flower, and of sassafras as the sap began to run; the pervading smell of October which settled for weeks upon the whole countryside, so heavy it seemed almost visible, almost like a mist, a potpourri of ripening walnuts, ripening wild grapes, leaves fallen and just beginning to decay. Each season, almost each day, each spot on the farm, had its special scent. All are still vivid to me. One bred on a farm knows that

> Smells are surer than sounds or sights
> To make your heart-strings crack.

Next to scents, my most vivid early memories are of sounds: the whir of the mowing machine in outlying fields in June; the two-note *clunk, clank* of the whetstone against the scythe, which we kept for mowing corners of the field and bits of hillside too steep for the mowing machine. Another two-note sound was of the ax cutting down a tree in the woods, a low-pitched *chug* from the level stroke that made the bottom of the incision, a higher-pitched note made by the downward chop—both followed, after a half-hour of chopping, by a moment of silence, having the effect of suspense, by which I knew my father had stepped hurriedly back, and then the swish of the falling tree against the twigs and limbs of its neighbors, the sound gathering volume and tempo until it became a roar, climaxing in a mighty crash as the tree struck the ground. The two-pitched whine of the crosscut saw, a high note as the faster of the two sawyers drew the blade toward him, a lower note made by the slower worker.

In the fields, as the sun told us noon was near, we listened for the dinner bells. On our farm we had none—we depended on my mother's voice. But on many of the neighboring farms was a huge bell, as big as a school or church bell—indeed, I think the makers of the bells did not differentiate in size between those designed to summon to spiritual refreshment Sunday mornings and those designed to announce the noonday meal of the flesh. The dinner bell hung from a tall post, with a chain attached to it. This the housewife pulled at a moment nicely chosen to enable the men to get back from the fields just as the dishes came hot from stove to table. The bells rang about the same time, their deep-toned voices a rude neighborhood carillon.

From the swamps and bottoms in early March came the chorus of the young frogs. They sounded hurried, breathless, as if passionately eager to bring the spring, of which they were the heralds. We called them "knee-deeps." For that name we had two explanations: one that the frogs were still knee-deep in the swamp, the other that their cry sounded like *knee-deep*—the first note low in pitch, the second high, almost a whistle. The knee-deep was not musical, much less so than the bobwhite or the dove; nor is the frog a glamorous creature, whether young or full-grown. Yet of all the sounds my childhood knew, the cry of the knee-deeps remains the most vivid, the most potent to evoke the past. During all the middle years of my life, wherever I was, in cities or in distant lands, I never saw March come on the calendar without thinking of the farm and wishing I could hear the knee-deeps.

One spring, while living in New York, my wife and I became troubled by the weedy pallor of the young children of the janitor who lived in the basement of our apartment house, shut off from the sunlight, and close to the street noises. We arranged that the children. with their mother, should go for some weeks into the country, a country not very remote, for it was Staten Island, with the Manhattan skyscrapers in sight. Our satisfaction over our good deed was brief. After two days mother and children were back in the noisy, gloomy basement. The mother explained she did not like the country, she could not stand "the noise of those little frogs at night." The incident was fruitful of many reflections, including that which says that one person's music may be another person's noise, one person's pleasure another's intolerable annoyance.

reminiscences of childhood

DYLAN THOMAS (1914–1953), one of the twentieth century's best-loved British poets, created "Reminiscences of
Childhood" for presentation on radio. This essay and the
texts of other Thomas broadcasts have been collected in a
volume called *Quite Early One Morning* (1954).

I like very much people telling me about their childhood, but
they'll have to be quick or else I'll be telling them about mine.

I was born in a large Welsh town at the beginning of the
Great War—an ugly, lovely town (or so it was and is to me), crawling, sprawling by a long and splendid curving shore where truant
boys and sand-field boys and old men from nowhere, beachcombed,
idled and paddled, watched the dock-bound ships or the ships
steaming away into wonder and India, magic and China, countries
bright with oranges and loud with lions; threw stones into the sea
for the barking outcast dogs; made castles and forts and harbours
and race tracks in the sand; and on Saturday summer afternoons
listened to the brass band, watched the Punch and Judy, or hung
about on the fringes of the crowd to hear the fierce religious speakers who shouted at the sea, as though it were wicked and wrong
to roll in and out like that, white-horsed and full of fishes.

One man, I remember, used to take off his hat and set fire to
his hair every now and then, but I do not remember what it
proved, if it proved anything at all, except that he was a very interesting man.

This sea-town was my world; outside a strange Wales, coal-
pitted, mountained, river-run, full, so far as I knew, of choirs and
football teams and sheep and story book tall hats and red flannel
petticoats, moved about its business which was none of mine.

Beyond that unknown Wales with its wild names like peals of

bells in the darkness, and its mountain men clothed in the skins of animals perhaps and always singing, lay England which was London and the country called the Front, from which many of our neighbours never came back. It was a country to which only young men travelled.

At the beginning, the only "front" I knew was the little lobby before our front door. I could not understand how so many people never returned from there, but later I grew to know more, though still without understanding, and carried a wooden rifle in the park and shot down the invisible unknown enemy like a flock of wild birds. And the park itself was a world within the world of the sea-town. Quite near where I lived, so near that on summer evenings I could listen in my bed to the voices of older children playing ball on the sloping paper-littered bank, the park was full of terrors and treasures. Though it was only a little park, it held within its borders of old tall trees, notched with our names and shabby from our climbing, as many secret places, caverns and forests, prairies and deserts, as a country somewhere at the end of the sea.

And though we would explore it one day, armed and desperate from end to end, from the robbers' den to the pirates' cabin, the highwayman's inn to the cattle ranch, or the hidden room in the undergrowth, where we held beetle races, and lit the wood fires and roasted potatoes and talked about Africa, and the makes of motor cars, yet still the next day, it remained as unexplored as the Poles—a country just born and always changing.

There were many secret societies but you could belong only to one; and in blood or red ink, and a rusty pocketknife, with, of course, an instrument to remove stones from horses' feet, you signed your name at the foot of a terrible document, swore death to all the other societies, crossed your heart that you would divulge no secret and that if you did, you would consent to torture by slow fire, and undertook to carry out by yourself a feat of either daring or endurance. You could take your choice: would you climb to the top of the tallest and most dangerous tree, and from there hurl stones and insults at grown-up passers-by, especially postmen, or any other men in uniform? Or would you ring every doorbell in the terrace, not forgetting the doorbell of the man with the red face who kept dogs and ran fast? Or would you swim in the reservoir, which was forbidden and had angry swans, or would you eat a whole old jam jar full of mud?

There were many more alternatives. I chose one of endurance and for half an hour, it may have been longer or shorter, held up off the ground a very heavy broken pram we had found in a bush. I thought my back would break and the half hour felt like a day, but I preferred it to braving the red face and the dogs, or to swallowing tadpoles.

We knew every inhabitant of the park, every regular visitor, every nursemaid, every gardener, every old man. We knew the hour when the alarming retired policeman came in to look at the dahlias and the hour when the old lady arrived in the Bath chair with six Pekinese, and a pale girl to read aloud to her. I think she read the newspaper, but we always said she read the *Wizard.* The face of the old man who sat summer and winter on the bench looking over the reservoir, I can see clearly now and I wrote a poem long long after I'd left the park and the sea-town called:

THE HUNCHBACK IN THE PARK

The hunchback in the park
A solitary mister
Propped between tree and water
From the opening of the garden lock
That lets the trees and water enter
Until the Sunday sombre ball at dark

Eating bread from a newspaper
Drinking water from the chained cup
That the children filled with gravel
In the fountain basin where I sailed my ship
Slept at night in a dog kennel
But nobody chained him up.

Like the park birds he came early
Like the water he sat down
And Mister they called Hey mister
The truant boys from the town
Running when he had heard them clearly
On out of sound

Past lake and rockery
Laughing when he shook his paper
Hunchbacked in mockery
Through the loud zoo of the willow groves
Dodging the park-keeper
With his stick that picked up leaves

And the old dog sleeper
Alone between nurses and swans
While the boys among willows
Made the tiger jump out of their eyes
To roar on the rockery stones
And the groves were blue with sailors

Made all day until bell-time
A woman figure without fault
Straight as a young elm
Straight and tall from his crooked bones
That she might stand in the night
After the locks and the chains

All night in the unmade park
After the railings and shrubberies
The birds the grass the trees and the lake
And the wild boys innocent as strawberries
Had followed the hunchback
To his kennel in the dark.

And that park grew up with me; that small world widened as
I learned its secrets and boundaries, as I discovered new refuges and
ambushes in its woods and jungles; hidden homes and lairs for the
multitudes of imagination, for cowboys and Indians, and the tall
terrible half-people who rode on nightmares through my bedroom.
But it was not the only world—that world of rockery, gravel path,
playbank, bowling green, bandstands, reservoir, dahlia garden, where
an ancient keeper, known as Smoky, was the whiskered snake in the
grass one must keep off. There was another world where with my
friends I used to dawdle on half holidays along the bent and Devon-
facing seashore, hoping for gold watches or the skull of a sheep or
a message in a bottle to be washed up with the tide; and another
where we used to wander whistling through the packed streets,
stale as station sandwiches, round the impressive gasworks and the
slaughter house, past by the blackened monuments and the museum
that should have been in a museum. Or we scratched at a kind of
cricket on the bald and cindery surface of the recreation ground, or
we took a tram that shook like an iron jelly down to the gaunt
pier, there to clamber under the pier, hanging perilously on to its
skeleton legs or to run along to the end where patient men with
the seaward eyes of the dockside unemployed capped and mufflered,
dangling from their mouths pipes that had long gone out, angled
over the edge for unpleasant tasting fish.

Never was there such a town as ours, I thought, as we fought
on the sandhills with rough boys or dared each other to climb up
the scaffolding of half-built houses soon to be called Laburnum
Beaches. Never was there such a town, I thought, for the smell of
fish and chips on Saturday evenings; for the Saturday afternoon
cinema matinees where we shouted and hissed our threepences away;
for the crowds in the streets with leeks in their hats on interna-
tional nights; for the park, the inexhaustible and mysterious,
bushy red-Indian hiding park where the hunchback sat alone and the

groves were blue with sailors. The memories of childhood have no order, and so I remember that never was there such a dame school as ours, so firm and kind and smelling of galoshes, with the sweet and fumbled music of the piano lessons drifting down from upstairs to the lonely schoolroom, where only the sometimes tearful wicked sat over undone sums, or to repeat a little crime—the pulling of a girl's hair during geography, the sly shin kick under the table during English literature. Behind the school was a narrow lane where only the oldest and boldest threw pebbles at windows, scuffled and boasted, fibbed about their relations—

"My father's got a chauffeur."

"What's he want a chauffeur for? He hasn't got a car."

"My father's the richest man in the town."

"My father's the richest man in Wales."

"My father owns the world."

And swapped gob-stoppers for slings, old knives for marbles, kite strings for foreign stamps.

The lane was always the place to tell your secrets; if you did not have any, you invented them. Occasionally now I dream that I am turning out of school into the lane of confidences when I say to the boys of my class, "At last, I have a real secret."

"What is it—what is it?"

"I can fly."

And when they do not believe me, I flap my arms and slowly leave the ground only a few inches at first, then gaining air until I fly waving my cap level with the upper windows of the school peering in until the mistress at the piano screams and the metronome falls to the ground and stops, and there is no more time.

And I fly over the trees and chimneys of my town, over the dockyards skimming the masts and funnels, over Inkerman Street, Sebastopol Street, and the street where all the women wear men's caps, over the trees of the everlasting park, where a brass band snakes the leaves and sends them showering down on to the nurses and the children, and the shouting boys: over the yellow seashore, and the stone-chasing dogs, and the old men, and the singing sea.

The memories of childhood have no order, and no end.

(1943, 1953)

from
the dark child

CAMARA LAYE (1928 –   ) published *The Dark Child* in
1954 while he was an engineering student in Paris. Marked
by dignity and a little sadness, the book tells of Laye's youth
in French Guinea before he left to study in France.

I was a little boy playing around my father's hut. How old would
I have been at that time? I can not remember exactly. I must
still have been very young: five, maybe six years old. My mother was
in the workshop with my father, and I could just hear their familiar voices above the noise of the anvil and the conversation of the
customers.

Suddenly I stopped playing, my whole attention fixed on a
snake that was creeping around the hut. After a moment I went
over to him. I had taken in my hand a reed that was lying in the
yard—there were always some lying around; they used to get broken
off the fence of plaited reeds that marked the boundary of our
concession—and I thrust it into his mouth. The snake did not try
to get away: he was beginning to enjoy our little game; he was
slowly swallowing the reed; he was devouring it, I thought, as if it
were some delicious prey, his eyes glittering with voluptuous bliss;
and inch by inch his head was drawing nearer to my hand. At last
the reed was almost entirely swallowed, and the snake's jaws were
terribly close to my fingers.

I was laughing. I had not the slightest fear, and I feel sure
that the snake would not have hesitated much longer before bury-
ing his fangs in my fingers if, at that moment, Damany, one of the
apprentices, had not come out of the workshop. He called my
father, and almost at once I felt myself lifted off my feet: I was
safe in the arms of one of my father's friends.

Around me there was a great commotion. My mother was shouting hardest of all, and she gave me a few sharp slaps. I wept, more upset by the sudden uproar than by the blows. A little later, when I was somewhat calmer and the shouting had ceased, my mother solemnly warned me never to play that game again. I promised, although the game still didn't seem dangerous to me.

My father's hut was near the workshop, and I often played beneath the veranda that ran around the outside. It was his private hut, and like all our huts built of mud bricks that had been pounded and moulded with water; it was round, and proudly helmeted with thatch. It was entered by a rectangular doorway. Inside, a tiny window let in a thin shaft of daylight. On the right was the bed, made of beaten earth like the bricks, and spread with a simple wicker-work mat on which lay a pillow stuffed with kapok. At the rear, right under the window where the light was strongest, were the tool-boxes. On the left were the *boubous* and the prayer-rugs. At the head of the bed, hanging over the pillow and watching over my father's slumber, stood a row of pots that contained extracts from plants and the bark of trees. These pots all had metal lids and were profusely and curiously garlanded with chaplets of cowry shells; it did not take me long to discover that they were the most important things in the hut; they contained magic charms—those mysterious liquids that keep the evil spirits at bay, and, if smeared on the body, make it invulnerable to every kind of black magic. My father, before going to bed, never failed to smear his body with a little of each liquid, first one, then another, for each charm had its own particular property: but exactly *what* property I did not know: I had left my father's house too soon.

From the veranda under which I played I could keep an eye on the workshop opposite, and the adults for their part could keep an eye on me. This workshop was the main building in our concession, and my father was generally to be found there, looking after the work, forging the most important items himself, or repairing delicate mechanisms; there he received his friends and his customers, and the place resounded with noise from morning to night. Moreover, everyone who entered or left our concession had to cross the workshop. There was a perpetual coming and going, though no one seemed to be in any particular hurry; each had his bit of gossip; each lingered at the forge to watch. Sometimes I came near the door, but I rarely went in; everyone there frightened me, and I would run away as soon as anyone tried to touch me. It was not until very much later that I got into the habit of crouching in a corner of the workshop to watch the fire blazing in the forge.

My private domain at that time was the veranda that encircled my father's hut, my mother's hut, and the orange tree that grew in the middle of the concession.

As soon as you crossed the workshop and went through the door at the back, you would see the orange tree. Compared with the giants of our native forests, the tree was not very big, but its mass of glossy leaves cast a dense shade that kept the heat at bay. When it was in flower a heady perfume pervaded the entire concession. When the fruit first appeared we were only allowed to look: we had to wait patiently until it was ripe. Then my father, who as head of the family—and a very large family it was—governed the concession, gave the order to pick the fruit. The men who did the picking brought their baskets one by one to my father, who portioned them out among the people who lived in the concession and among his neighbors and customers. After that we were permitted to help ourselves from the baskets and we were allowed as much as we liked! My father was open-handed; in fact, a lavish giver. Any visitor, no matter who he was, shared our meals; since I could never keep up with the speed at which such guests ate I might have remained forever hungry if my mother had not taken the precaution of putting my share aside.

"Sit here," she would say, "and eat, for your father's mad."

She did not look upon such guests with a kindly eye. There were too many for her liking, all bent on filling their bellies at her expense. My father, for his part, ate very little; he was an extremely temperate man.

We lived beside a railroad. The trains skirted the reed fence of the concession so closely that sparks thrown off from the locomotive set fire to it every now and then which had to be quickly extinguished so that the whole concession would not go up in smoke. These alarms, frightening yet exciting, made me aware of the passing trains. And even where there were no trains—for in those days the railroad was dependent on a most irregular water traffic—much of my time was spent watching the iron rails. They glistened cruelly in a light which nothing in that place could relieve. Baking since dawn, the roadbed was so hot that oil which dropped from the locomotives evaporated immediately, leaving no trace. Was it the oven-like heat or the smell of oil—for the smell remained in spite of everything—which attracted the snakes? I do not know. But often I came upon them crawling in that hot roadbed. It would have been fatal if they had gotten into the concession.

Ever since the day when I had been forbidden by my mother to play with snakes I ran to her as soon as I saw one.

"There's a snake!" I would cry.

"What? Another?"

And she would come running to see what sort of snake it was. If it was just a snake like any other snake—actually they were all quite different—she would immediately beat it to death; and, like all the women of our country, she would work herself into a frenzy, beating the snake to a pulp. The men contented themselves with a single hard blow, neatly struck.

One day, however, I noticed a little black snake with a strikingly marked body. He was proceeding slowly in the direction of the workshop. I ran to warn my mother, as usual. But as soon as she saw the black snake she said to me gravely:

"My son, this one must not be killed: he is not like other snakes, and he will not harm you; you must never interfere with him."

Everyone in our concession knew that this snake must not be killed—everyone except myself, and, I suppose, my little playmates, who were still ignorant children.

"This snake," my mother added, "is your father's guiding spirit."

I gazed dumbfounded at the little snake. He was proceeding calmly toward the workshop, gracefully, very sure of himself, and almost as if conscious of his immunity; his body, black and brilliant, glittered in the harsh light of the sun. When he reached the workshop, I noticed for the first time a small hole in the wall, cut out level with the ground. The snake disappeared through this hole.

"Look," said my mother, "the snake is going to pay your father a visit."

Although I was familiar with the supernatural, this sight filled me with such astonishment that I was struck dumb. What business would a snake have with my father? And why this particular snake? No one was to kill him because he was my father's guiding spirit! At any rate, that was the explanation my mother had given me. But what exactly *was* a "guiding spirit"? What were these guiding spirits that I encountered almost everywhere, forbidding one thing, commanding another to be done? I could not understand it at all, though their presences surrounded me as I grew to manhood. There were good spirits, and there were evil ones; and more evil than good ones, it seemed. And how was I to know that this snake was harmless? He was a snake like the others: black, to be sure, with extraordinary markings—but for all that a snake. I was completely perplexed, but I did not question my mother: I had decided that I must ask my father about it, as if this were a mystery to be discussed only between men, a mystery in which women had no part. I decided to wait until evening to speak to him.

Immediately after the evening meal, when the palavers were over, my father bade his friends farewell and sat under the veranda of his hut; I seated myself near him. I began questioning him in a dilatory manner, as all children do, regarding every subject under the sun. Actually I was no more talkative than on other evenings. Only this evening I withheld what troubled me, waiting for the opportunity when—my face betraying nothing—I might ask the question which had worried me so deeply from the moment when I first saw the black snake going toward the workshop. Finally, unable to restrain myself any longer, I asked:

"My father, what is that little snake that comes to visit you?"

"What snake do you mean?"

"Why, the little black snake that my mother forbids us to kill."

"Ah!" he said.

He gazed at me for a long while. He seemed to be considering whether to answer or not. Perhaps he was thinking about how old I was, perhaps he was wondering if it was not a little too soon to confide such a secret to a twelve-year-old boy. Then suddenly he made up his mind.

"That snake," he said, "is the guiding spirit of our race. Can you understand that?"

"Yes," I answered, although I did not understand very well.

"That snake," he went on, "has always been with us; he has always made himself known to one of us. In our time, it is to me that he has made himself known."

"Yes," I said.

And I said it with all my heart, for it seemed obvious to me that the snake could have made himself known to no one but my father. Was not my father the head man in our concession? Was it not my father who had authority over all the blacksmiths in our district? Was he not the most skilled? Was he not, after all, my father?

"How did he make himself known?" I asked.

"First of all, he made himself known in the semblance of a dream. He appeared to me several times in sleep and told me the day on which he would appear to me in reality: he gave me the precise time and place. But when I really saw him for the first time, I was filled with fear. I took him for a snake like any other snake, and I had to keep myself under control or I would have tried to kill him. When he saw that I did not receive him kindly, he turned away and departed the way he had come. And there I stood, watching him depart, wondering all the time if I should not simply have killed him there and then; but a power greater than I stayed my hand and prevented me from pursuing him. I stood watching him disappear. And even then, at that very moment, I could easily have overtaken him; a few swift strides would have been enough; but I was struck motionless by a kind of paralysis. Such was my first encounter with the little black snake."

He was silent a moment, then went on:

"The following night, I saw the snake again in my dream. 'I came as I foretold,' he said, 'but thou didst not receive me kindly; nay, rather I did perceive that thou didst intend to receive me unkindly: I did read it thus in thine eyes. Wherefore dost thou reject me? Lo, I am the guiding spirit of thy race, and it is even as the guiding spirit of thy race that I make myself known to thee, as to the most worthy. Therefore forbear to look with fear upon me, and beware that thou dost not reject me, for behold, I bring thee good fortune.' After that, I received the snake kindly when he made himself known to me a second time; I received him without fear, I received him with loving kindness, and he brought me nothing but good."

My father again was silent for a moment, then he said:

"You can see for yourself that I am not more gifted than other men, that I have nothing which other men have not also, and even that I have less than others, since I give everything away, and would even give away the last thing I had, the shirt on my back. Nevertheless I am better known. My name is on everyone's tongue, and it is I who have authority over all the blacksmiths in the five cantons. If these things are so, it is by virtue of this snake alone, who is the guiding spirit of our race. It is to this snake that I owe everything; it is he who gives me warning of all that is to happen. Thus I am never surprised, when I awake, to see this or that person waiting for me outside my workshop: I already know that he will be there. No more am I suprised when this or that motorcycle or bicycle breaks down, or when an accident happens to a clock: because I have had foreknowledge of what would come to pass. Everything is transmitted to me in the course of the night, together with an account of all the work I shall have to perform, so that from the start, without having to cast about in my mind, I know how to repair whatever is brought to me. These things have established my renown as a craftsman. But all this—let it never be forgotten—I owe to the snake, I owe it to the guiding spirit of our race."

He was silent; and then I understood why, when my father came back from a walk he would enter the workshop and say to the apprentices: "During my absence, this or that person has been here, he was dressed in such and such a way, he came from such and such a place and he brought with him such and such a piece of work to be done." And all marveled at this curious knowledge. When I raised my eyes, I saw that my father was watching me.

"I have told you all these things, little one, because you are my son, the eldest of my sons, and because I have nothing to hide from you. There is a certain form of behavior to observe, and certain ways of acting in order that the guiding spirit of our race may approach you also. I, your father, was observing that form of behavior which persuades our guiding spirit to visit us. Oh, perhaps not consciously: but nevertheless it is true that if you desire the guiding spirit of our race to visit you one day, if you desire to inherit it in your turn, you will have to conduct yourself in the selfsame manner; from now on, it will be necessary for you to be more and more in my company."

He gazed at me with burning eyes, then suddenly he heaved a sigh.

"I fear, I very much fear, little one, that you are not often enough in my company. You are all day at school, and one day you will depart from that school for a greater one. You will leave me, little one . . ."

And again he heaved a sigh. I saw that his heart was heavy within him. The hurricane-lamp hanging on the veranda cast a harsh glare on his face. He suddenly seemed to me an old man.

"Father!" I cried.

"Son . . ." he whispered.

And I was no longer sure whether I ought to continue to attend school or whether I ought to remain in the workshop: I felt unutterably confused.

"Go now," said my father.

I went to my mother's hut. The night was full of sparkling stars; an owl was hooting nearby. Ah! what was the right path for me? Did I know yet where that path lay? My perplexity was boundless as the sky, and mine was a sky, alas, without any stars . . . I entered my mother's hut, which at that time was mine also, and went to bed at once. But sleep did not come and I tossed restlessly on my bed.

"What's the matter with you?" asked my mother.

"Nothing."

No. I couldn't find anything to say.

"Why don't you go to sleep?" my mother continued.

"I don't know."

"Go to sleep!" she said.

"Yes," I said.

"Sleep . . . Nothing can resist sleep," she said sadly.

Why did she, too, appear so sad? Had she divined my distress? Anything that concerned me she sensed very deeply. I was trying to sleep, but I shut my eyes and lay still in vain: the image of my father under the hurricane-lamp would not leave me: my father who had suddenly seemed so old and who was so young, so lively—younger and livelier than the rest of us, a man no one could outrun, who was swifter of limb than any of us . . . "Father! . . . Father! . . . !" I kept repeating. "What must I do if I am to do the right thing?" And I wept silently and fell asleep still weeping.

After that we never mentioned the little black snake again: my father had spoken to me about him for the first and last time. But from that time on, as soon as I saw the little snake, I would run and sit in the workshop. I would watch him glide through the little hole in the wall. As if informed of his presence, my father at that very instant would turn his eyes to the hole and smile. The snake would go straight to him, opening his jaws. When he was within reach my father would stroke him and the snake would accept the caress with a quivering of his whole body. I never saw the little snake attempt to do the slightest harm to my father. That caress and the answering tremor—but I ought to say: that appealing caress and that answering tremor—threw me each time into an inexpressible confusion. I imagined I know not what mysterious conversations: the hand inquired and the tremor replied. . . .

Yes. It was like a conversation. Would I too converse that way some day? No. I would continue to attend school. Yet I should have liked so much to place my hand, my own hand, on that snake, and to understand and listen to that tremor too; but I did not know whether the snake would have accepted my hand, and I felt now that he would have nothing to tell me. I was afraid that he would never have anything to tell me.

When my father felt that he had stroked the snake enough he left him alone. Then the snake coiled himself under the edge of one of the sheepskins on which my father, facing his anvil, was seated.

from
Black Elk speaks

JOHN G. NEIHARDT (1881–1973), an American poet who
had lived for years among the Plains Indians, made a visit
in 1930 to Black Elk, an aged holy man of the Oglala Sioux.
By talking with the old man, Neihardt hoped to add to his
knowledge of Indian history. Their first meeting was marked
by a long silence, after which Black Elk said in Sioux: "As
I sit here, I can feel in this man beside me a strong desire
to know the things of the Other World. He has been sent
to learn what I know, and I will teach him." Neihardt's *Black
Elk Speaks* (1932) records the holy man's subsequent account of his visions and his efforts to act them out in life.

Neihardt has also published several volumes of poetry
about the American West. Notable among them is *A Cycle
of the West* (1949), a collection of five epic poems.

I am a Lakota of the Ogalala band. My father's name was Black Elk,
and his father before him bore the name, and the father of his
father, so that I am the fourth to bear it. He was a medicine man
and so were several of his brothers. Also, he and the great Crazy
Horse's father were cousins, having the same grandfather. My
mother's name was White Cow Sees; her father was called Refuse-
to-Go, and her mother, Plenty Eagle Feathers. I can remember my
mother's mother and her father. My father's father was killed by
the Pawnees when I was too little to know, and his mother, Red
Eagle Woman, died soon after.

I was born in the Moon of the Popping Trees (December) on
the Little Powder River in the Winter When the Four Crows
Were Killed (1863), and I was three years old when my father's
right leg was broken in the Battle of the Hundred Slain.[1] From

[1] The Fetterman Fight, commonly described as a "massacre," in which Captain Fetterman and 81 men were wiped out on Peno Creek near Fort Phil Kearney, December 21, 1866.

that wound he limped until the day he died, which was about the
time when Big Foot's band was butchered on Wounded Knee
(1890). He is buried here in these hills.

I can remember that Winter of the Hundred Slain as a man
may remember some bad dream he dreamed when he was little, but
I cannot tell just how much I heard when I was bigger and how
much I understood when I was little. It is like some fearful thing
in a fog, for it was a time when everything seemed troubled and
afraid.

I had never seen a Wasichu[2] then, and did not know what
one looked like; but every one was saying that the Wasichus were
coming and that they were going to take our country and rub us
all out and that we should all have to die fighting. It was the
Wasichus who got rubbed out in that battle, and all the people
were talking about it for a long while; but a hundred Wasichus was
not much if there were others and others without number where
those came from.

I remember once that I asked my grandfather about this. I
said: "When the scouts come back from seeing the prairie full of bison somewhere, the people say the Wasichus are coming; and when
strange men are coming to kill us all, they say the Wasichus are
coming. What does it mean?" And he said, "That they are many."

When I was older, I learned what the fighting was about that
winter and the next summer. Up on the Madison Fork the Wasichus had found much of the yellow metal that they worship and
that makes them crazy, and they wanted to have a road up
through our country to the place where the yellow metal was; but
my people did not want the road. It would scare the bison and
make them go away, and also it would let the other Wasichus come
in like a river. They told us that they wanted only to use a little
land, as much as a wagon would take between the wheels; but our
people knew better. And when you look about you now, you can
see what it was they wanted.

Once we were happy in our own country and we were seldom
hungry, for then the two-leggeds and the four-leggeds lived together like relatives, and there was plenty for them and for us. But
the Wasichus came, and they have made little islands for us and
other little islands for the four-leggeds, and always these islands are
becoming smaller, for around them surges the gnawing flood of the
Wasichu; and it is dirty with lies and greed.

A long time ago my father told me what his father told him,
that there was once a Lakota holy man, called Drinks Water, who

[2] A term used to designate the white man, but having no reference to the color
of his skin.

dreamed what was to be; and this was long before the coming of
the Wasichus. He dreamed that the four-leggeds were going back into the earth and that a strange race had woven a spider's web all
around the Lakotas. And he said: "When this happens, you shall
live in square gray houses, in a barren land, and beside those square
gray houses you shall starve." They say he went back to Mother
Earth soon after he saw this vision, and it was sorrow that killed
him. You can look about you now and see that he meant these
dirt-roofed houses we are living in, and that all the rest was true.
Sometimes dreams are wiser than waking.

And so when the soldiers came and built themselves a town
of logs there on the Piney Fork of the Powder, my people knew
they meant to have their road and take our country and maybe kill
us all when they were strong enough. Crazy Horse was only about
19 years old then, and Red Cloud was still our great chief. In the
Moon of the Changing Season (October) he called together all the
scattered bands of the Lakota for a big council on the Powder River, and when we went on the warpath against the soldiers, a horseback could ride through our villages from sunrise until the day was
above his head, so far did our camp stretch along the valley of the
river; for many of our friends, the Shyela[3] and the Blue Clouds,[4]
had come to help us fight.

And it was about when the bitten moon was delayed (last
quarter) in the Time of the Popping Trees when the hundred were
rubbed out. My friend, Fire Thunder here, who is older than I, was
in that fight and he can tell you how it was.

Fire Thunder speaks: I was 16 years old when this happened, and after the big council on the Powder we had moved over to the
Tongue River where we were camping at the mouth of Peno Creek.
There were many of us there. Red Cloud was over all of us, but the
chief of our band was Big Road. We started out on horseback just
about sunrise, riding up the creek toward the soldiers' town on the
Piney, for we were going to attack it. The sun was about half way
up when we stopped at the place where the Wasichu's road came
down a steep, narrow ridge and crossed the creek. It was a good
place to fight, so we sent some men ahead to coax the soldiers
out. While they were gone, we divided into two parts and hid in
the gullies on both sides of the ridge and waited. After a long
while we heard a shot up over the hill, and we knew the soldiers
were coming. So we held the noses of our ponies that they might
not whinny at the soldiers' horses. Soon we saw our men coming

[3] Cheyennes.
[4] Arapahoes.

back, and some of them were walking and leading their horses, so that the soldiers would think they were worn out. Then the men we had sent ahead came running down the road between us, and the soldiers on horseback followed, shooting. When they came to the flat at the bottom of the hill, the fighting began all at once. I had a sorrel horse, and just as I was going to get on him, the soldiers turned around and began to fight their way back up the hill. I had a six-shooter that I had traded for, and also a bow and arrows. When the soldiers started back, I held my sorrel with one hand and began killing them with the six-shooter, for they came close to me. There were many bullets, but there were more arrows—so many that it was like a cloud of grasshoppers all above and around the soldiers; and our people, shooting across, hit each other. The soldiers were falling all the while they were fighting back up the hill, and their horses got loose. Many of our people chased the horses, but I was not after horses; I was after Wasichus. When the soldiers got on top, there were not many of them left and they had no place to hide. They were fighting hard. We were told to crawl up on them, and we did. When we were close, some-one yelled: "Let us go! This is a good day to die. Think of the help-less ones at home!" Then we all cried, "Hoka hey!" and rushed at them. I was young then and quick on my feet, and I was one of the first to get in among the soldiers. They got up and fought very hard until not one of them was alive. They had a dog with them, and he started back up the road for the soldiers' town, howling as he ran. He was the only one left. I did not shoot at him because he looked too sweet;[5] but many did shoot, and he died full of arrows. So there was nobody left of the soldiers. Dead men and horses and wounded Indians were scattered all the way up the hill, and their blood was frozen, for a storm had come up and it was very cold and getting colder all the time. We left all the dead lying there, for the ground was solid, and we picked up our wounded and started back; but we lost most of them before we reached our camp at the mouth of the Peno. There was a big bliz-zard that night; and some of the wounded who did not die on the way, died after we got home. This was the time when Black Elk's father had his leg broken.

Black Elk continues: I am quite sure that I remember the time when my father came home with a broken leg that he got from killing so many Wasichus, and it seems that I can remember all about the battle too, but I think I could not. It must be the

[5] Because of its current colloquial usage as a vapid sentimentalism, the expression may well seem off key in the mouth of the grizzled old warrior.

fear that I remember most. All this time I was not allowed to play very far away from our tepee, and my mother would say, "If you are not good the Wasichus will get you."

We must have broken camp at the mouth of the Peno soon after the battle, for I can remember my father lying on a pony drag with bison robes all around him, like a baby, and my mother riding the pony. The snow was deep and it was very cold, and I remember sitting in another pony drag beside my father and mother, all wrapped up in fur. We were going away from where the soldiers were, and I do not know where we went, but it was west.

It was a hungry winter, for the deep snow made it hard to find the elk; and also many of the people went snowblind. We wandered a long time, and some of the bands got lost from each other. Then at last we were camping in the woods beside a creek somewhere, and the hunters came back with meat.

I think it was this same winter when a medicine man, by the name of Creeping, went around among the people curing snowblinds. He would put snow upon their eyes, and after he had sung a certain sacred song that he had heard in a dream, he would blow on the backs of their heads and they would see again, so I have heard. It was about the dragonfly that he sang, for that was where he got his power, they say.

When it was summer again we were camping on the Rosebud, and I did not feel so much afraid, because the Wasichus seemed farther away and there was peace there in the valley and there was plenty of meat. But all the boys from five or six years up were playing war. The little boys would gather together from the different bands of the tribe and fight each other with mud balls that they threw with willow sticks. And the big boys played the game called Throwing-Them-Off-Their-Horses, which is a battle all but the killing; and sometimes they got hurt. The horsebacks from the different bands would line up and charge upon each other, yelling; and when the ponies came together on the run, they would rear and flounder and scream in a big dust, and the riders would seize each other, wrestling until one side had lost all its men, for those who fell upon the ground were counted dead.

When I was older, I, too, often played this game. We were always naked when we played it, just as warriors are when they go into battle if it is not too cold, because they are swifter without clothes. Once I fell off on my back right in the middle of a bed of prickly pears, and it took my mother a long while to pick all the stickers out of me. I was still too little to play war that summer, but I can remember watching the other boys, and I thought that when we all grew up and were big together, maybe we could kill all the Wasichus or drive them far away from our country.

It was in the Moon When the Cherries Turn Black (August) that all the people were talking again about a battle, and our warriors came back with many wounded. It was The Attacking of the Wagons,[6] and it made me afraid again, for we did not win that battle as we did the other one, and there was much mourning for the dead. Fire Thunder was in that fight too, and he can tell you how it was that day.

Fire Thunder speaks: It was very bad. There is a wide flat prairie with hills around it, and in the middle of this the Wasichus had put the boxes of their wagons in a circle, so that they could keep their mules there at night. There were not many Wasichus, but they were lying behind the boxes and they shot faster than they ever shot at us before. We thought it was some new medicine of great power that they had, for they shot so fast that it was like tearing a blanket. Afterwards I learned that it was because they had new guns that they loaded from behind, and this was the first time they used these guns.[7] We came on after sunrise. There were many, many of us, and we meant to ride right over them and rub them out. But our ponies were afraid of the ring of fire the guns of the Wasichus made, and would not go over. Our women were watching us from the hills and we could hear them singing and mourning whenever the shooting stopped. We tried hard, but we could not do it, and there were dead warriors and horses piled all around the boxes and scattered over the plain. Then we left our horses in a gulch and charged on foot, but it was like green grass withering in a fire. So we picked up our wounded and went away. I do not know how many of our people were killed, but there were very many. It was bad.

Black Elk continues: I do not remember where we camped that winter but it must have been a time of peace and of plenty to eat.

Standing Bear speaks: I am four years older than Black Elk, and he and I have been good friends since boyhood. I know it was on the Powder that we camped where there were many cottonwood trees. Ponies like to eat the bark of these trees and it is good for them. That was the winter when High Shirt's mother was killed by a big

[6]The Wagon Box Fight, which took place about six miles west of Fort Phil Kearney on August 2, 1867.
[7]Breech-loading Springfields.

tree that fell on her tepee. It was a very windy night and there were noises that 'woke me, and then I heard that an old woman had been killed, and it was High Shirt's mother.

Black Elk continues: I was four years old then, and I think it must have been the next summer that I first heard the voices. It was a happy summer and nothing was afraid, because in the Moon When the Ponies Shed (May) word came from the Wasichus that there would be peace and that they would not use the road any more and that all the soldiers would go away. The soldiers did go away and their towns were torn down; and in the Moon of Falling Leaves (November), they made a treaty with Red Cloud that said our country would be ours as long as grass should grow and water flow. You can see that it is not the grass and the water that have forgotten.

Maybe it was not this summer when I first heard the voices, but I think it was, because I know it was before I played with bows and arrows or rode a horse, and I was out playing alone when I heard them. It was like somebody calling me, and I thought it was my mother, but there was nobody there. This happened more than once, and always made me afraid, so that I ran home.

It was when I was five years old that my Grandfather made me a bow and some arrows. The grass was young and I was horseback. A thunder storm was coming from where the sun goes down, and just as I was riding into the woods along a creek, there was a kingbird sitting on a limb. This was not a dream, it happened. And I was going to shoot at the kingbird with the bow my Grandfather made, when the bird spoke and said: "The clouds all over are one-sided." Perhaps it meant that all the clouds were looking at me. And then it said: "Listen! A voice is calling you!" Then I looked up at the clouds, and two men were coming there, headfirst like arrows slanting down; and as they came, they sang a sacred song and the thunder was like drumming. I will sing it for you. The song and the drumming were like this:

> Behold, a sacred voice is calling you;
> All over the sky a sacred voice is calling.

I sat there gazing at them, and they were coming from the place where the giant lives (north). But when they were very close to me, they wheeled about toward where the sun goes down, and suddenly they were geese. Then they were gone, and the rain came with a big wind and a roaring.

I did not tell this vision to any one. I liked to think about it, but I was afraid to tell it.

a tin butterfly

MARY McCARTHY (1912–   ) is the author of several
recent books, including *The Group* (1963), *Birds of America*
(1971), and *The Seventeenth Degree* (1974), a collection of
essays about the war in Vietnam. "A Tin Butterfly," the
McCarthy piece presented here, is one of the eight
autobiographical essays in her *Memories of a Catholic Girlhood* (1957), a volume that offers a revealing look at the
process of remembering and writing. McCarthy's introduction
to the book and her comments between essays provide can-
did snapshots of the writer at work.

The man we had to call Uncle Myers was no relation to us. This
was a point on which we four orphan children were very firm. He
had married our great-aunt Margaret shortly before the death of
our parents and so became our guardian while still a benedict—not
perhaps a very nice eventuality for a fat man of forty-two who has
just married an old maid with a little income to find himself summoned overnight from his home in Indiana to be the hired parent
of four children, all under seven years old.

When Myers and Margaret got us, my three brothers and me,
we were a handful; on this there were no two opinions in the
McCarthy branch of the family. The famous flu epidemic of 1918,
which had stricken our little household en route from Seattle to
Minneapolis and carried off our parents within a day of each other,
had, like all God's devices, a meritorious aspect, soon discovered by
my grandmother McCarthy: a merciful end had been put to a regi-
men of spoiling and coddling, to Japanese houseboys, iced cakes, pic-
nics, upset stomachs, diamond rings (imagine!), an ermine muff and
neckpiece, furred hats and coats. My grandmother thanked her stars
that Myers and her sister Margaret were available to step into the
breach. Otherwise, we might have had to be separated, an idea
that moistened her hooded grey eyes, or been taken over by "the

Protestants"—thus she grimly designated my grandfather Preston, a respectable Seattle lawyer of New England antecedents who, she many times declared with awful emphasis, had refused to receive a Catholic priest in his house! But our Seattle grandparents, coming on to Minneapolis for the funeral, were too broken up, she perceived, by our young mother's death to protest the McCarthy arrangements. Weeping, my Jewish grandmother (Preston, born Morganstern), still a beauty, like her lost daughter, acquiesced in the wisdom of keeping us together in the religion my mother had espoused. In my sickbed, recovering from the flu in my grandmother McCarthy's Minneapolis house, I, the eldest and the only girl, sat up and watched the other grandmother cry, dampening her exquisite black veil. I did not know that our parents were dead or that my sobbing grandmother—whose green Seattle terraces I remembered as delightful to roll down on Sundays—had just now, downstairs in my grandmother McCarthy's well-heated sun parlor, met the middle-aged pair who had come on from Indiana to undo her daughter's mistakes. I was only six years old and had just started school in a Sacred Heart convent on a leafy boulevard in Seattle before the fatal November trek back east, but I was sharp enough to see that Grandmother Preston did not belong here, in this dour sickroom, and vain enough to pride myself on drawing the inference that something had gone awry.

We four children and our keepers were soon installed in the yellow house at 2427 Blaisdell Avenue that had been bought for us by my grandfather McCarthy. It was situated two blocks away from his own prosperous dwelling, with its grandfather clock, tapestries, and Italian paintings, in a block that some time before had begun to "run down." Flanked by two-family houses, it was simply a crude box in which to stow furniture, and lives, like a warehouse; the rooms were small and brownish and for some reason dark, though I cannot think why, since the house was graced by no ornamental planting; a straight cement driveway ran up one side; in the back, there was an alley. Downstairs, there were a living room, a "den," a dining room, a kitchen, and a lavatory; upstairs, there were four bedrooms and a bathroom. The dingy wallpaper of the rooms in which we children slept was promptly defaced by us; bored without our usual toys, we amused ourselves by making figures on the walls with our wet tongues. This was our first crime, and I remember it because the violence of the whipping we got surprised us; we had not known we were doing wrong. The splotches on the walls remained through the years to fix this first whipping and the idea of badness in our minds; they stared at us in the evenings when, still bored but mute and tamed, we learned to make shadow figures on the wall—the swan, the rabbit with its ears wiggling—to while away the time.

It was this first crime, perhaps, that set Myers in his punitive mold. He saw that it was no sinecure he had slipped into. Child-less, middle-aged, he may have felt in his slow-turning mind that his inexperience had been taken advantage of by his wife's grandilo-quent sister, that the vexations outweighed the perquisites; in short, that he had been sold. This, no doubt, was how it must have really looked from where he sat—in a brown leather armchair in the den, wearing a blue work shirt, stained with sweat, open at the neck to show an undershirt and lion-blond, glinting hair on his chest. Below this were workmen's trousers of a brownish-gray material, straining at the buttons and always gaping slightly, just below the belt, to show another glimpse of underwear, of a yellow-ish white. On his fat head, frequently, with its crest of bronze cur-ly hair, were the earphones of a crystal radio set, which he some-times, briefly, in a generous mood, fitted over the grateful ears of one of my little brothers.

A second excuse for Myers' behavior is manifest in this descrip-tion. He had to contend with Irish social snobbery, which looked upon him dispassionately from four sets of green eyes and set him down as "not a gentleman." "My father was a gentleman and you're not"—what I meant by these categorical words I no longer know precisely, except that my father had had a romantic temperament and was a spendthrift; but I suppose there was also included some notion of courtesy. Our family, like many Irish Catholic new-rich families, was filled with aristocratic delusions; we children were always being told that we were descended from the kings of Ireland and that we were related to General "Phil" Sheridan, a dream of my great-aunt's. More precisely, my great-grandfather on this side had been a streetcar conductor in Chicago.

But at any rate Myers (or Meyers) Shriver (or Schreiber—the name had apparently been Americanized) was felt to be beneath us socially. Another count against him in our childish score was that he was a German, or, rather, of German descent, which made us glance at him fearfully in 1918, just after the armistice. In Minnea-polis at that time, there was great prejudice among the Irish Catholics, not only against the Protestant Germans, but against all the northern bloods and their hateful Lutheran heresy. Luther-anism to us children was, first of all, a religion for servant girls and, secondly, a sort of yellow corruption associated with original sin and with Martin Luther's tongue rotting in his mouth as God's pun-ishment. Bavarian Catholics, on the other hand, were singled out for a special regard; we saw them in an Early Christian light, bru-

nette and ringleted, like the Apostles. This was due in part to the
fame of Oberammergau and the Passion Play, and in part to the
fact that many of the clergy in our diocese were Bavarians; all
through this period I confided my sins of disobedience to a handsome, dark, young Father Elderbush. Uncle Myers, however, was a
Protestant, although, being too indolent, he did not go to
church; he was not one of us. And the discovery that we could
take refuge from him at school, with the nuns, at church, in the
sacraments, seemed to verify the ban that was on him; he was
truly outside grace. Having been impressed with the idea that our
religion was a sort of logical contagion, spread by holy books and
good example, I could never understand why Uncle Myers, bad as he
was, had not caught it; and his obduracy in remaining at home in
his den on Sundays, like a somnolent brute in its lair, seemed to
me to go against nature.

Indeed, in the whole situation there was something unnatural
and inexplicable. His marriage to Margaret, in the first place: he
was younger than his wife by three years, and much was made of this
difference by my grandmother McCarthy, his wealthy sister-in-law,
as though it explained everything in a slightly obscene way, Aunt
Margaret, née Sheridan, was a well-aged quince of forty-five, with
iron-gray hair shading into black, a stiff carriage, high-necked
dresses, unfashionable hats, a copy of *Our Sunday Visitor* always
under her arm—folded, like a flail—a tough dry skin with soft color-
less hairs on it, like dust, and furrowed and corrugated, like the
prunes we ate every day for breakfast. It could be said of her that
she meant well, and she meant especially well by Myers, all two
hundred and five pounds, dimpled double chin, and small, glinting,
gross blue eyes of him. She called him "Honeybunch," pursued him
with attentions, special foods, kisses, to which he responded with
tolerance, as though his swollen passivity had the character of a
male thrust or assertion. It was clear that he did not dislike her,
and that poor Margaret, as her sister said, was head over heels in
love with him. To us children, this honeymoon rankness was in-
comprehensible; we could not see it on either side for, quite apart
from everything else, both parties seemed to us very old, as indeed
they were, compared to our parents, who had been young and handsome. That he had married her for her money occurred to us inevitably, though it may not have been so; very likely it was his power
over her that he loved, and the power he had to make her punish
us was perhaps her strongest appeal to him. They slept in a bare,
ugly bedroom with a tall, cheap pine chiffonier on whch Myers' black
wallet and his nickels and dimes lay spread out when he was at
home—did he think to arouse our cupidity or did he suppose that

this stronghold of his virility was impregnable to our weak desires? Yet, as it happened, we did steal from him, my brother Kevin and I—rightfully, as we felt, for we were allowed no pocket money (two pennies were given us on Sunday morning to put into the collection plate) and we guessed that the money paid by our grandfather for the household found its way into Myers' wallet.

And here was another strange thing about Myers. He not only did nothing for a living but he appeared to have no history. He came from Elkhart, Indiana, but beyond this fact nobody seemed to know anything about him—not even how he had met my aunt Margaret. Reconstructed from his conversation, a picture of Elkhart emerged for us that showed it as a flat place consisting chiefly of ball parks, poolrooms, and hardware stores. Aunt Margaret came from Chicago, which consisted of the Loop, Marshall Field's, assorted priests and monsignors, and the black-and-white problem. How had these two worlds impinged? Where our family spoke freely of its relations, real and imaginary, Myers spoke of no one, not even a parent. At the very beginning, when my father's old touring car, which had been shipped on, still remained in our garage, Myers had certain seedy cronies whom he took riding in it or who simply sat in it in our driveway, as if anchored in a houseboat; but when the car went, they went or were banished. Uncle Myers and Aunt Margaret had no friends, no couples with whom they exchanged visits—only a middle-aged, black haired, small, emaciated woman with a German name and a yellowed skin whom we were taken to see one afternoon because she was dying of cancer. This protracted death had the aspect of a public execution, which was doubtless why Myers took us to it; that is, it was a spectacle and it was free, and it inspired restlessness and depression. Myers was the perfect type of rootless municipalized man who finds his pleasures in the handouts or overflow of an industrial civilization. He enjoyed standing on a curbstone, watching parades, the more nondescript the better, the Labor Day parade being his favorite, and next to that a military parade, followed by the commercial parades with floats and girls dressed in costumes; he would even go to Lake Calhoun or Lake Harriet for doll-carriage parades and competitions of children dressed as Indians. He liked bandstands, band concerts, public parks devoid of grass; skywriting attracted him; he was quick to hear of a department-store demonstration where colored bubbles were blown, advertising a soap, to the tune of "I'm Forever Blowing Bubbles," sung by a mellifluous soprano. He collected coupons and tinfoil, bundles of newspaper for the old rag-and-bone man (thus interfering seriously with our school paper drives), free samples of cheese at Donaldson's, free tickets given out by a neighborhood

movie house to the first installment of a serial—in all the years
we lived with him, we never saw a full-length movie but only those
truncated beginnings. He was also fond of streetcar rides (could the
system have been municipally owned?), soldiers' monuments, ceme-
teries, big, coarse flowers like cannas and cockscombs set in beds by
city gardeners. Museums did not appeal to him, though we did go
one night with a large crowd to see Marshal Foch on the steps of
the Art Institute. He was always weighing himself on penny weighing machines. He seldom left the house except on one of these pur-
poseless errands, or else to go to a ball game, by himself. In the winter, he spent the days at home in the den, or in the kitchen,
making candy. He often had enormous tin trays of decorated fon-
dants cooling in the cellar, which leads my brother Kevin to think
today that at one time in Myers' life he must have been a pastry
cook or a confectioner. He also liked to fashion those little figures
made of pipe cleaners that were just then coming in as favors in
the better candy shops, but Myers used old pipe cleaners, stained
yellow and brown. The bonbons, with their pecan or almond topping, that he laid out in such perfect rows were for his own use;
we were permitted to watch him set them out, but never—and
my brother Kevin confirms this—did we taste a single one.

In the five years we spent with Myers, the only candy I ever
had was bought with stolen money and then hidden in the bottom layer of my paper-doll set; the idea of stealing to buy candy
and the hiding place were both lifted from Kevin. Opening my
paper-doll box one day, I found it full of pink and white soft-sugar
candies, which it seemed to me God or the fairies had sent me in
response to my wishes and prayers, until I realized that Kevin was
stealing, and using my paper-doll box for a cache; we had so few possessions that he had no place of his own to hide things in. Underneath the mattress was too chancy, as I myself found when I tried
to secrete magazines of Catholic fiction there; my aunt, I learned,
was always tearing up the bed and turning the mattress to find
out whether you had wet it and attempted to hide your crime by
turning it over. Reading was forbidden us, except for schoolbooks,
and, for some reason, the funny papers and magazine section of the
Sunday Hearst papers, where one read about leprosy, the affairs of
Count Boni de Castellane, and a strange disease that turned
people to stone creepingly from the feet up.

This prohibition against reading was a source of scandal to the
nuns who taught me in the parochial school, and I think it was
due to their intervention with my grandmother that finally,
toward the end, I was allowed to read openly the Camp Fire Girls
series, *Fabiola*, and other books I have forgotten. Myers did not

read; before the days of the crystal set, he passed his evenings listening to the phonograph in the living room: Caruso, Harry Lauder, "Keep the Home Fires Burning," "There's a Sweet Little Nest," and "Listen to the Mocking Bird." It was his pleasure to make the four of us stand up in a line and sing to him the same tunes he had just heard on the phonograph, while he laughed at my performance, for I tried to reproduce the staccato phrasing of the sopranos, very loudly and off key. Also, he hated long words, or, rather, words that he regarded as long. One summer day, in the kitchen, when I had been ordered to swat flies, I said, "They disappear so strangely," a remark that he mimicked for years whenever he wished to humiliate me, and the worst of this torture was that I could not understand what was peculiar about the sentence, which seemed to me plain ordinary English, and, not understanding, I knew that I was in perpetual danger of exposing myself to him again.

So far as we knew, he had never been in any army, but he liked to keep smart military discipline. We had frequently to stand in line, facing him, and shout answers to his questions in chorus. "Forward *march!*" he barked after every order he gave us. The Fourth of July was the only holiday he threw himself into with geniality. Anything that smacked to him of affectation or being "stuck-up" was subject to the harshest reprisals from him, and I, being the oldest, and the one who remembered my parents and the old life best, was the chief sinner, sometimes on purpose, sometimes unintentionally.

When I was eight, I began writing poetry in school: "Father Gaughan is our dear parish priest / And he is loved from west to east." And "Alas, Pope Benedict is dead, / The sorrowing people said." Pope Benedict at that time was living, and, as far as I know, in good health; I had written this opening couplet for the rhyme and the sad idea; but then, very conveniently for me, about a year later he died, which gave me a feeling of fearsome power, stronger than a priest's power of loosing and binding. I came forward with my poem and it was beautifully copied out by our teacher and served as the school's elegy at a memorial service for the Pontiff. I dared not tell that I had had it ready in my desk. Not long afterward, when I was ten, I wrote an essay for a children's contest on "The Irish in American History," which won first the city and then the state prize. Most of my facts I had cribbed from a series on Catholics in American history that was running in *Our Sunday Visitor.* I worked on the assumption that anybody who was Catholic must be Irish, and then, for good measure, I went over the signers of the Declaration of Independence and added any name that sounded Irish to my ears. All this was clothed in rhetoric invoking "the lilies of France"—God knows why, except that I was in love with France and somehow, through Marshal MacMahon, had made Lafayette out an Irishman. I believe that even Kosciusko figured as an Irishman *de coeur*. At any rate, there was a school ceremony, at which I was presented with the city prize (twenty-five dollars, I think, or perhaps that was the state prize); my aunt was in the audience in her best mallard-feathered hat, looking, for once, proud and happy. She spoke kindly to me as we walked home, but when we came to our ugly house, my uncle silently rose from his chair, led me into the dark downstairs lavatory, which always smelled of shaving cream, and furiously beat me with the razor strop—to teach me a lesson, he said, lest I become stuck-up. Aunt Margaret did not intervene. After her first look of discomfiture, her face settled into folds of approval; she had been too soft. This was the usual tribute she paid Myers' greater discernment—she was afraid of losing his love by weakness. The money was taken, "to keep for me," and that, of course, was the end of it. Such was the fate of anything considered "much too good for her," a category that was rivaled only by its pendant, "plenty good enough."

We were beaten all the time, as a matter of course, with the hairbrush across the bare legs for ordinary occasions, and with the razor strop across the bare bottom for special occasions, like the prize-winning. It was as though these ignorant people, at sea with four frightened children, had taken a Dickens novel—*Oliver Twist*, perhaps, or *Nicholas Nickleby*—for a navigation chart. Sometimes our punishments were earned, sometimes not; they were administered gratuitously, often, as preventive medicine. I was whipped more frequently than my brothers, simply by virtue of seniority; that is, every time one of them was whipped, I was whipped also, for not having set a better example, and this was true for all four of us in a descending line. Kevin was whipped for Preston's misdeeds and for Sheridan's, and Preston was whipped for Sheridan's, while Sheridan, the baby and the favorite, was whipped only for his own. This naturally made us fear and distrust each other, and only between Kevin and myself was there a kind of uneasy alliance. When Kevin ran away, as he did on one famous occasion, I had a feeling of joy and defiance, mixed with the fear of punishment for myself, mixed with something worse, a vengeful anticipation of the whipping *he* would surely get. I suppose that the two times I ran away, his feelings were much the same—envy, awe, fear, admiration, and a certain evil thrill, collusive with my uncle, at the thought of the strop ahead. Yet, strange to say, nobody was beaten on these historic days. The culprit, when found, took refuge at my grandmother's, and a fearful hush lay over the house on Blaisdell Avenue at the thought of the monstrous daring and deceitfulness of the runaway; Uncle Myers, doubtless, was shaking in his boots at the prospect of explanations to the McCarthy family council. The three who remained at home were sentenced to spend the day upstairs, in strict silence. But if my uncle's impartial application of punishment served to make us each other's enemies very often, it did nothing to establish discipline, since we had no incentive to behave well, not knowing when he might be punished for something we had not done or even for something that by ordinary standards would be considered good. We knew not when we would offend, and what I learned from this, in the main, was a policy of lying and concealment; for several years after we were finally liberated, I was a problem liar.

Despite Myers' quite justified hatred of the intellect, of reading and education (for he was right—it *was* an escape from him), my uncle, like all dictators, had one book that he enjoyed. It was *Uncle Remus,* in a red cover—a book I detested—which he read aloud to us in his den over and over again in the evenings. It seemed to me that this reduction of human life to the level of talking animals and this corruption of language to dialect gave my uncle some very personal relish. He knew I hated it and he rubbed it in, trotting my brother Sheridan on his knee as he dwelt on some exploit of Br'er Fox's with many chuckles and repetitions. In *Uncle Remus,* he had his hour, and to this day I cannot read anything in dialect or any fable without some degree of repugnance.

A distinction must be made between my uncle's capricious brutality and my aunt's punishments and repressions, which seem to have been dictated to her by her conscience. My aunt was not a bad woman; she was only a believer in method. Since it was the family theory that we had been spoiled, she undertook energetically to remedy this by quasi-scientific means. Everything we did proceeded according to schedule and in line with an over-all plan. She was very strong, naturally, on toilet-training, and everything in our life was directed toward the after-breakfast session on "the throne." Our whole diet—not to speak of the morning orange juice with castor oil in it that was brought to us on the slightest pretext of "paleness"—was centered around this levee. We had prunes every day for breakfast, and corn-meal mush, Wheatena, or farina, which I had to eat plain, since by some medical whim it had been decided that milk was bad for me. The rest of our day's menu consisted of parsnips, turnips, rutabagas, carrots, boiled potatoes, boiled cabbage, onions, Swiss chard, kale, and so on; most green vegetables, apparently, were too dear to be appropriate for us, though I think that, beyond this, the family had a sort of moral affinity for the root vegetable, stemming, perhaps, from everything fibrous, tenacious, watery, and knobby in the Irish peasant stock. Our desserts were rice pudding, farina pudding, overcooked custard with little air holes in it, prunes, stewed red plums, rhubarb, stewed pears, stewed dried peaches. We must have had meat, but I have only the most indistinct recollection of pale lamb stews in which the carrots outnumbered the pieces of white, fatty meat and bone and gristle; certainly we did not have steak or roasts or turkey or fried chicken, but perhaps an occasional boiled fowl was served to us with its vegetables (for I do remember the neck, shrunken in its collar of puckered skin, coming to me as my portion, and the fact that if you sucked on it, you could draw out an edible white cord), and doubtless there was meat loaf and beef stew. There was no ice cream, cake, pie, or butter, but on rare mornings we had johnnycake or large woolly pancakes with Karo syrup.

We were not allowed to leave the table until every morsel was finished, and I used to sit through half a dark winter afternoon staring at the cold carrots on my plate, until, during one short snowy period, I found that I could throw them out the back window if I raised it very quietly. (Unfortunately, they landed on the tar roofing of a sort of shed next to the back porch, and when the snow finally melted, I met a terrible punishment.) From time to time, we had a maid, but the food was so wretched that we could not keep "girls," and my aunt took over the cooking, with sour enthusiasm, assisted by her sister, Aunt Mary, an arthritic, white-haired, wan, devout old lady who had silently joined our household and earned her keep by helping with the sewing and dusting and who tried to stay out of Myers' way. With her gentle help, Aunt Margaret managed to approximate, on a small scale, the conditions prevailing in the orphan asylums we four children were always dreaming of being let into.

Myers did not share our diet. He sat at the head of the table, with a napkin around his neck, eating the special dishes that Aunt Margaret prepared for him and sometimes putting a spoonful on the plate of my youngest brother, who sat next to him in a high chair. At breakfast, he had corn flakes or shredded wheat with bananas or fresh sliced peaches, thought by us to be a Lucullan treat. At dinner, he had pigs' feet and other delicacies I cannot remember. I only know that he shared them with Sheridan, who was called Herdie, as my middle brother was called Pomps, or Pompsie—childish affectionate nicknames inherited from our dead parents that sounded damp as gravemold in my aunt Margaret's flannelly voice, which reminded one of a chest rag dipped in asafetida to ward off winter throat ailments.

In addition to such poultices, and mustard plasters, and iron pills to fortify our already redoubtable diet, we were subject to other health fads of the period and of my great-aunt's youth. I have told elsewhere of how we were put to bed at night with our mouths sealed with adhesive tape to prevent mouth-breathing; ether, which made me sick, was used to help pull the tape off in the morning, but a grimy, gray, rubbery remainder was usually left on our upper lips and in the indentations of our pointed chins when we set off for school in our heavy outer clothes, long underwear, black stockings, and high shoes. Our pillows were taken away from us; we were given a sulphur-and-molasses spring tonic, and in the winter, on Saturdays and Sundays, we were made to stay out three hours in the morning and three in the afternoon, regardless of the temperature. We had come from a mild climate, in Seattle, and at fifteen, twenty, or twenty-four below zero we could not play, even if we had had something to play with, and used simply to stand in the snow, crying, and beating sometimes on the window with our frozen mittens, till my aunt's angry face would appear there and drive us away.

No attempt was made to teach us a sport, winter or summer; we were forbidden to slide in Fairoaks Park nearby, where in winter the poorer children made a track of ice down a hill, which they flashed down sitting or standing, but I loved this daring sport and did it anyway, on the way home from school, until one day I tore my shabby coat on the ice and was afraid to go home. A kind woman named Mrs. Corkerey, who kept a neighborhood candy store across from our school, mended it for me, very skillfully, so that my aunt never knew; nevertheless, sliding lost its lure for me, for I could not risk a second rip.

The neighbors were often kind, surreptitiously, and sometimes they "spoke" to the sisters at the parochial school, but everyone, I think, was afraid of offending my grandparents, who diffused an air of wealth and pomp when they entered their pew at St. Stephen's Church on Sunday. Mrs. Corkerey, in fact, got herself and me in trouble by feeding me in the mornings in her kitchen above the candy store when I stopped to pick up her daughter, Clarazita, who was in my class. I used to lie to Mrs. Corkerey and say that I had had no breakfast (when the truth was that I was merely hungry), and she went to the nuns finally in a state of indignation. The story was checked with my aunt, and I was obliged to admit that I had lied and that they did feed me, which must have disillusioned Mrs. Cockerey forever with the pathos of orphaned childhood. It was impossible for me to explain to her then that what I needed was her pity and her fierce choleric heart. Another neighbor, Mr. Harrison, a well-to-do old bachelor or widower who lived in the corner house, used sometimes to take us bathing, and it was thanks to his lessons that I learned to swim—a strange anti-quated breast stroke—copied from an old man with a high-necked bathing suit and a beard. In general, we were not supposed to have anything to do with the neighbors or with other children. It was a rule that other children were not allowed to come into our yard or we to go into theirs, nor were we permitted to walk to school with another boy or girl. But since we were in school most of the day, five days a week, our guardians could not prevent us from mak-ing friends despite them; other children were, in fact, very much attracted to us, pitying us for our woebegone condition and res-pecting us because we were thought to be rich. Our grandmother's chauffeur, Frank, in her winter Pierce-Arrow and summer Locomo-bile, was well known in the neighborhood, waiting outside church on Sunday to take her home from Mass. Sometimes we were taken, too, and thus our miserable clothes and underfed bodies were asso-ciated with high financial status and became a sort of dubious priv-ilege in the eyes of our classmates.

We both had enviable possessions and did not have them. In the closet in my bedroom, high on the top shelf, beyond my reach even standing on a chair, was a stack of cardboard doll boxes, con-taining wonderful French dolls, dressed by my Seattle grandmother in silks, laces, and satins, with crepe-de-Chine underwear and shoes with high heels. These and other things were sent us every year at Christmastime, but my aunt had decreed that they were all too good for us, so they remained in their boxes and wrappings, *verboten*, except on the rare afternoon, perhaps once in a twelve-month or so, when a relation or a friend of the family would come through from the West, and then down would come the dolls, out would come the baseball gloves and catchers' masks and the watches and the shiny cars and the doll houses, and we would be set to playing with these things on the floor of the living room while the visitor tenderly looked on. As soon as the visitor left, bearing a good re-port of our household, the dolls and watches and cars would be whisked away, to come out again for the next emergency. If we had been clever, we would have refused this bait and paraded our misery, but we were too simple to do anything but seize the moment and play out a whole year's playtime in this gala hour and a half. Such techniques, of course, are common in concentration camps and pen-al institutions, where the same sound calculation of human nature is made. The prisoners snatch at their holiday; they trust their guards and the motto *"Carpe diem"* more than they do the strangers who have come to make the inspection. Like all people who have been mistreated, we were wary of being taken in; we felt uneasy about these visitors—Protestants from Seattle—who might be much worse than our uncle and aunt. The latter's faults, at any rate, we knew. Moreover, we had been subjected to propaganda: we had been threatened with the Seattle faction, time and again, by our uncle, who used to jeer and say to us, *"They"*d make you toe the chalk line."

The basis, I think, of my aunt's program for us was in truth totalitarian: she was idealistically bent on destroying our privacy. She imagined herself as enlightened in comparison with our parents, and a super-ideal of health, cleanliness, and discipline softened in her own eyes the measures she applied to attain it. A nature not unkindly was warped by bureaucratic zeal and by her subservience to her husband, whose masterful autocratic hand cut through our nonsense like a cleaver. The fact that our way of life resembled that of an orphan asylum was not a mere coincidence; Aunt Margaret strove purposefully toward a corporate goal. Like most heads of institutions, she longed for the eyes of Argus. To the best of her ability, she saw to it that nothing was hidden from her. Even her health measures had this purpose. The aperients we were continually dosed with guaranteed that our daily processes were open to her inspection, and the monthly medical checkup assured her, by means of stethoscope and searchlight and tongue depressor, that nothing was happening inside us to which she was not privy. Our letters to Seattle were written under her eye, and she scrutinized our homework sharply, though her arithmetic, spelling, and grammar were all very imperfect. We prayed, under supervision, for a prescribed list of people. And if we were forbidden companions, candy, most toys, pocket money, sports, reading, entertainment, the aim was not to make us suffer but to achieve efficiency. It was simpler to interdict other children than to inspect all the children with whom we might want to play. From the standpoint of efficiency, our lives, in order to be open, had to be empty; the books we might perhaps read, the toys we might play with figured in my aunt's mind, no doubt, as what the housewife calls "dust catchers"— around these distractions, dirt might accumulate. The inmost folds of consciousness, like the belly button, were regarded by her as unsanitary. Thus, in her spiritual outlook, my aunt was an early functionalist.

Like all systems, my aunt's was, of course, imperfect. Forbidden to read, we told stories, and if we were kept apart, we told them to ourselves in bed. We made romances out of our schoolbooks, even out of the dictionary, and read digests of novels in the *Book of Knowledge* at school. My uncle's partiality for my youngest brother was a weakness in him, as was my aunt Mary's partiality for me. She was supposed to keep me in her room, sewing on squares of cheap cotton, making handkerchiefs with big, crude, ugly hems, and ripping them out and making them over again, but though she had no feeling for art or visual beauty (she would not even teach me to darn, which is an art, or to do embroidery, as the nuns did later on, in the convent), she liked to talk of the old days in Chicago and to read sensational religious fiction in a magazine called the *Extension,* which sometimes she let me take to my room, with a caution against being caught. And on the Sunday walks that my uncle headed, at the end of an interminable streetcar ride, during which my bigger brothers had to scrunch down to pass for under six, there were occasions on which he took us (in military order) along a wooded path, high above the Mississippi River, and we saw late-spring harebells and, once, a coral-pink snake. In Minnehaha Park, a favorite resort, we were allowed to play on the swings and to examine the other children riding on the ponies or on a little scenic railway. Uncle Myers always bought himself a box of Cracker Jack, which we watched him eat and delve into, to find the little favor at the bottom—a ritual we deeply envied, for, though we sometimes had popcorn at home (Myers enjoyed popping it) and even, once or twice, homemade popcorn balls with molasses, we had never had more than a taste of this commercial Cracker Jack, with peanuts in it, which seemed to us the more valuable because *he* valued it and would often come home eating a box he had bought at a ball game. But one Sunday, Uncle Myers, in full, midsummer mood, wearing his new pedometer, bought my brother Sheridan a whole box for himself.

Naturally, we envied Sheridan—the only blond among us, with fair red-gold curls, while the rest of us were all pronounced brunets, with thick black brows and lashes—as we watched him, the lucky one, munch the sticky stuff and fish out a painted tin butterfly with a little pin on it at the bottom. My brothers clamored around him, but I was too proud to show my feelings. Sheridan was then about six years old, and this butterfly immediately became his most cherished possession—indeed, one of the few he had. He carried it about the house with him all the next week, clutched in his hand or pinned to his shirt, and my two other brothers followed him, begging him to be allowed to play with it, which slightly disgusted me, at the age of ten, for I knew that I was too sophisticated to care for tin butterflies and I felt in this whole affair the instigation of my uncle. He was relishing my brothers' performance and saw to it, strictly, that Sheridan clung to his rights in the butterfly and did not permit anybody to touch it. The point about this painted tin butterfly was not its intrinsic value; it was the fact that it was virtually the only toy in the house that had not been, so to speak, socialized, but belonged privately to one individual. Our other playthings—a broken-down wooden swing, an old wagon, a dirty sandbox, and perhaps a fire engine or so and some defaced blocks and twisted second-hand train tracks in the attic—were held by us all in common, the velocipedes we had brought with us from Seattle having long ago foundered, and the skipping rope, the jacks, the few marbles, and the pair of rusty roller skates that were given us being decreed to be the property of all. Hence, for a full week this butterfly excited passionate emotions, from which I held myself stubbornly apart, refusing even to notice it, until one afternoon, at about four o'clock, while I was doing my weekly chore of dusting the woodwork, my white-haired aunt Mary hurried softly into my room and, closing the door behind her, asked whether I had seen Sheridan's butterfly.

The topic wearied me so much that I scarcely lifted my head, answering no, shortly, and going on with my dusting. But Aunt Mary was gently persistent: Did I know that he had lost it? Would I help her look for it? This project did not appeal to me but in response to some faint agitation in her manner, something almost pleading, I put down my dustcloth and helped her. We went all over the house, raising carpets, looking behind curtains, in the kitchen cupboards, in the Victrola, everywhere but in the den, which was closed, and in my aunt's and uncle's bedroom. Somehow— I do not know why—I did not expect to find the butterfly, partly, I imagine, because I was indifferent to it and partly out of the fatalism that all children have toward lost objects, regarding them as irretrievable, vanished into the flux of things. At any rate I was right: we did not find it and I went back to my dusting, vindicated. Why should *I* have to look for Sheridan's stupid butterfly, which he ought to have taken better care of? "Myers is upset," said Aunt Mary, still hovering, uneasy and diffident, in the doorway. I made a slight face, and she went out, plaintive, remonstrant, and sighing, in her pale, high-necked, tight-buttoned dress.

It did not occur to me that I was suspected of stealing this toy, even when Aunt Margaret, five minutes later, burst into my room and ordered me to come and look for Sheridan's butterfly. I protested that I had already done so, but she paid my objections no heed and seized me roughly by the arm. "Then do it again, Miss, and mind that you find it." Her voice was rather hoarse and her whole furrowed iron-gray aspect somewhat tense and disarrayed, yet I had the impression that she was not angry with me but with something in outer reality—what one would now call fate or contingency. When I had searched again, lackadaisically, and again found nothing, she joined in with vigor, turning everything upside down. We even went into the den, where Myers was sitting, and searched all around him, while he watched us with an ironical expression, filling his pipe from a Bull Durham sack. We found nothing, and Aunt Margaret led me upstairs to my room, which I ransacked while she stood and watched me. All at once, when we had finished with my bureau drawers and my closet, she appeared to give up. She sighed and bit her lips. The door cautiously opened and Aunt Mary came in. The two sisters looked at each other and at me. Margaret shrugged her shoulders. "She hasn't got it, I do believe," she said.

She regarded me then with a certain relaxing of her thick wrinkles, and her heavy-skinned hand, with its wedding ring, came down on my shoulder. "Uncle Myers thinks you took it," she said in a rusty whisper, like a spy or a scout. The consciousness of my own innocence, combined with a sense of being let into the confederacy of the two sisters, filled me with excitement and self-importance. "But I didn't, Aunt Margaret," I began proclaiming, making the most of my moment. "What would I want with his silly old butterfly?" The two sisters exchanged a look. "That's what I said, Margaret!" exclaimed old Aunt Mary sententiously. Aunt Margaret frowned; she adjusted a bone hairpin in the coiled rings of her unbecoming coiffure. "Mary Therese," she said to me, solemnly, "if you know anything about the butterfly, if one of your brothers took it, tell me now. If we don't find it, I'm afraid Uncle Myers will have to punish you." "He *can't* punish me, Aunt Margaret," I insisted, full of righteousness. "Not if I didn't do it and *you* don't think I did it." I looked up at her, stagily trustful, resting gingerly on this solidarity that had suddenly appeared between us. Aunt Mary's pale old eyes watered. "You mustn't let Myers punish her, Margaret, if you don't think she's done wrong." They both glanced up at the Murillo Madonna that was hanging on my stained wall. Intelligence passed between them and I was sure that, thanks to our Holy Mother, Aunt Margaret would save me. "Go along, Mary Therese," she said hoarsely. "Get yourself ready for dinner. And don't you say a word of this to your uncle when you come downstairs."

When I went down to dinner, I was exultant, but I tried to hide it. Throughout the meal, everyone was restrained; Herdie was in the dumps about his butterfly, and Preston and Kevin were silent, casting covert looks at me. My brothers, apparently, were wondering how I had avoided punishment, as the eldest, if for no other reason. Aunt Margaret was rather flushed, which improved her appearance slightly. Uncle Myers had a cunning look, as though events would prove him right. He patted Sheridan's golden head from time to time and urged him to eat. After dinner, the boys filed into the den behind Uncle Myers, and I helped Aunt Margaret clear the table. We did not have to do the dishes, for at this time there was a "girl" in the kitchen. As we were lifting the white tablecloth and the silence pad, we found the butterfly — pinned to the silence pad, right by my place.

My hash was settled then, though I did not know it. I did not catch the significance of its being found at *my* place. To Margaret, however, this was grimly conclusive. She had been too "easy," said her expression; once again Myers had been right. Myers went through the formality of interrogating each of the boys in turn ("No, sir," "No, sir," "No, sir") and even, at my insistence, of calling in the Swedish girl from the kitchen. Nobody knew how the butterfly had got there. It had not been there before dinner, when the girl set the table. My judges therefore concluded that I had had it hidden on my person and had slipped it under the tablecloth at dinner, when nobody was looking. This unanimous verdict maddened me, at first simply as an indication of stupidity—how could they be so dense as to imagine that I would hide it by my own place, where it was sure to be discovered? I did not really believe that I was going to be punished on such ridiculous evidence, yet even I could form no theory of how the butterfly had come there. My first base impulse to accuse the maid was scoffed out of my head by reason. What would a grownup want with a silly six-year-old's toy? And the very unfairness of the condemnation that rested on me made me reluctant to transfer it to one of my brothers. I kept supposing that the truth somehow would out, but the interrogation suddenly ended and every eye avoided mine.

Aunt Mary's dragging step went up the stairs, the boys were ordered to bed, and then, in the lavatory, the whipping began. Myers beat me with the strop, until his lazy arm tired; whipping is hard work for a fat man, out of condition, with a screaming, kicking, wriggling ten-year-old in his grasp. He went out and heaved himself, panting, into his favorite chair and I presumed that the whipping was over. But Aunt Margaret took his place, striking harder than he, with a hairbrush, in a businesslike, joyless way, repeating, "Say you did it, Mary Therese, say you did it." As the blows fell and I did not give in, this formula took on an intercessory note, like a prayer. It was clear to me that she was begging me to surrender and give Myers his satisfaction, for my own sake, so that the whipping could stop. When I finally cried out "All right!" she dropped the hairbrush with a sigh of relief; a new doubt of my guilt must have been visiting her, and my confession set everything square. She led me in to my uncle, and we both stood facing him, as Aunt Margaret, with a firm but not ungentle hand on my shoulder, whispered, "Just tell him, 'Uncle Myers, I did it,' and you can go to bed." But the sight of him, sprawling in his leather chair, complacently waiting for this, was too much for me. The words froze on my tongue. I could not utter them to *him*. Aunt Margaret urged me on, reproachfully, as though I were breaking our compact, but as I looked straight at him and assessed his ugly nature, I burst into yells. "I didn't! I didn't!" I gasped, between screams. Uncle Myers shot a vindictive look at his wife, as though he well understood that there had been collusion between us. He ordered me back to the dark lavatory and symbolically rolled up his sleeve. He laid on the strop decisively, but this time I was beside myself, and when Aunt Margaret hurried in and tried to reason with me, I could only answer with wild cries as Uncle Myers, gasping also, put the strop back on its hook. "You take her," he articulated, but Aunt Margaret's hairbrush this time was perfunctory, after the first few angry blows that punished me for having disobeyed her. Myers did not take up the strop again; the whipping ended, whether from fear of the neighbors or of Aunt Mary's frail presence upstairs or sudden guilty terror, I do not know; perhaps simply because it was past my bedtime.

I finally limped up to bed, with a crazy sense of inner victory, like a saint's, for I had not recanted, despite all they had done or could do to me. It did not occur to me that I had been unchristian in refusing to answer a plea from Aunt Margaret's heart and conscience. Indeed, I rejoiced in the knowledge that I had *made* her continue to beat me long after she must have known that I was innocent; this was her punishment for her condonation of Myers. The next morning, when I opened my eyes on the Murillo Madonna and the Baby Stuart, my feeling of triumph abated; I was afraid of what I had done. But throughout that day and the next, they did not touch me. I walked on air, incredulously and, no doubt, somewhat pompously, seeing myself as a figure from legend: my strength was *as* the strength of ten because my *heart* was pure! Afterward, I was beaten, in the normal routine way, but the question of the butterfly was closed forever in that house.

In my mind, there was, and still is, a connection between the butterfly and our rescue, by our Protestant grandfather, which took place the following year, in the fall or early winter. Already defeated, in their own view, or having ceased to care what became of us, our guardians, for the first time, permitted two of us, my brother Kevin and me, to be alone with this strict, kindly lawyer, as we walked the two blocks between our house and our grandfather McCarthy's. In the course of our walk, between the walls of an early snow, we told Grandpa Preston everything, overcoming our fears and fixing our minds on the dolls, the baseball gloves, and the watches. Yet, as it happened, curiously enough, albeit with a certain aptness, it was not the tale of the butterfly or the other atrocities that chiefly impressed him as he followed our narration with precise legal eyes but the fact that I was not wearing my glasses. I was being punished for breaking them in a fall on the school playground by having to go without; and I could not see why my account of this should make him flush up with anger—to me it was a great relief to be free of those disfiguring things. But he shifted his long, lantern jaw and, settling our hands in his, went straight as a writ up my grandfather McCarthy's front walk. Hence it was on a question of health that this good American's alarms finally alighted; the rest of what we poured out to him he either did not believe or feared to think of, lest he have to deal with the problem of evil.

On health grounds, then, we were separated from Uncle Myers, who disappeared back into Elkhart with his wife and Aunt Mary. My brothers were sent off to the sisters in a Catholic boarding school, with the exception of Sheridan, whom Myers was permitted to bear away with him, like a golden trophy. Sheridan's stay, however, was of short duration. Very soon, Aunt Mary died, followed by Aunt Margaret, followed by Uncle Myers; within five years, still in the prime of life, they were all gone, one, two, three, like ninepins. For me, a new life began, under a happier star. Within a few weeks after my Protestant grandfather's visit, I was sitting in a compartment with him on the train, watching the Missouri River go westward to its source, wearing my white-gold wrist watch and a garish new red hat, a highly nervous child, fanatical against Protestants, who, I explained to Grandpa Preston, all deserved to be burned at the stake. In the dining car, I ordered greedily, lamb chops, pancakes, sausages, and then sat, unable to eat them. "Her eyes," observed the waiter, "are bigger than her stomach."

Six or seven years later, on one of my trips east to college, I stopped in Minneapolis to see my brothers, who were all together now, under the roof of a new and more indulgent guardian, my uncle Louis, the handsomest and youngest of the McCarthy uncles. All the old people were dead; my grandmother McCarthy, but recently passed away, had left a fund to erect a chapel in her name in Texas, a state with which she had no known connection. Sitting in the twilight of my uncle Louis' screened porch, we sought a common ground for our reunion and found it in Uncle Myers. It was then that my brother Preston told me that on the famous night of the butterfly, he had seen Uncle Myers steal into the dining room from the den and lift the tablecloth, with the tin butterfly in his hand.

AFTERWORD

A mother pinches the arm of her young child as their nation's president rides by in a limousine, and she says almost harshly, "Remember this!" Or a normally shy man visiting Washington, D.C., hands his camera to a stranger and asks to be photographed in front of the Lincoln Memorial. Both these acts reflect a widely shared concern with memory. To forget an important experience is to think and act, consciously, at least, as though it never happened. When a mother pinches her child to help him remember the day he saw the president, she obviously believes it important to save the memory from oblivion. We might quarrel with her choice of memories and her method, but all of us know of events, people, and places we want never to forget. That is surely one reason we take photographs, relate stories, and, in lesser numbers, keep journals and diaries. Indeed, one objective of early education, even in our age of computerized memory banks, is to help children select significant parts of their experience to remember.

Memory is especially important to a writer. It is sometimes said that great writers have pipelines to their childhoods, that they have special powers for recalling the sights, sounds, smells, and emotions of their early lives. And many good writers tell of sitting down to write about an event and discovering that they remember much more about it than they thought possible. The process of writing about a memory sometimes has the effect of bringing it alive in the writer's mind.

There is another, more mysterious, aspect of the memory process; namely, that a writer sometimes finds important blank spots in a memory. Mary McCarthy acknowledges several such blank spots in *Memories of a Catholic Girlhood,* and she tells of filling them with information gathered from her brothers and other fairly reliable sources. Sometimes, however, she suspects that some of these memory holes have been filled by means of her imagination. Commenting on "A Tin Butterfly," for example, she says: "An awful suspicion occurred to me as I was reading it over the other day. I suddenly remembered that in college I had started writing a play on this subject. Could the idea that Uncle Myers put the butterfly at my place have been suggested to me by teacher?" McCarthy tells then of having asked her brothers about the tin butterfly episode. When they proved as uncertain as she, she realized that she would probably never know whether she had remembered or imagined that her Uncle Myers was so obviously a villain.

Such a doubt might torture a historian, but for the autobiographical writer it is not a great problem. We know our minds filter past experiences, and for various reasons we are able to recall only part of what we have known. To admit that fact, as McCarthy and Black Elk do, often makes those details that can be dredged up out of the past especially convincing. When we speak of *honesty* and *candor* in autobiographical writing, we are not primarily concerned with factual accuracy; rather, we are conveying our belief that the writer has attempted to tell as fully as possible what he knows of his past, including doubts as well as certainties.

This belief is particularly important when the writer's world is unfamiliar to us, as the childhood world of Camara Laye's is to most of his readers. It is a measure of his skill as a narrator that we can become engaged in the experiences he describes. There are a number of ways he might have handled the memories he includes in the opening chapter of *Dark Child*. His attitude toward the memory of the snake visiting his father, for example, was probably tinged with skepticism by the time Laye wrote about it; but, although he might have focused on some of his more recent thoughts about this childhood experience, Laye chose to present it unequivocally without analysis or later doubts. Laye's ability to recall rather long speeches by his father may seem farfetched; but it can be explained, in part, by the fact that he comes from a culture in which oral tradition and memory play much more important roles than they do in most societies.

But in all societies, and for writers and nonwriters, memories have at least one major role: they serve as bridges between people. Consider this example: two middle-aged Americans on a tour of Paris meet and find they have both lived in Kingdom City, Missouri. It is surely not difficult to imagine that, in their delight at this discovery, they live imaginatively for a time more intensely in their shared memories of Kingdom City than in their experience of Paris. Perhaps they spend an afternoon talking and find something that feels like instant friendship. Observing that conversation—and experiences like it are not uncommon among travelers—a psychologist might suggest that it grew out of rather special conditions. The tourists were probably feeling lonely and uncertain in Paris, uncomfortably alien in their new environment. Perhaps they had even observed other American tourists who seemed to be much more at ease than they were. The discovery of someone interested in stories about Kingdom City, then, was a welcome antidote for a sense of loneliness and isolation: contemporaries who have lived in Kingdom City, the tourists probably sensed, must have much in common.

This situation is not so different from that of a writer who wants to communicate well. He must somehow convince his reader that they have something in common, and vividly described early memories can help to make that point. A paragraph from Mark Sullivan's *The Education of an American* offers a clear example:

Next to scents, my most vivid early memories are of sounds: the whir of the mowing machine in outlying fields in June; the two-note *clunk, clank* of the whetstone against the scythe, which we kept for mowing corners of the field and bits of hillside too steep for the mowing machine. Another two-note sound was of the ax cutting down a tree in the woods, a low-pitched *chug* from the level stroke that made the bottom of the incision, a higher-pitched note made by the downward chop—both followed, after a half-hour of chopping, by a moment of silence, having the effect of suspense, by which I knew my father had stepped hurriedly back, and then the swish of the falling tree against the twigs and limbs of its neighbors, the sound gathering volume and tempo until it became a roar, climaxing in a mighty crash as the tree struck the ground. The two-pitched whine of the crosscut saw, a high note as the faster of the two sawyers drew the blade toward him, a lower note made by the slower worker.

I did not grow up on a farm, as Mark Sullivan did, but his description of sounds from his childhood gives me a sense of shared experience nevertheless. He helps me to recall a time when simple sensory experiences had a clarity and meaning they seldom have for me any longer. He accomplishes this in part by relating his memory in compelling detail. For instance, recounting the same memory, most of us would probably describe the sounds of tree cutting much more sparsely than Sullivan does, if we mentioned them at all. Sullivan, in one sentence, distinguishes a sequence of sounds and joins them to a picture in his mind's eye, the picture the sounds created for the little boy as he imagined his father in the woods. That is how sensory experiences often come to us in childhood—as news of what might be happening in a rather mysterious, often inaccessible, adult world. For example, due probably to Sullivan's influence, I now recall that a drawn-out staccato of hacking coughs produced by our next door neighbor sounded through the window of my bedroom nearly every morning when I was seven or eight. I cannot remember ever actually seeing the man cough, but I have a picture of him in my mind—red-faced in his sleeveless, yellowed undershirt, angered by the pain but proud to be awake and coughing so loudly before most of those around him were out of bed. That is the way sounds used to strike my imagination, and Sullivan's ability to describe a similar memory in detail helps to bridge the gulf between his world and mine.

Suggested writing assignments

1. Choose a memory from your early childhood and use it as the subject for a short essay. The fact that you remember a particular happening in some detail can be reason enough to choose it. Do not worry very much about whether you understand the significance of the memory in your own development; both Camara Laye, in the excerpt from *Dark Child,* and Dylan Thomas, in "Reminiscences of Childhood," are fascinated by memories they cannot understand. As you work the memory out in all the fullness you can recall, consider how you happen to remember it. Have you discussed it with others who were there? Did your parents ever tell you about it, or have you seen photographs that might have helped to fix it in your mind? Be sure to acknowledge any large blank spots in the memory.

2. Most good storytellers have unusually good memories, and it is often interesting to ask such a person to recall a very early memory in some detail. Make such an interview the basis for an essay. Remember that it is important to find an interviewing technique with which you and your subject are comfortable. A tape recorder has obvious advantages, but they are diminished if either the interviewer or his subject is bothered by its presence. Taking notes unobtrusively is an alternative method; John G. Neihardt based *Black Elk Speaks* on shorthand notes taken by his daughter during the many days that Black Elk told his story. But sometimes any means of transcription visible to the subject is a handicap. When Truman Capote researched *In Cold Blood,* he trained himself to talk with people without taking notes and to retain even long conversations in memory until it was convenient to put them on paper.

3. Set aside two hours when you expect to be undisturbed, and simply allow yourself to write whatever comes into your mind. It is possible to learn a number of things about writing in this experiment. You will probably discover that you have a built-in censor that often convinces you to refrain from writing much of what you think, including some very effective prose. If you can bypass that censor occasionally and capture language and details you were tempted to discard, you may well find some memories worth exploring in a more fully developed essay. Upon reading through a passage of their "uncensored," or "automatic," writing, a good many students find that their experimental prose is more colorful and more engaging than they ever thought possible.

three: person and place

from

the armies
of the night

NORMAN MAILER (1923 –   ) assured himself of a place
in American literature with the publication of his war novel
The Naked and the Dead (1948). Since then he has become
a controversial author and celebrity, alternately outraging and
then endearing himself to the American literary public.
Increasingly, he is referred to as a journalist rather than a
novelist, for his recent literary works map his journey through
an astonishing range of modern life. *The Armies of the Night*
(1968), a Pulitzer Prize-winning book and the source of the
following excerpt, is Mailer's profoundly autobiographical
statement about the 1967 March on the Pentagon. Among
his many other published works are *The Deer Park* (1955),
Advertisements for Myself (1959), *An American Dream*
(1965), and *Marilyn* (1973).

Since the parking lot was huge as five football fields, and just
about empty, for they were the first arrivals, the terminus of the
March was without drama. Nor was the Pentagon even altogether
visible from the parking lot. Perhaps for that reason, a recollection
returned to Mailer of that instant (alive as an open nerve) when
they had seen it first, walking through the field, just after the
March had left the road on the Virginia side of the Potomac;
there, topping a rise, it appeared, huge in the near distance, not
attractive. Somehow, Mailer had been anticipating it would look
more impressive than its pictures, he was always expecting corporation land to surprise him with a bit of wit, an unexpected turn
of architectural grace—it never did. The Pentagon rose like an anom-
aly of the sea from the soft Virginia fields (they were crossing a
park), its pale yellow walls reminiscent of some plastic plug coming

out of the hole made in flesh by an unmentionable operation. There, it sat, geometrical aura complete, isolated from anything in nature surrounding it. Eras ago had corporation land begun by putting billboards on the old post roads?—now they worked to clean them up—just as the populace had finally succeeded in depositing comfortable amounts of libido on highway signs, gasoline exhaust, and oil-stained Jersey macadam—now corporation land, here named Government, took over state preserves, straightened crooked narrow roads, put up government buildings, removed unwelcome signs till the young Pop eye of Art wept for unwelcome signs—where are our old friends?—and corporation land would succeed, if it hadn't yet, in making nature look like an outdoor hospital, and the streets of U.S. cities, grace of Urban Renewal, would be difficult to distinguish when drunk from pyramids of packaged foods in the aisles of a supermarket.

For years he had been writing about the nature of totalitarianism, its need to render populations apathetic, its instrument—the destruction of mood. Mood was forever being sliced, cut, stamped, ground, excised, or obliterated; mood was a scent which rose from the acts and calms of nature, and totalitarianism was a deodorant to nature. Yes, and by the logic of this metaphor, the Pentagon looked like the five-sided tip on the spout of a spray can to be used under the arm, yes, the Pentagon was spraying the deodorant of its presence all over the fields of Virginia.

The North Parking Lot was physically separated from the Pentagon by a wide four-lane highway. Corporate wisdom had been at work—they might have been rattling about in the vast and empty parking lot of a modern stadium when no game is being played. Being among the first hundred to arrive, they found themselves in a state of confusion. No enemy was visible, nor much organization. In the reaches of the parking lot where they had entered was some sort of crane, with what appeared to be a speaker's platform on the end of its arm, and that was apparently being gotten ready for more speeches. Lowell, Macdonald, and Mailer discussed whether to remain there. They were hardly in the mood for further addresses, but on the other hand, combat was getting nearer—one could tell by the slow contractions of the gut. It was not that they would lose their courage, so much as that it would begin to seep away; so the idea of listening to speeches was not intolerable. There would be at least company.

But a pleasant young woman accompanied by her child had come up to greet Lowell, and she now mentioned that the hippies were going to have a play at the other end of the parking lot and music seemed by far the better preparation for all battle, and music was indeed coming from that direction. So they set out, a modest group in the paved empty desert of the North Parking Area, and strolled toward the sounds of the band which were somehow medieval in sound, leaving behind the panorama of marchers slowly flowing in. On the way, they agreed again that they would be arrested early. That seemed the best way to satisfy present demands and still get back to New York in time for their dinners, parties, weekend parts. The desire to get back early is not dishonorable in Lowell and Macdonald; they had stayed on today, and indeed probably had come this far because Mailer had helped to urge them, but Mailer! with his apocalyptic visions at Lincoln Memorial and again on the March, his readiness to throw himself, breast against breast, in any charge on the foe, why now in such a rush? Did he not respect his visions?

Well the party that night looked to be the best coming up in some time; he simply hated to miss it. Besides, he had no position here; it was not his March on the Pentagon in conception or execution; he was hardly required to remain for days or even hours on the scene. His function was to be arrested—his name was expendable for the cause. He did not like the idea of milling about for hours while the fine line of earlier perception (and Vision!) got mucked in the general confusion. Besides, he was a novelist, and there is no procurer, gambler, adventurer or romantic lover more greedy for experience in great gouts—a part of the novelist wished to take the cumulative rising memories of the last three days and bring them whole, intact, in sum, as they stood now, to cast, nay—shades of Henry James—to *fling* on the gaming tables of life resumed in New York, and there amass a doubling and tripling again. He was in fact afraid that within the yawning mute concrete of the parking lot this day which had begun with such exultation would dissipate into leaderless armies wandering about, acting like clowns and fools before the face of the authority; or worse, raw massacres, something more than bones broken: actual disasters— that was also in the air. He did not know if he was secretly afraid too much would happen or too little, but one thing he knew he hated—that would be to wait, and wait again, and nerve up to the point of being arrested, and get diverted and wait again while the light of the vision went out of the day and out of his head until hungry and cold they would all shamble off shamefacedly to New York on a late plane, too late for everything all around. One could not do that to this day. Great days demanded as much respect as great nights—Victorian, no Edwardian, were Mailer's more courtly sentiments.

And in his defense, one decent motive. He had the conviction that his early arrest might excite others to further effort: the early battles of a war wheel on the hinge of their first legends—perhaps his imagination, in lockstep to many a montage in many an old movie, saw the word going out from mouth to ear to mouth to ear, linking the troops—in fact cold assessment would say that was not an inaccurate expectation. Details later.

Yes, Mailer had an egotism of curious disproportions. With the possible exception of John F. Kennedy, there had not been a President of the United States nor even a candidate since the Second World War whom Mailer secretly considered more suitable than himself, and yet on the first day of a war which he thought might go on for twenty years, his real desire was to be back in New York for a party. Such men are either monumental fools or excruciatingly practical since it may be wise to go to every party you can if the war is to contine for two decades. Of course, the likelihood is that the government—old corporation land—knew very well how wise it was to forge an agreement in negotiation to stage (dump) the marchers on arrival in the North Area's parking—coming off the March and into the face of a line of troops at the Pentagon, Mailer along with a good many others would not have been diverted with thoughts of New York whereas the parking area was so large and so empty that any army would have felt small in its expanse.

the flow of the river

LOREN C. EISELEY (1907–   ) is both a poet and an an-
thropologist. He grew up in Nebraska, and his continuing affection for the high plains of the Midwest is apparent in much
of his literary work. In addition to *The Immense Journey*
(1957), from which the following essay is taken, Eiseley is
the author of *Darwin's Century* (1958), *Firmament of Time*
(1960), *The Mind as Nature* (1962), *Francis Bacon and the
Modern Dilemma* (1963), *The Invisible Pyramid* (1970), and
Notes of an Alchemist (1972).

If there is magic on this planet, it is contained in water. Its least
stir even, as now in a rain pond on a flat roof opposite my office,
is enough to bring me searching to the window. A wind ripple may
be translating itself into life. I have a constant feeling that some
time I may witness that momentous miracle on a city roof, see life
veritably and suddenly boiling out of a heap of rusted pipes and old
television aerials. I marvel at how suddenly a water beetle has come
and is submarining there in a spatter of green algae. Thin vapors,
rust, wet tar and sun are an alembic remarkably like the mind; they
throw off odorous shadows that threaten to take real shape when
no one is looking.

Once in a lifetime, perhaps, one escapes the actual confines of
the flesh. Once in a lifetime, if one is lucky, one so merges with
sunlight and air and running water that whole eons, the eons that
mountains and deserts know, might pass in a single afternoon without discomfort. The mind has sunk away into its beginnings among
old roots and the obscure tricklings and movings that stir inani-
mate things. Like the charmed fairy circle into which a man once
stepped, and upon emergence learned that a whole century had
passed in a single night, one can never quite define this secret; but
it has something to do, I am sure, with common water. Its substance reaches everywhere; it touches the past and prepares the fu-

ture; it moves under the poles and wanders thinly in the heights of air. It can assume forms of exquisite perfection in a snowflake, or strip the living to a single shining bone cast up by the sea.

Many years ago, in the course of some scientific investigations in a remote western county, I experienced, by chance, precisely the sort of curious absorption by water—the extension of shape by osmosis—at which I have been hinting. You have probably never experienced in yourself the meandering roots of a whole watershed or felt your outstretched fingers touching, by some kind of clairvoyant extension, the brooks of snow-line glaciers at the same time that you were flowing toward the Gulf over the eroded debris of worndown mountains. A poet, MacKnight Black, has spoken of being "limbed . . . with waters gripping pole and pole." He had the idea, all right, and it is obvious that these sensations are not unique, but they are hard to come by; and the sort of extension of the senses that people will accept when they put their ear against a sea shell, they will smile at in the confessions of a bookish professor. What makes it worse is the fact that because of a traumatic experience in childhood, I am not a swimmer, and am inclined to be timid before any large body of water. Perhaps it was just this, in a way, that contributed to my experience.

As it leaves the Rockies and moves downward over the high plains towards the Missouri, the Platte River is a curious stream. In the spring floods, on occasion, it can be a mile-wide roaring torrent of destruction, gulping farms and bridges. Normally, however, it is a rambling, dispersed series of streamlets flowing erratically over great sand and gravel fans that are, in part, the remnants of a mightier Ice Age stream bed. Quicksands and shifting islands haunt its waters. Over it the prairie suns beat mercilessly throughout the summer. The Platte, "a mile wide and an inch deep," is a refuge for any heat-weary pilgrim along its shores. This is particularly true on the high plains before its long march by the cities begins.

The reason that I came upon it when I did, breaking through a willow thicket and stumbling out through ankle-deep water to a dune in the shade, is of no concern to this narrative. On various purposes of science I have ranged over a good bit of that country on foot, and I know the kinds of bones that come gurgling up through the gravel pumps, and the arrowheads of shining chalcedony that occasionally spill out of water-loosened sand. On that day, however, the sight of sky and willows and the weaving net of water murmuring a little in the shallows on its way to the Gulf stirred me, parched as I was with miles of walking, with a new idea: I was going to float. I was going to undergo a tremendous adventure.

The notion came to me, I suppose, by degrees. I had shed my

clothes and was floundering pleasantly in a hole among some reeds
when a great desire to stretch out and go with this gently insist-
ent water began to pluck at me. Now to this bronzed, bold, modern generation, the struggle I waged with timidity while standing
there in knee-deep water can only seem farcical; yet actually for me
it was not so. A near-drowning accident in childhood had scarred
my reactions; in addition to the fact that I was a nonswimmer,
this "inch-deep river" was treacherous with holes and quicksands.
Death was not precisely infrequent along its wandering and illusory
channels. Like all broad wastes of this kind, where neither water
nor land quite prevails, its thickets were lonely and untraversed.
A man in trouble would cry out in vain.

I though of all this, standing quietly in the water, feeling the
sand shifting away under my toes. Then I lay back in the floating
position that left my face to the sky, and shoved off. The sky
wheeled over me. For an instant, as I bobbed into the main channel, I had the sensation of sliding down the vast tilted face of the
continent. It was then that I felt the cold needles of the alpine
springs at my fingertips, and the warmth of the Gulf pulling me
southward. Moving with me, leaving its taste upon my mouth and
spouting under me in dancing springs of sand, was the immense body
of the continent itself, flowing like the river was flowing, grain by
grain, mountain by mountain, down to the sea. I was streaming
over ancient sea beds thrust aloft where giant reptiles had once
sported; I was wearing down the face of time and trundling cloud-
wreathed ranges into oblivion. I touched my margins with the deli-
cacy of a crayfish's antennae, and felt great fishes glide about their
work.

I drifted by stranded timber cut by beaver in mountain fast-
nesses; I slid over shallows that had buried the broken axles of prairie schooners and the mired bones of mammoth. I was streaming
alive through the hot and working ferment of the sun, or oozing
secretively through shady thickets. I *was* water and the unspeak-
able alchemies that gestate and take shape in water, the slimy jel-
lies that under the enormous magnification of the sun writhe and
whip upward as great barbeled fish mouths, or sink indistinctly back
into the murk out of which they arose. Turtle and fish and the
pinpoint chirpings of individual frogs are all water projections,
concentrations—as man himself is a concentration—of that
indescribable and liquid brew which is compounded in varying proportions of salt and sun and time. It has appearances, but at its
heart lies water, and as I was finally edged gently against a sand bar
and dropped like any log, I tottered as I rose. I knew once more the
body's revolt against emergence into the harsh and unsupporting

air, its reluctance to break contact with that mother element which still, at this late point in time, shelters and brings into being nine tenths of everything alive.

As for men, those myriad little detached ponds with their own swarming corpuscular life, what were they but a way that water has of going about beyond the reach of rivers? I, too, was a microcosm of pouring rivulets and floating driftwood gnawed by the mysterious animalcules of my own creation. I was three fourths water, rising and subsiding according to the hollow knocking in my veins: a minute pulse like the eternal pulse that lifts Himalayas and which, in the following systole, will carry them away.

Thoreau, peering at the emerald pickerel in Walden Pond, called them "animalized water" in one of his moments of strange insight. If he had been possessed of the geological knowledge so laboriously accumulated since his time, he might have gone further and amusedly detected in the planetary rumblings and eructations which so delighted him in the gross habits of certain frogs, signs of that dark interior stress which has reared sea bottoms up to mountainous heights. He might have developed an acute inner ear for the sound of the surf on Cretaceous beaches where now the wheat of Kansas rolls. In any case, he would have seen, as the long trail of life was unfolded by the fossil hunters, that his animalized water had changed its shapes eon by eon to the beating of the earth's dark millennial heart. In the swamps of the low continents, the amphibians had flourished and had their day; and as the long skyward swing—the isostatic response of the crust—had come about, the era of the cooling grasslands and mammalian life had come into being.

A few winters ago, clothed heavily against the weather, I wandered several miles along one of the tributaries of that same Platte I had floated down years before. The land was stark and ice-locked. The rivulets were frozen, and over the marshlands the willow thickets made such an array of vertical lines against the snow that tramping through them produced strange optical illusions and dizziness. On the edge of a frozen backwater, I stopped and rubbed my eyes. At my feet a raw prairie wind had swept the ice clean of snow. A peculiar green object caught my eye; there was no mistaking it.

Staring up at me with all his barbels spread pathetically, frozen solidly in the wind-ruffled ice, was a huge familiar face. It was one of those catfish of the twisting channels, those dwellers in the yellow murk, who had been about me and beneath me on the day of my great voyage. Whatever sunny dream had kept him paddling there while the mercury plummeted downward and that Che-

shire smile froze slowly, it would be hard to say. Or perhaps he was
trapped in a blocked channel and had simply kept swimming until
the ice contracted around him. At any rate, there he would lie
till the spring thaw.

At that moment I started to turn away, but something in
the bleak, whiskered face reproached me, or perhaps it was the river
calling to her children. I termed it science, however—a convenient
rational phrase I reserve for such occasions—and decided that I
would cut the fish out of the ice and take him home. I had no
intention of eating him. I was merely struck by a sudden impulse
to test the survival qualities of high-plains fishes, particularly
fishes of this type who get themselves immured in oxygenless ponds
or in cut-off oxbows buried in winter drifts. I blocked him out as
gently as possible and dropped him, ice and all, into a collecting can
in the car. Then we set out for home.

Unfortunately, the first stages of what was to prove a remarkable resurrection escaped me. Cold and tired after a long drive, I de-
posited the can with its melting water and ice in the basement.
The accompanying corpse I anticipated I would either dispose of or
dissect on the following day. A hurried glance had revealed no signs
of life.

To my astonishment, however, upon descending into the basement several hours later, I heard stirrings in the receptacle and
peered in. The ice had melted. A vast pouting mouth ringed with
sensitive feelers confronted me, and the creature's gills labored slowly. A thin stream of silver bubbles rose to the surface and popped.
A fishy eye gazed at me protestingly.

"A tank," it said. This was no Walden pickerel. This was a
yellow-green, mud-grubbing, evil-tempered inhabitant of floods and
droughts and cyclones. It was the selective product of the high
continent and the waters that pour across it. It has outlasted
prairie blizzards that left cattle standing frozen upright in the
drifts.

"I'll get the tank," I said respectfully.

He lived with me all that winter, and his departure was totally in keeping with his sturdy, independent character. In the
spring a migratory impulse or perhaps sheer boredom struck him.
Maybe, in some little lost corner of his brain, he felt, far off, the
pouring of the mountain waters through the sandy coverts of the
Platte. Anyhow, something called to him, and he went. One
night when no one was about, he simply jumped out of his tank.
I found him dead on the floor next morning. He had made his gamble like a man—or, I should say, a fish. In the proper place it would
not have been a fool's gamble. Fishes in the drying shallows of inter-

mittent prairie streams who feel their confinement and have the impulse to leap while there is yet time may regain the main channel and survive. A million ancestral years had gone into that jump, I thought as I looked at him, a million years of climbing through prairie sunflowers and twining in and out through the pillared legs of drinking mammoth.

"Some of your close relatives have been experimenting with air breathing," I remarked, apropos of nothing, as I gathered him up. "Suppose we meet again up there in the cottonwoods in a million years or so."

I missed him a little as I said it. He had for me the kind of lost archaic glory that comes from the water brotherhood. We were both projections out of that timeless ferment and locked as well in some greater unity that lay incalculably beyond us. In many a fin and reptile foot I have seen myself passing by—some part of myself, that is, some part that lies unrealized in the momentary shape I inhabit. People have occasionally written me harsh letters and castigated me for a lack of faith in man when I have ventured to speak of this matter in print. They distrust, it would seem, all shapes and thoughts but their own. They would bring God into the compass of a shopkeeper's understanding and confine Him to those limits, lest He proceed to some unimaginable and shocking act—create perhaps, as a casual afterthought, a being more beautiful than man. As for me, I believe nature capable of this, and having been part of the flow of the river, I feel no envy—any more than the frog envies the reptile or an ancestral ape should envy man.

Every spring in the wet meadows and ditches I hear a little shrilling chorus which sounds for all the world like an endlessly reiterated "We're here, we're here, we're here." And so they are, as frogs, of course. Confident little fellows. I suspect that to some greater ear than ours, man's optimistic pronouncements about his role and destiny may make a similar little ringing sound that travels a small way out into the night. It is only its nearness that is offensive. From the heights of a mountain, or a marsh at evening, it blends, not too badly, with all the other sleepy voices that, in croaks or chirrups, are saying the same thing.

After a while the skilled listener can distinguish man's noise from the katydid's rhythmic assertion, allow for the offbeat of a rabbit's thumping, pick up the autumnal monotone of crickets, and find in all of them a grave pleasure without admitting any to a place of preëminence in his thoughts. It is when all these voices cease and the waters are still, when along the frozen river nothing cries, screams or howls, that the enormous mindlessness of space settles down upon the soul. Somewhere out in that waste of crushed ice and reflected stars, the black waters may be running, but they appear to be running without life toward a destiny in which the whole of space may be locked in some silvery winter of dispersed radiation.

It is then, when the wind comes straitly across the barren marshes and the snow rises and beats in endless waves against the traveler, that I remember best, by some trick of the imagination, my summer voyage on the river. I remember my green extensions, my catfish nuzzlings and minnow wrigglings, my gelatinous materializations out of the mother ooze. And as I walk on through the white smother, it is the magic of water that leaves me a final sign.

Men talk much of matter and energy, of the struggle for existence that molds the shape of life. These things exist, it is true; but more delicate, elusive, quicker than the fins in water, is that mysterious principle known as "organization," which leaves all other mysteries concerned with life stale and insignificant by comparison. For that without organization life does not persist is obvious. Yet this organization itself is not strictly the product of life, nor of selection. Like some dark and passing shadow within matter, it cups out the eyes' small windows or spaces the notes of a meadow lark's song in the interior of a mottled egg. That principle—I am beginning to suspect—was there before the living in the deeps of water.

The temperature has risen. The little stinging needles have given way to huge flakes floating in like white leaves blown from some great tree in open space. In the car, switching on the lights, I examine one intricate crystal on my sleeve before it melts. No utilitarian philosophy explains a snow crystal, no doctrine of use or disuse. Water has merely leapt out of vapor and thin nothingness in the night sky to array itself in form. There is no logical reason for the existence of a snowflake any more than there is for evolution. It is an apparition from that mysterious shadow world beyond nature, that final world which contains—if anything contains— the explanation of men and catfish and green leaves.

Yellowstone Park

MARY McCARTHY

The summer I was fifteen I was invited to go to Montana by Ruth and Betty Bent, a pair of odd sisters who had come that year to our boarding school in Tacoma from a town called Medicine Springs, where their father was a federal judge. The answer from my grandparents was going to be no, I foresaw. I was too young (they would say) to travel by train alone, just as I was too young (they said) to go out with boys or accept rides in automobiles or talk to male callers on the telephone. This notion in my grandparents' minds was poisoning my life with shame, for mentally I was old for my age—as I was also accustomed to hearing from grownups in the family circle. I was so much older in worldly wisdom than *they* were that when my grandmother and my great-aunt read *The Well of Loneliness,* they had to come to ask me what the women in the book "did." "Think of it," nodded my great-aunt, reviewing the march of progress, "nowadays a fifteen-year-old girl knows a thing like that." At school, during study hall, I wrote stories about prostitutes with "eyes like dirty dishwater," which my English teacher read and advised me to send to H. L. Mencken for criticism. Yet despite all this—or possibly because of it—I was still being treated as a child who could hardly be trusted to take a streetcar without a grownup in attendance. The argument that "all the others did it" cut no ice with my grandfather, whose lawyer's mind was too precise to deal in condonation. He conceived that he had a weighty trust in my upbringing, since I had come to him as an orphan, the daughter of his only daughter.

Yet like many old-fashioned trustees, he had a special, one might say an occupational, soft spot. Anything educational was a lure to him. Salesmen of encyclopedias and stereopticon sets and Scribner's classics found him an easy prey in his Seattle legal offices, where he rose like a trout to the fly or a pickerel to the spoon.

He reached with alacrity for his pocketbook at the sight of an extra on the school bill. I had had music lessons, special coaching in
Latin, tennis lessons, riding lessons, diving lessons; that summer,
he was eager for me to have golf lessons. Tickets for civic pageants,
theater and concert subscription series, library memberships were
treated by him as necessities, not to be paid for out of my allow-
ance, which I was free to devote to freckle creams and Christmas
Night perfume. Some of the books I read and plays I saw made other
members of the family raise their eyebrows, but my grandfather
would permit no interference. He looked tolerantly over his glasses
as he saw me stretched out on the sofa with a copy of *Count Bruga*
or *The Hard Boiled Virgin.* I had been styling myself an atheist and
had just announced, that spring, that I was going east to college.
The right of the mind to develop according to its own lights was
a prime value to my grandfather, who was as rigid in applying this
principle as he was strait-laced in social matters.

The previous summer had been made miserable for me by his
outlandish conduct. At the resort we always went to in the
Olympic Mountains (my grandmother, who did not care for the
outdoors, always stayed home in Seattle), he and I had suddenly become a center of attention. The old judges and colonels, the young
married women whose husbands came up for the week end, the
young college blades, the hostess with the Sweetheart haircut who
played the piano for dancing, the very prep-school boys were looking
on me, I knew, with pity because of the way my grandfather was
acting—never letting me out of his sight, tapping me on the
dance floor to tell me it was my bedtime, standing on the dock
with a pair of binoculars when a young man managed to take me
rowing for fifteen clocked minutes on the lake. One time, when a
man from New York named Mr. Jones wanted me to take his picture with a salmon, my grandfather had leapt up from the bridge
table and thundered after us down the woodland path. And what
did he discover?—me snapping Mr. Jones' picture on a rustic bridge,
that was all. What did he think could have happened, anyway, at
eleven o'clock in the morning, fifty feet from the veranda where he
and his cronies were playing cards? The whole hotel knew what he
thought and was laughing at us. A boy did imitations of Mr. Jones
holding the salmon with one hand and hugging me with the other,
then dropping the salmon and fleeing in consternation when my
grandfather appeared.

My grandfather did not care; he never cared what people
thought of him, so long as he was doing his duty. And he expected
me to be perfectly happy, taking walks up to the waterfall with
him and the judges' and colonels' ladies; measuring the circumference
of Douglas firs; knocking the ball around the five-hole golf course;

doing the back dive from the springboard while he looked on, approving, with folded arms; playing the player piano by myself all afternoon: torn rolls of "Tea for Two" and "Who" and one called "Sweet Child" that a young man with a Marmon roadster had sung into my radiant ear on the dance floor until my grandfather scared him off.

Sweet child, indeed! I felt I could not stand another summer like that. I had to go to Montana, and my grandfather, I knew, would let me if only I could persuade him that the trip would be broadening and instructive; that is, if in my eyes it would be profoundly boring.

It did not take divination on my part to guess what would fit these requirements: Yellowstone Park. The very yawn I had to stifle at the thought of geysers, Old Faithful, colored rock formations, Indians, grizzly bears, pack horses, tents, rangers, parties of tourists with cameras and family sedans, told me I had the bait to dangle before his kindly-severe grey eyes. It was too bad, I remarked casually, in the course of my last school letter home, that the trip was out of the question: the girls had been planning to take me on a tour of Yellowstone Park. That was all that was needed. It was as simple as selling him a renewal of his subscription to the *National Geographic*. The ease of it somehow depressed me, casting a pall over the adventure; one of the most boring things about adolescence is the knowledge of how people can be worked.

I *ought* to go to Montana, said my grandfather decidedly, after he had looked up Judge Bent in a legal directory and found that he really existed: a thing which slightly surprised me, for in my representations to my grandparents, I always had the sensation of lying. Whatever I told them was usually so blurred and glossed, in the effort to meet their approval (for, aside from anything else, I was fond of them and tried to accommodate myself to their perspective), that except when answering a direct question I hardly knew whether what I was saying was true or false. I really tried, or so I thought, to avoid lying, but it seemed to me that they forced it on me by the difference in their vision of things, so that I was always transposing reality for them into terms they could understand. To keep matters straight with my conscience, I shrank, whenever possible, from the lie absolute, just as, from a sense of precaution, I shrank from the plain truth. Yellowstone Park was a typical instance. I had not utterly lied when I wrote that sentence. I entertained, let us say, a vague hope of going there and had spoken to the Bent girls about it in a tentative, darkling manner, *i.e.*, "My family hopes we can see Yellowstone." To which the girls replied, with the same discreet vagueness, "Umm."

At home, it was settled for me to entrain with the girls

shortly after school closed, stay three weeks, which would give us
time to "do" the Park, and come back by myself. It would only be
two nights, my grandfather pointed out to my grandmother; and
Judge Bent could put me on the train in care of the conductor.
The two girls nodded demurely, and Ruth, the elder, winked at me,
as my grandfather repeated these instructions.

I was mortified. As usual, my grandfather's manner seemed calculated to expose me in front of my friends, to whom I posed as
a practiced siren. My whole life was a lie, it often appeared to me,
from beginning to end, for if I was wilder than my family knew, I
was far tamer than my friends could imagine, and with them, too,
as with my family, I was constantly making up stories, pretending
that a ring given me by a great-aunt was a secret engagement ring,
that I went out dancing regularly to the Olympic Hotel, that a
literary boy who wrote to me was in love with me—the usual
tales, but I did not know that. All I knew was that there was
one central, compromising fact about me that had to be hidden
from my friends and that burned me like the shirt of the Centaur:
I could not bear to have anyone find out that I was considered too
young to go out with boys.

But every word, every gesture of my grandfather's seemed designed to proclaim this fact. I perceived an allusion to it in the
fussy way he saw us off at the Seattle depot, putting us in our
drawing room with many cautions not to speak to strangers, tip-
ping the Pullman porter and having a "word" with the conductor,
while my grandmother pressed a lacy handkerchief to her eyes and
my uncle grinned and the old family gardener and handy man advised
me not to take any wooden nickels. During this degrading ordeal,
the Bent girls remained polite and deferential, agreeing to everything (it was always my tendency to argue). But as soon as the
train pulled out of the station, Ruth Bent coolly summoned the
conductor and exchanged our drawing room for two upper berths.
They always did this on boarding the train, she explained; two
could fit very comfortably into an upper, and the money they got
back was clear profit.

Ruth Bent was the boldest person, for her age, I had ever met.
She was seventeen, two years older than her sister, and she looked,
to me, about forty. She had reddish-brown frizzy hair and she wore
earrings, eyeglasses, picture hats, printed chiffon dresses, a deep pur-
plish red lipstick, and Golliwog perfume. Her voice was deep, like a
man's; her skin was swarthy and freckled; her eyebrows, shaped with
tweezers, were a dark chocolate color. She had a good figure, small,
with a sort of shimmying movement to it. In school she had the
name of being fast, which was based partly on her clothes and part-

ly on the direct stare of her reddish-brown eyes, very wide open and rounded by the thick lenses of her glasses so that the whites had the look of boiled eggs. She made me think of a college widow.

Actually, she was a serious girl, in her own inscrutable way; she sang in the choir and was respected by the school principal. No one knew quite what to make of her. It was argued that she was common (I could not help thinking this myself) and that her sister, Betty, was more the school type. Betty was a boyish girl with a short haircut, a wide thin face, high cheekbones, and clear grey-green eyes. She had a broad flat mouth and a big elastic Western smile that disclosed shining teeth. Her lipstick was Tangee. She had a lighter voice than her sister's and a light, scherzo touch on the piano; she played at school recitals.

Both girls were very good dancers. And they both liked to ride, which was how we had become friends. In the pocket of her black riding habit (Betty wore jodhpurs), Ruth always had a package of cigarettes, which she calmly took out as soon as we were mounted, right in front of the English major who was the school riding master. The major liked both girls and let them have the best horses and ride wherever they pleased. The Bent girls had some quality— levelheadedness, I suppose—that reassured older people. They never got into trouble, no matter what they did, while I was either in high favor or on the verge of being expelled. Unlike me, they did not seek to make a point; they merely did what they wanted, in a bald, impersonal way, like two natural forces—a sultry dark-browed wind and a light playful breeze. Their self-possession, I felt, must rest on an assured social position at home. In Montana, they said, they had a very lively crowd and their family gave them complete freedom. Their town was small, but there was always a party going, and they had friends all over the state. I would have plenty of dates, they promised me, in Medicine Springs.

Geography, in those days, left me cold; it reminded me of grade school, slide lectures, and the stereopticon. Consequently, I had not bothered to look up Medicine Springs on the map. It had once been a spa, the girls said, and this was enough for me to place it up in the north, near Canada, where I supposed the mountains were; I thought vaguely of Saratoga Springs, horse races, big rambling hotels in Victorian architecture, gamblers, mining men from roaring Butte. It astonished me to learn, in mid-journey, that Medicine Springs was in the center of the state and that we were going to have to change trains to get there. It was nowhere near Yellowstone Park, I discovered with a guilty tremor; in fact, it was not near any place I had heard of. It did not even figure on the railroad map on our timetable.

We changed—I forget where—and took a dusty little branch

train with hard board seats. I had never seen a train like this, and a gloomy premonition overtook me as we jolted along across a prairie, the two girls in high spirits at the prospect of getting home. I kept looking out the window for scenery, but there was nothing, not a river, not a hill, not a tree—just a flat expanse of dry grass and gopher mounds, with a few houses strung along at the rare stations. Medicine Springs, when we reached it, was a small, flat, yellowish town set in the middle of nowhere. There was one wide dusty main street with a drugstore and a paintless hotel; several smaller streets crossed it, ran for a block or two, and then stopped. You could take it in at a glance. Behind the hotel there were the "springs" alluded to in the town's name; they consisted of a dirty, sulphurous, cement swimming pool with one half-dead tree leaning over it. The heat was awful, and the only shade apparent was provided by telephone poles. I could not believe that my friends lived here and supposed, to myself, that we must be going to a ranch somewhere out of sight on the prairie.

Judge Bent was at the depot, a sallow, middle-aged man with dark hair and a modified cowboy hat; he put our bags in his car, and I got set for a long drive. But in a trice we had arrived at the Bent home. It was somewhat larger than the other houses we had passed and it had a front porch and a tree. Another dwelling with a tree was identified by the girls as "The Manse"; I looked in vain for mosses. These two frame houses and one other, which professed to be haunted, constituted the town's "residential" quarter.

Mrs. Bent came to the door, and I tried to put on a pleased and excited expression. But everything I saw shocked and almost frightened me; the modest size of the house, the thin walls, the absence of books and pictures, the lack of any ornament or architectural feature, the table already set in the middle of the afternoon without a flower or a centerpiece, the fact that Mrs. Bent evidently did her own work, that there was no guest room and that I was to share a room and closet with Betty and a bath with the whole family. This feeling on my part was not precisely a snobbish reaction; if the Bents had been poor, I would not have felt so ill-at-ease and indeed paralyzed. What struck me here was a sense of disorientation. Knowing the Bents not to be poor, I could not "place" them. The girls, I perceived, were unaware of my difficulties. They did not catch even a glimpse of their home refracted from my glazed eyes. This was a relief, but at the same time it amazed me. In their place, I would have died of mortification.

This disregard was typical of the Bent household. The two girls, while perfectly affectionate, took no notice of their parents, who might as well have been a pair of mutes at the family board.

I had been trained not to talk at table until drawn out by my hosts, but neither Judge nor Mrs. Bent appeared conscious of a social duty to find out who I was, where I came from, what my parents did. I was there, simply, and they accepted my presence. The only fact I ever elicited about them was that Judge Bent had taken his law degree at Madison, Wisconsin. My provenance, theirs, were as indifferent to them as that of the baked potato that the judge silently helped onto my plate.

Mrs. Bent's function seemed to be to answer the telephone and iron the girls' summer dresses. She never wanted to know who was calling or where the dresses were to be worn. I wished she *would* ask, that first night at dinner, for this was a question that interested me. Despite what I had seen of Medicine Springs, my hopes began to stir again when I perceived that we were to have dates that night. The girls were talking of a dance, out of town, on the prairie; someone named Frank was coming to call for us with his car. I was too uppity to dream of cowboys, even if the girls had not warned me that they were all dirty, spitting old men. But from casual bits dropped by the girls, I was piecing together, once more, an image of what the true West must have in store for me— smooth, sleek boys whose fathers owned sheep or cattle ranches, who wore white linen suits and drove roadsters and probably went east to college. I imagined a long piazza, a barbecue pit, and silver flasks glinting in the moonlight.

But there were no boys in Medicine Springs; all the men in Medicine Springs were married.

This bitter news came to me slowly, and it was prefaced by other information that slightly blunted its effect, like a preliminary dose of Novocain. They were not *all* married; there was one dim exception, the "Frank" who had come to fetch us in an old Ford. He was a young man of twenty with glasses and hair that stood straight up; he clerked in the hotel in the summer and in the winter he went to the state college at Bozeman. His father, Mr. Hoey, was the hotelkeeper. The Hoeys and the Bents and the people who owned the drugstore made up the local aristocracy. That was all there was. There had once been a clergyman, but he had died, and a circus family, but they had gone away. I now say to myself that there must have been a doctor, at least, and an undertaker, but memory shakes its head. No. Probably the pharmacist combined these functions.

At any rate, I was so dashed by this lesson in small-town sociology, which the girls imparted on the way down to the hotel, and by the sight of the hotel lobby, which contained three straight-backed chairs, three cuspidors, a desk with a register, some flypaper, and Mr. Hoey in his shirtsleeves, that I could hardly take in the next tidings: on my first official date, I was going to have to go out with a married man. Betty too. There they stood, the husbands, waiting for us beside their cars: a small black-haired man called "Acey," who did automobile repairs (he was Betty's), and a tall wavy-haired blond named Bob Berdan, who worked in the drugstore (he was mine).

Later, Ruth explained that the men here married early or else went away to work. That winter there had been several marriages, which left only Frank, who belonged to her, as the elder sister, and Acey, who belonged to Betty and was practically single since he was getting divorced from a wife who had run away from him. Usually, there were boys staying in the town, but this summer they had been lucky to get Bob Berdan, whose wife was away visiting her relations. Every single girl was after him; he was the handsomest man in Medicine Springs and very hard to please.

Of the three men, he was certainly the best looking; I had to admit that, as he put out a large hand with a ring on it and stood looking down into my eyes. He was common; his hair was too wavy; his skin was too dark for his hair; and he had a white toothpaste-ad smile that made me think of his work in the drugstore. But from a distance he could pass. He had an old touring car, which he was waiting for me to get into; Betty had already joined Acey in his salesman's coupé.

What was I to do? My grandfather would have told me to say good night, politely, and ask to be taken home. Just because the others had fixed it up for me was no reason for me to fall in with their plans. Today, in my grandfather's place, I would give the same counsel, which shows how out of touch, how impractical, older people are. In reality, I had no choice but to get into the car, which I did, seating myself nervously in the far corner. The three cars, with Frank and Ruth in the lead, started out in procession across the prairie. I could see that in the car ahead of us Betty's head was on Acey's shoulder. Was I expected to follow this example too? My date, I was glad to find, was busy manipulating the wheel and singing last year's love songs in a croony voice. Peering at his arrow-cut profile, I began to feel a little less terrified.

Before long, the first car stopped and we all followed suit. I thought there was something wrong; the road was very bad, almost a wagon trail. But it seemed that we were pausing to have a drink. Frank got out of the first car and came back with a pint bottle, which he passed to Acey and Betty and then to Bob and me. I took a mouthful and gagged. It was the first time I had ever tasted hard liquor, but I did not want them to guess that; the few sips of champagne and half-glass of Canadian beer that had been allowed me at home, on special occasions, had prompted me to boast of my drinking prowess. With Frank and Bob watching, I tried once more to swallow the burning stuff in my mouth; instead, I gagged again and the liquor spilled out all over my face and neck. Bob got out a handkerchief and advised me to try again. I could not get it down. By this time, the whole party had joined us. "Is that whisky?" I asked cautiously; it did not smell like the whisky my grandfather drank. It was moonshine, they said; corn whisky, but the very best; Bob always tested it at the drugstore. One by one, they tilted the bottle and drank, to show me how to do it. It was no use. My throat simply rejected it; I gagged until the tears came. Ruth proposed that I should hold my nose, and in this way I managed to get down a large gulp, which made my stomach rock.

I did not like it at all; the lift they spoke of did not come; I would rather have had my throat painted with Argyrol by the doctor. But they kept passing me the bottle; we stopped repeatedly on the way to the dance to have another swig; eventually, to my horror (for I thought at last it was over), Bob produced a fresh pint from the side pocket of the car. They did not force me to drink; I was free to refuse, as my grandfather could have pointed out. They just watched while I did it and they noticed if I merely put my lips to the bottle. I was ashamed to keep holding my nose, but there seemed to be no other way to swallow, until at length I discovered that I could take a gulp and hold it in my mouth and work it down gradually, when no one was looking, a few drops at a time. This prevented me from talking for long periods. Bob Berdan sang, and I rode along tight-lipped beside him, with a mouth full of unswallowed moonshine, which washed around my teeth as the car bumped along the rutted road. After a while he threw his arm lightly over the back of the seat.

I must have choked down more than I would have thought possible for I can hardly remember the dance. It was in a sort of shed—not even a barn; and there were a lot of rough-looking, unshaven, coatless men pushing and grabbing and yelling while an old woman played the piano. I was frightened, and we did not stay there very long. There was nobody of our own sort or age present, only hands from a ranch and a few older women. The men in our party seemed very white and civilized and out of place in this setting. I stuck close to Bob Berdan, who appeared much more attractive than he had an hour or so before. I could almost imagine that he had been to college.

Perhaps we bought another pint there.

Some hours later, I woke up in a strange room and found there was a man in bed with me. It took me a minute or two to recall who he was: Bob Berdan, of course. My date. We were in a double bed; overhead, hanging from a cord, an unshaded electric light bulb was burning. I had no idea what time it was; probably it was morning, the morning after. And I had no recollection of the room or how we had got there. As everything whirled around me, I felt a wan relief in being able to recognize *him* at least. I had only known him a few hours, but at any rate I knew him. *And it could have been anybody.* I was undressed, I could tell from the touch of the sheet on my bare shoulders, and I was afraid to raise the covers to explore any further. I lay absolutely still, staring up at the unfinished beams of the ceiling. In the next room, I could hear a phonograph and voices. I felt that my life was over. Bob was asleep; one of his arms was around me. As I lay there, grimly taking stock, he woke up and his arm tightened; he started muttering tenderly. Men, I had heard, were like that after. . . . I was too horror-stricken to finish the thought. The *very* first night, the *very* first man, I said to myself, paying no attention to him, absorbed in my own stolid woe. I did not blame him, but I would have blotted him out if I could.

He was offering me reassurances, I slowly realized. Nothing had happened, he kept murmuring; he had not harmed me. I dared not believe him. But he pulled off the blankets to show me and, sure enough, I was not really undressed. It was only my dress and shoes that were gone. I was in my slip and underclothes, and he was dressed too, except for his coat and shoes.

I had been sick, he explained, and the girls had taken my dress to try to wash it. We were in his house; they had put me to bed and I had passed out there. This was not all, I was certain; it did not explain what *he* was doing there, with his arms around me. I decided not to inquire. If there had been a certain amount of necking (which now began to come back to me, hazily), I did not want to hear about it. The main thing, the miraculous thing, was that my age had spared me. His voice was full of emotion as he told me that he would never take advantage of a sweet kid like me. He had fallen for me, the girls declared, teasing; the sound of our voices had brought them in from the next room to corroborate what he was telling me. Nothing had happened, they attested; they had been there all the time.

Had I drawn a blank, they inquired, solicitously. I had to ask the meaning of this expression. Was it different, I wished to know, from "passing out"? Oh, very different, replied Ruth: you walked around and did and said things which you could not remember afterward. A peculiar smile, reminiscent, flitted across the assembled faces; I buried my head in the covers. It was all right, said Ruth, kindly: Betty used to draw blanks too, when she was younger. ("Younger?" I cried to myself. How much younger? Twelve?)

Matter-of-factly, just as though this happened every day, the girls helped me into my dress, which they had sponged out and ironed. Wasn't it lucky, they commented, that Bob was a married man? Bob kissed me good night, tenderly, and Frank Hoey, who seemed a trifle embarrassed, drove us home in the dawn. I was nerving myself to face Judge and Mrs. Bent, irate, on the stairway, in their night clothes, but no one was up at the Bent house. When we came down to breakfast, finally, Mrs. Bent was busy with the iron. The only question she asked was an absent one: "Did you have a good time?" "Bob Berdan took a tumble for Mary," Ruth vouchsafed, with a laugh. "Oh," said Mrs. Bent, incuriously. "Bob's a nice fellow; is his wife still away?"

During the next weeks, I worried about what Mrs. Bent thought. She must have known that Betty was with Acey and that I was with Bob Berdan nearly every night. But in her mind, apparently, we were out with what she called "the crowd," which included Frank Hoey's sister and the pharmacist's daughters. She must have felt there was safety in numbers or that a married man was a chaperon; that seemed to be how she viewed Bob Berdan, who was nearly twenty-five. Yet what did she suppose the crowd did, from eight until three in the morning? She must have heard me being sick, time and again, in the Bent bathroom and noted my green face at breakfast.

That was the awful thing. Virtually every night was a repetition of the first one. I could not learn to drink their liquor, but I would not stop trying, so that I was either passed out or sick on every one of our dates. We were forever driving somewhere (or, rather, nowhere), and the parade of cars was forever halting for me to throw up by the roadside. As soon as I had done so, the bottle would be passed again. When I was conscious, I was frequently speechless, owing to the fact that there was a gulp of moonshine in my mouth that I had not yet been able to swallow it; it would sometimes take ten minutes to work it down. It was all a matter of practice I told myself; look at Ruth and Betty. They never got sick or passed out. And they were always able to tell me what I had done during the hours I could not remember, or rather what I had *not* done, which was all I cared about hearing. Half the town, I think, knew about me and Bob Berdan, down to the detail that he was not "taking advantage" of me, on account of my age and inexperience. He was sweet on me, everyone said, and I accepted it, though I could not imagine why he should be, considering.

It seemed to me, often, that I was taking advantage of *him*. I grew a little tired of his kisses, which did not excite me, perhaps because they were always the same, leading nowhere but to more kisses. I felt he was sentimental, which made me impatient. When I saw him in the drugstore, with his white coat and ripply hair, I was embarrassed for him, just because I could see him so clearly *from the outside*, as a clerk, who would always be a clerk, limited, like his kisses, flat, like the town.

And yet I liked him. I think it was that I was sorry for him, in some faraway part of myself, the part that was already back in Seattle while the rest of me was locked in his arms. I really looked on him, though I was not aware of it, as I did on other adults, seeing him as circumscribed and finite and yet encumbered, like all the rest of them, with a mysterious burden of feeling. In the back of my mind, I had a child's certainty that I was moving, going somewhere, while the grownups around me were standing still. I was only precocious mentally and lived in deadly fear of losing my virtue, not for moral reasons, but from the dread of being thought "easy." Bob's restraint on this score was his sole source of fascination for me, paradoxically. Here, his being older and married put him somehow beyond me.

Yet I was glad, I know, of the respite, when, after ten days of Medicine Springs, the girls grew restless and we went off with Frank and his sister on overnight trips to Helena and Great Falls. I had suggested Yellowstone, hopefully, but the girls temporized. If we went to Yellowstone, they said, the family would want to go too. We could do that later, when we got back. The idea of sightseeing had begun to appeal to me. In Medicine Springs, the only things we had done that would bear repeating were an afternoon visit to a sheep ranch, where they were slaughtering some lambs, and a morning visit to a cow ranch, where I rode for five minutes on a mutinous old horse and tried in vain to trot in a Western saddle. One night, in the car's headlights, we had seen the red eyes of a loco horse reflected. That was all, except for the thunderstorms that took place every evening at dinner time and left the sky on the horizon a pale green. In a word, nothing to write home about.

In Helena and Great Falls, we stayed at hotels, ordering gin from the bellboy to drink in our rooms. I liked the gin quite well, mixed with lemon soda and ice. Nothing to write home about, either, though on the ride up to Helena I had had an odd experience. As usual, we had a bottle of moonshine with us when we started out and we passed it back and forth, as usual, while we drove along. The road was rough and once, when it was my turn, I spilled a few drops on my silk stockings. That night when we were changing for dinner I found little holes in my stockings everywhere the liquor had spattered. I showed them to the girls, who positively could not understand it. The liquor, they pointed out, had been analyzed by Bob in the drugstore.

We made jokes about it and kept the stockings for a trophy; yet the incident, so to speak, burned a hole in our minds. In Great Falls, Ruth suddenly decided that she did not like the looks of the bellboy who had brought us the gin. It tasted all right; it smelled all right; but Ruth remained suspicious, her dark brows drawn together, as we had one drink and started on a second. About halfway through the second, with one accord we set down our glasses. Ruth packed the bottle to take back to Medicine Springs for analysis. It was wood alcohol, sure enough, Bob Berdan told us a few days later. If so, we should have been dead, since we had each had two or three ounces of it. In fact, we felt no ill effects; perhaps the local moonshine had developed a tolerance in us—a tolerance not shared by my stockings. But the two incidents made us warier and tamer. That night, in Great Falls, we went respectably to the movies and then back to bed. The next morning I found a book store and while the others waited in the car I hurried in to make a purchase: the latest volume, in a boxed de luxe edition, of James Branch Cabell.

I was tremendously excited by this act. It was the first expensive book I had ever bought with my own money. The whole trip to Montana for a moment seemed worthwhile, as I stood in the wide dull main street with the book, wrapped, in my hands. I was in love with Cabell and had written him many letters that I had not had the courage to mail. Why, it would change my grandmother's whole life, I used to tell her, if she would only let herself read a few pages of Cabell or listen to me recite them. Now, as the owner of a limited edition, I felt proudly close to him, far closer than to Bob Berdan or to the girls, who were already honking the horn for me to get in and join the party. They could never understand—only Cabell could, I supposed—what finding this book in this out-of-the-way place meant to me. That was the way it went, in Cabell; horns honked, alarm clocks shrilled, cocks crowed, to bring the ardent dreamer back to the drab, mean routines of middle-class reality.

And yet a strange thing happened when I finally opened the book, taking it carefully from its waxy wrapper. I was disappointed. I told myself that it was not a very *good* Cabell; perhaps he had written himself out (I knew about that, of course). But all the while I suspected that it was not the book, which was no different from other Cabells; it was me. I had "outgrown" Cabell, just as older people had said I would. For the second time in Montana, I felt that my life was over. I put the book aside quietly and now I cannot remember whether I ever finished it.

The next thing I recall is being on the train, going home. We had never got to Yellowstone, naturally, and my conscience was bothering me. I felt I had nothing to show for the visit—not even a proper array of lies, for the Bent household possessed no encyclopedia in which I could have boned up on the Park, while the girls, for their part, had only the haziest memories of Old Faithful and bears. My grandfather, in his youth, had been a geodetic surveyor during college vacations, and he would be bound to ask a lot of questions that I had no means of answering. Were there mountains there, for instance? What tribes of Indians? What kind of rock? Did we stay in a hotel or camp out and if so, where? Yellowstone was a big place. The paucity of my information made me conscious of the enormity of the deception I was going to have to put over. It was not the fear of being found out, even, that was troubling me as the train brought home nearer and nearer. Not being the kind of person who took refuge in monosyllables, I felt I owed my grandparents the courtesy of a well-put-together and decently documented lie.

Fortunately, a party of tourists, two men and two women, fresh out of Yellowstone, boarded the train. They had a bottle with them in the observation car and were very lively and friendly, treating me as an equal, though they must have been around thirty. They were able to help me a little, when I explained my predicament, but they did not have the grasp of detail that my grandfather expected from a narrative. To my critical ear it sounded as if they had hardly been in Yellowstone at all. I attributed it to drinking; they were having too good a time, on the train, to put their minds on scenery and Indians and what kind of bears.

A fatherly old conductor kept watching them as they bought me lemonades. On the second day out I was sitting with them in the observation car when the conductor stuck his head in the doorway and beckoned to me. He led me into an empty drawing room, asked me to sit down and, looking at me gravely through steel-rimmed glasses, told me that I must not talk to those people any more. "Steer clear of them," he said. "Give them a wide berth." Why, I wanted to know; but instead of answering this question he swerved off on a tangent and announced that he had been studying me and that I was one of the cleanest, sweetest, truest young girls it had ever been his pleasure to observe. It was because of this he was speaking to me now, as he would to one of his own daughters or granddaughters. There were tears in his eyes, I saw, as he warmed to his subject. "Stay that way," he said. "Clean and sweet and wholesome." I dropped my eyes, abashed and yet touched by this notion. I did not get exactly what he was driving at, but I supposed my friends in the observation car must be cardsharps or something of the kind. Even so, I did not see what harm they could do me and my curiosity was roused. "What's wrong with them?" I said bluntly. "Don't ask me," said the old conductor. "Just take my word for it and stay away from them." I persisted, and at last he told me, lowering his voice and glancing away from me. "They changed berths," he said. "Last night." I did not take in his point at first, for I had supposed they were married. Thinking it was my innocence, he elucidated. When they had got on at the Park, he said solemnly, the two women were together and the two men were together. "During the night . . ." He broke off.

"Oh," I said, flatly, meaning, "Is that all?" "Do you understand?" he asked. I nodded. "So you see why you mustn't talk to them?" I supposed I did, from his point of view, and I nodded again, reluctantly. A month before I might have argued the issue, for how could I have been safer than with two men and two women who only had designs on each other? Or I might have defied him. But now I did not have the heart to go against his instructions. It would crush him if he caught me talking to them after what he had told me; he would see that he had been duped in me. And I felt too old and weary to explain why I was not shocked.

On the other hand, it seemed rather mean to drop my new friends out of hand just to spare the conductor's feelings. I felt caught in a dilemma that was new to me then but which since has become horribly familiar: the trap of adult life, in which you are held, wriggling, powerless to act because you can see both sides. On that occasion, as generally in the future, I compromised. That is, I steered a zigzag course between the conductor and the two couples, talking to them when the conductor was not looking and leaving them abruptly, with some unlikely excuse, when I would glance up and find his old eyes on me. This jerky behavior, and the copious, dazzling smiles with which I tried to mitigate it, must have made both parties think I was deranged.

Back in Seattle, I found myself still serving out my sentence of childhood, which had three more years to run yet: I was eighteen, a freshman home from college, before I was able to sweep down the staircase, dressed in the height of fashion, and find a boy waiting, in uneasy conversation with my grandparents. Even then, my grandfather, as he raised his soft cheek for a kiss, would mortify me by the inevitable question: "Home by eleven?"

The trip to Montana left no outward scars. Indeed, it was educational, in that I could not bear the taste of whisky for years afterward; even now I cannot take it straight—I gag. And my ardor for dates was somewhat subdued, for the time being; more than a year passed before I began meeting boys on the sly, in the afternoons. I do not know whether my grandparents guessed that I had never been to Yellowstone. I think they must have, eventually, for they did not ask too many questions. In a gloomy way, I was happy to be home again. At home, at least I could be romantic, lying on the sofa in the evenings, reading and dreaming, and looking out across our terraces to where the moon made a path on the lake, a path that beckoned to suicide, as I wrote in a school composition. Across the room, my grandparents played double solitaire, and when my grandmother lost she would send me upstairs to fetch her petit-point handbag out of the drawer that contained her handkerchiefs, her pearl opera glasses, and her pearl-handled revolver. The phone seldom rang, and I was almost glad of it, because if it were a boy, I would have to make some excuse to explain why I could not go out that night or any other night he proposed. At home, nothing ever happened, but it was an atmosphere in which one could think that the unknown, the improbable, might occur in the depths of the familiar, like the treasures I could find in my grandmother's bureau drawer.

And in fact this proved to be true. Two summers later, when I was going to drama school, I first beheld what we then called my Dream Man (an actor whom I later married), at, of all places, a Bar Association pageant on the Magna Charta that my grandfather had made me go to, sulky and protesting. As for the Bent girls, I do not know what has become of them. The last time I saw Ruth Bent was when I was a junior at Vassar and she telephoned me from a small town in the Hudson River Valley to ask me to come and see her. She was twenty-one then and a widow, very well to do; she was running a chocolate factory which her husband, who had been killed in a plane crash, had left her. I had the sense that she had fulfilled her destiny: she still looked about forty, a poised, competent executive, with a furrow between her brows. And she was not a bit wild any more.

a good climbing tree
is hard to find

BARBARA ANDERSON (1952–   ) wrote the following essay while a student at Denison University, where she majored
in American Studies.

Our backyard was the approximate geographical center of a residential neighborhood located on the western edge of the small community of Wooster, Ohio. It was in our backyard that most of my
growing up (or at least most of the important parts) took place.
For ten years it offered all the ground I needed; its boundaries were
the edges of my planet, and the larger neighborhood lay on all sides
like the nebulous expanse of the universe.

I was very conscious of boundaries and property lines in those
years. I could sense a sort of silent agreement, or rather silent an-
tagonism, among the grownups that the kids in the
neighborhood—which meant mostly me and my friend Mark, and my
brother David and his handful of friends—wouldn't be allowed to go
trampling through other people's shrubs and into their backyards.
Luckily for my parents, and luckily for my behind parts too, our
backyard was big enough and contained so many different areas, each
with its own atmosphere and mood, that I never felt the need to
wander off into other people's property. And besides, most of the
other houses on the block were owned by old people without any
children; so I wouldn't have any reason to play around in their yards
anyway.

When I think back, it wasn't the space in these older people's
yards that was off-limits to our play: it was the boundaries themselves that were forbidden. Certain things came to symbolize
boundaries—the edge of a driveway, a row of tulips, a line of bushes
a clothesline, even a change in the color of the grass. And we were
expected to be aware of these and of what they meant—that to
cross them or to trample on them or to lose your baseball over
them was to intrude on someone's privacy. We could only look at
these people's houses and wonder what they were like inside or look

107

at their trees and imagine how it would feel to climb in their branches or look at the grass and wonder if it would be cool when you lay on it or whether it would be scratchy like the people in the houses.

The editor of the town's newspaper lived in the big white-pillared house just across the street from us. He must have owned that half of the block because his was the only house on that side of the street. He had the most unusual trees in his yard—ginkgoes and flowering oriental trees. But we never got a chance to climb in them or touch them or even get a good look at them because his backyard was hidden all around by a five-foot hedge. My friend Mark and I never once dared to cross this boundary into this world of beautiful trees. But we were brave enough to ride our bicycles around the driveway just to get a look at what we weren't allowed to touch. The editor's house had a driveway that went all the way around in back of the house and then came out again on the other side. One day Mark and I were particularly brave and were riding furiously around and around the house. On one of our laps, the editor's wife came out and stopped us. She offered us cookies from a plate and asked us not to ride around in back of their house anymore. I can remember the cookies—they were oatmeal—and I nearly gagged on them I was so scared. I was never so glad as when she withdrew the plate and went back inside, and Mark and I could quietly walk our bicycles back into the familiarity of the street.

Mrs. McCoy, a middle-aged widow who ran the Gift Corner downtown on the square, lived alone in the red brick house next to ours. Our driveway served as the only boundary between our lots, so naturally there were a lot of violations due to runaway basketballs and baseballs. But Mrs. McCoy was one of the few who didn't mind much—or at least she didn't say anything, even when Mark and I, on those afternoons when we would sit and move about quietly in the grass looking for four-leaf clovers, would move unknowingly into her yard. One summer I remember we came across a whole patch of four-leaf clovers on the edge of Mrs. McCoy's lawn. We were pretty excited with our find and even told her about it so she could take some for herself. She did and then invited us inside her house to show us how to press them in a Bible so that they would keep for our grandchildren.

Next to Mrs. McCoy lived Mr. and Mrs. Winger. For some reason, Mark and I never tried to go past the crabapple trees that bounded their lawn. They didn't have any children, and we never found out much about them, even though we would always see them outside, busily trimming the grass and working with their trees and shrubs.

Next to the Wingers and at the corner of the block was a chocolate brown, two-family apartment house. No one ever stayed there for longer than a season or two; it seemed like there was always a moving van out front. And I sensed each time a new family moved in that my parents didn't want me to run around with their kids, so I stayed away from that place as much as I could.

On the other side of us was a pure white, two-story house with a backyard that stretched itself out beside ours. In ten years, three different families occupied that house, and our family became close friends with all of them. It has always been unusual for our family to share itself with anyone or anything. I think perhaps it was because our backyards merged that we were able to share ourselves so well with these three families.

I didn't have much contact with the rest of the people who lived on down the street because they were elderly and had no children. About the only contact I ever had with them was on Halloween when Mark and I would knock on their doors and ask for candy and then peek past the doorway to see stuffy Victorian furniture that was always some shade of pink or gray, with yellowed lace doilies on the arms and headrests.

Around the corner of the block lived Old Man Pim, the director of the funeral parlor. My parents never liked Mr. Pim, and therefore I grew to dislike him too. We had two dogwood trees and some forsythia bushes that formed the boundary between our backyard and Mr. Pim's, and I remember that he used to cut off their branches when they grew over into his property. He had a garden too, and was always yelling at us kids to stay out of it. I guess that's why we were always tromping through it—just to irritate him—and just to see if he would really use that shotgun full of buckshot that was rumored to hang by his back door.

Next door to Old Man Pim was Mark's house, and its yard marked the borderline past which the families on the block became successively poorer. On down the street from Mark's, the houses became progressively smaller, and when you turned the corner on to Oak Hill, there were just a few lower-income, run-down houses. There were two houses on Oak Hill that were especially scary looking. They were two-story houses, with tall narrow windows, many of which had fallen victim to rocks thrown from without or kitchen utensils thrown from within. One in its day had been olive green, the other had been a subdued yellow; but now they were faded, and the rotten wood had begun to show from under the peeling paint. Both houses sagged in the middle, and this made them look like two ghastly old faces with leering grins. Both houses had the remains of a porch, and on each porch was the rusty frame

of a metal couch with a few ratty cushions. I remember walking by
these houses and seeing two fat ladies sitting on the couches. They
would usually be yelling at each other across the cluttered lawn.

Oak Hill was a place our parents never let us go to on Halloween. They never knew, though, that we sometimes played with the
kids that lived there. We would meet them in the shallow woods
that separated our orchard from their backyard trash piles. Sometimes they had dirty pictures they'd found in the magazines their
parents had discarded. But most often they would tell dirty jokes
and dirty stories which I could never understand because I didn't
understand the terms they used, and I knew better than to ask
for definitions.

We were all scared of the Oak Hill kids; we generally stayed out
of the woods and out of their yards, except to make forays on their
trash piles. These were a goldmine of old lumber and old cardboard
for the clubhouse we built. We had sort of an undeclared war with
the Oak Hill kids. They knew we were stealing their trash, and
they knew what we were using it for. They would come at night
and remove parts of our clubhouse, but the next day we would
sneak back to the trash piles and steal it back again.

All the kids in our neighborhood seemed to gravitate toward
trees. I guess that was why most of them generally ended up in our
backyard, where all the good climbing trees were. We had nearly a
quarter of an acre, and a tree for every purpose. There were about
twenty yards out front bordering the properly cemented street
with its regulation curbs and regulation sidewalks on each side. Besides the rhododendrons and slender hemlocks that landscaped the
front of our orange brick house, there were two rather prickly and
unfriendly pin oak trees, one on either side of the front yard. The
yard, about twenty yards by twenty yards, was raised like a platform and sloped down about four yards to the street. It was a
great place to run around and play tree tag and show off to the
rest of the neighborhood and to that white cement street. Somehow, as much as I disliked that street and the fact that its sidewalks had eaten up part of our playground, I felt a sort of security
when I played where it could watch me and I could watch it. It
was public, and nothing terrifying or unfamiliar could happen to me
while I was in its sight.

Out back was different. Immediately backing the house was a
calm, sort of neutralized fifteen yards of deep green grass. This was
my parents' area. Here were the picnic table, the charcoal grill, the
lawn chairs, and the radio on Saturday afternoons. It was bordered
on one side by the garage and driveway and on the other side by
a white board fence. This fence was the backdrop for my mother's

rose garden, a spot that had conflicting appeal for me. The colors were magnificent, my mother being partial to the deep burgundies and the light, nearly white pinks. I would collect the velvety petals when they fell, mix them all together and crush as many as I could hold in my hands until they squeezed out through my fingers; or I would take one at a time and roll it back and forth until the dark colors came off on my hands. I loved the colors and the touching, but the garden was always filled with Japanese beetles and smelled of bug powder. I usually kept away unless my mother were there working. It was her place, and the tools and the bugs and the flowers were her secrets.

Besides the landscape shrubs that hid the bare right angle between the house and the yard, there was only one tree in this part of the backyard. It was a big maple, probably no more than fifty or sixty feet high, but which, by my youthful estimate, seemed at least a hundred yards tall. This tree was pretty remarkable to me because, unlike all the other trees in our yard, whose leaves were bright green and usually tasty for an afternoon snack, this tree's leaves were dark, bluish green, and when you ate them you got this horrible heavy squelching taste on the back of your tongue and in your throat.

There was a bit of danger involved in this tree. I always felt a sense of panic when I climbed it, but I would never ever have admitted that it was beyond my climbing capabilities. Its thick branches didn't start till ten feet up on the trunk, which meant that I had to shinny all that way just to get a hand- or a leg-hold—a pretty painful undertaking since my legs couldn't quite fit around the knobby trunk. Once into the body of the tree, the trunk forked into two branches that tapered up and up and up until you couldn't tell which was more powerful, the branch or the air currents. I would climb up as close to this point as I dared, swaying more and more with each higher reach, until finally I would have to stop because I was clutching the branch too tightly to let go for another reach.

It was pretty obvious to me why my brother picked this tree as the one for his tree house. He knew when I was scared, and he knew I was scared of this tree; so he figured he'd have less trouble keeping me out of his house if he built it there. My brother was good at figuring me out that way, and he would protect himself from my annoying presence by setting up obstacles—challenges to my strength or courage or ingenuity—that I had to overcome before he would grudgingly let me take part in his activities.

Beyond the square of grass and garden that belonged to my parents, there was a small step-rise of about three feet onto another platform of yard. It was a comfortably enclosed place about twenty-five yards by twenty yards. It was bordered on the east, or bottom side, by the step-rise and the garage. Along the left side was a hedge of poison berry bushes the height of a grownup, and along the right, or north side, was a row of forsythia bushes. It was the top, western boundary that was outstanding though, because on its right side there was the swing set, backed by two handsome but aloof dogwood trees. On the right side was the sandbox, backed by a row of bushes and shaded by a small maple tree from whose low branches we would make parachute leaps onto the sand castles we built. The sandbox and the bushes on the left and the swing set and dogwoods on the right formed the opening to an aisleway that extended back for twenty or thirty yards and then opened out into the orchard. At the farthest end of the orchard there were groupings of fertile apple trees, just far enough away from the house so that mom couldn't see the apple fights that went on. There were peach trees, too, from which we would scrape the sticky globs of sap that oozed out of the bark and rub them in each other's hair. There were pear trees that weren't good for much of anything, and a huge black-barked cherry tree where we'd climb and gorge ourselves and have cherry fights with what we couldn't eat.

Along the right, the aisleway leading to the orchard passed four or five rows of a small grape arbor, and along the left, it passed a garden plot—again my mother's world. I especially enjoyed working with my mother in the garden and among the grape vines. There was no DDT here, only moist, worm-filled earth, and dozens of different greens, all smelling as I thought they were meant to smell. There were a thousand questions I had to ask my mother about this place, like: when to dig up the ground, how to tell a young stalk from a weed, why we had to pull the weeds, why did the carrots grow down instead of up like the cabbages, and how you could tell when a carrot was done growing. And there were a thousand things to learn, like: if I stepped on the tomato seedlings, they wouldn't come back up again, and if I ate the grapes before they were ripe, I'd get miserably sick. I think it was from the garden and the grapes, my mother's world, that I developed a sense of seasons and of time passing. For a long time I had known the names—summer, spring, winter, fall—but was unable to link them to events or grasp their rhythm. My mother would say to me, "Spring, then summer, then fall, then winter, then spring again, just like that." But it never stuck. For me, it wasn't something that anybody could explain. It was all a matter of time, of experiencing the rhythm over and over again until the pattern was established.

It was from the trees that I learned the rhythm; and from

one particular tree that I think I sensed the links and learned the pattern. This tree, which stood in the center of the backyard, the center of the neighborhood, was also the center of my world. It was just the right height, with just the right type branches, which formed a sort of spiral ladder to the top—not so dangerous that you couldn't swing around in it, yet enough of a challenge that you didn't grow tired of it. It was a comfortable tree. I would spend hours in that fine tree, climbing over and over again from the ground to the very top, some fifteen or twenty yards up, trying to improve my speed, trying to find the combination of branches and foot placement that would get me to the top the fastest. We used to call that tree the monkey tree because we would take bananas and fruit up into the tree and eat them and then swing around and dare each other to jump from the branch that, when you hung from it, left your feet dangling about seven feet off the ground. I would watch the tree, or rather I would watch its leaves, move calmly through the cycle of birth and change and death, and I came to realize that the games I could play in the tree were all dependent on which stage of the cycle those leaves were in.

There were times when my parents wouldn't let us climb in the trees because they said we would break off all the buds and that if we did that, there wouldn't be any leaves in the summer. So we stayed out of the trees and played football or kites and looked at the trees and waited. With summer came freedom to do whatever we wanted with the trees—climb them, hide in them, jump from them, build tents and houses in them, eat their leaves—they were indestructible. When it came time for school to start, we found that we couldn't spend as much time in the trees as we wanted. But that was all right because the most exciting things that happen to a tree in the fall happen not inside its branches but outside, where you can see all the changes and colors at once, and on the ground where the leaves are raked into piles deep enough to hide in.

But I can remember some depressing times when there were no games, and I would sit with my elbows on the ledge of the picture window that looked out over the back yard, and stare blankly and hopelessly at the snow and the bare dead tips of the branches. It was a desolate time, and my parents would try to reassure me that the leaves would come back again; but I could never trust them, as I could the trees, to reassure me that life and green would come again after such a long time of death and cold.

I used to think a lot about trees in those days—trees and the seasons and leaves that changed color all by themselves. There were other trees besides the maple that were special in one way or another, and the dogwoods were in this special group. Each one of us had a dogwood tree that was his very own. I had planted mine out by the garden and used to watch how it grew, each year getting larger and stronger and thicker in its branches. I used to await the day when it would finally be big enough to show the changes of the seasons. The two giant dogwoods by the swing set were able to do this. These two trees held a special fascination for me when in the spring they would blaze pure white with perfectly shaped four-petal blossoms. In the summer their leaves would be a fresh soft green, and then in the fall they would turn a magnificent scarlet. They would turn first of all along the edges, leaving the veins green, and then the veins would go, hardening into a rich chocolate brown. In the late fall, the leaves would drop, leaving the tight clusters of red berries and revealing a delicate lacelike pattern of branches. No other tree was like those dogwoods, which were able to change colors three times a year instead of just two. There was a sort of majesty or aloofness in those two trees that I deeply respected, and I waited for that majesty to develop in my own small dogwood tree.

But that never happened. When I was ten years old, and when my tree was three, we moved to a new house. My tree was the only one of the three which we tried to move. I helped my parents dig up my tree and helped them transplant it in our new yard. But it didn't even last the winter. I was sure it had died as we dug it up from its original ground. Well, what do you do with a dead tree? I watched my father axe it down with a few quick chops—too few, I thought, to be in keeping with the potential character of that tree—and then throw it on the leaf pile to become compost with all the dead leaves from those common, two-color trees.

I knew I wasn't going to like the new house. Something had died there. There were no climbing trees, not a single one. There was a ring of thirteen maples around the house, but not a single one had a branch that was within reaching distance. We would have had to use a twelve-foot ladder to get started. Out back were dozens of huge black pines that cast dark shadows over everything, and made the ground wet and spongy. Not even the grass grew under them. The ground was decades deep in browned-out pine needles. My mother and father loved this new house; it was somber. There was a certain aged, unchanging quality about it that appealed to them. I thought it was gloomy. For me it meant that my childhood days of climbing and galloping wildly down aisles of trees were over. Here I kept bumping into trees and tripping over the tunnels that the moles had burrowed in the soft ground.

The only event that we celebrated with the yard was the season of fall, when all those tons of leaves from all those anonymous trees would come falling down, and we would have to rake them up so that the yard would "look nice." After one or two seasons, I began to refuse to take part in the family leaf-raking. The raking was every weekend for two months beginning in September and ending with the first snows in November. I told my parents I thought it was senseless to rake everything clear one week, only to have to rake it all over again the following week. My parents were angry with me because they said it was one of the few things that we did as a family and that I should feel obliged to take part. But I couldn't stand that weekly, yearly, celebration of death. I would tell my parents that I had to study or had made plans to play with a friend, but mostly I would just go on long walks or long bike rides. One time I rode over to the neighborhood where we used to live. I rode my bike back and forth in front of the house and tried to decide whether or not I should try to sneak into the back yard. It would have been easy enough to do; all I would have had to do was go around the corner to Mark's house and sneak in through the orchard. But I couldn't do it. I was afraid Mark or someone might recognize me, and I wanted to be alone when I would see the trees again after four years. I rode on down the street and around the corner and on out to the country road that marked the western edge of town. It was dark by the time I got home.

AFTERWORD

A sense of place seems to be very important to most successful writers. Of the Americans, William Faulkner is perhaps the best-known example of a writer whose life and work are closely tied to a specific region; but there are many others. Mark Twain, for example, was unable to finish his masterpiece, *The Adventures of Huckleberry Finn,* until he returned to the land along the Mississippi River where he had lived as a boy. Similarly, Wendell Berry explains in *The Hidden Wound* (see page 162) how his own writing was influenced by his return to Kentucky, the scene of his childhood.

A sense of place is important to the average person as well. I remember an afternoon six years ago when my father and I revisited his boyhood home in Pennsylvania. We walked in the yard of the farmhouse in which he was raised, and we looked out across a patch of berries at the darkly weathered barn. This was his first return to the site in forty years, and it touched off memories so rapidly that he could barely tell me one before another clicked into focus. As we walked among his memories, he stumbled. We both looked down at the freshly cut grass and saw that there was nothing there to stumble on, and then he looked over toward the house and laughed. He proceeded to explain that, where we now stood on smooth-cut grass, there had once been a wooden drain used for dumping waste water from the kitchen. As a boy, he told me, he had often stumbled painfully on that drain while running through the yard. Now, more than forty years later, he had nearly fallen on the sudden, intense memory of a drain that was no longer really there.

Writers value such stumbling on the past because it can provide the sort of concrete, immediate details that help to bring literature to life. Mary McCarthy's "Yellowstone Park," for example, is built around a concrete sense of place—although one might say that the essay is no more about Medicine Springs, the small town it describes, than it is about Yellowstone Park. But, while the piece is really the tale of a strange initiation rite for a bright, over-protected young woman, its sharp edge is surely due to the concreteness with which McCarthy evokes the disappointing little town: "Behind the hotel there were the 'springs' alluded to in the town's name; they consisted of a dirty, sulphurous, cement swimming pool with one half-dead tree leaning over it. The heat was awful, and the only shade apparent was provided by telephone poles."

Writers make various uses of place in their work. In "The Flow of the River," for example, Loren Eiseley shows obvious affection for the Platte River and the high plains of Nebraska; but his purpose is to reflect upon man's relationship to nature and the process of evolution. What makes the essay fascinating, I think, is the way Eiseley offers these rather abstract observations in the midst of carefully detailed, concrete description—the way he roots his ideas to a place.

Norman Mailer's description of the Pentagon's north parking area in *The Armies of the Night* is similarly indirect. It is not the parking lot that interests Mailer, but its influence on his own mood as he prepares to commit an act of civil disobedience. His descriptions of the parking lot, the Pentagon, and surrounding landscape alternate with passages that trace his thinking as he stands at the end of the March on the Pentagon. And beyond that, in the way he describes this place, Mailer offers his reasons for participating in the March. Throughout, he is more concerned with communicating an attitude than with providing a precise image, as, for example, when he says that "the Pentagon looked like the five-sided tip on the spout of a spray can to be used under the arm, yes, the Pentagon was spraying the deodorant of its presence all over the fields of Virginia."

In "A Good Climbing Tree Is Hard to Find," Barbara Anderson focuses more directly on place, describing her childhood in Wooster, Ohio, in terms of a particular back yard. Place works two ways in this short essay: it is the stimulus for concrete early memories as well as the structure for describing them. Within the context of this anthology, the essay is also a reminder that the inclusion of a piece in one chapter does not necessarily mean that it is unsuited to others. Anderson's essay is obviously appropriate both for "Person and Place" and for "Early Memory"; many of the book's other selections exhibit similar overlaps.

Suggested writing assignments

1. Write an essay that focuses on a place of some significance in your own experience. It might be a place you visited only once or the place where you played out your childhood. Try to describe the place so fully that its importance to you will be conveyed to the reader.

2. Sometimes you can learn a good deal about people from their surroundings. The way a person furnishes a room in which he lives, for example, often tells thoughtful observers much about his interests and attitudes. Thus in "Yellowstone Park," for example, McCarthy's description of the Bent house provides an indirect but convincing characterization of its occupants. The relationship between people and places exists on a large scale as well, for it is possible to say a good deal about communities or whole societies by describing the architecture they choose and their modifications of the land they inhabit. Write an essay in which your description of a place provides a valid characterization of a person or group associated with it.

four: selfhood and event

from
narrative of the life
of Frederick Douglass

FREDERICK DOUGLASS (1817–1895), who had escaped
from slavery in 1838, electrified an antislavery convention in
Nantucket in 1841 with a speech about his life as a slave.
Soon thereafter he became associated with the Massachusetts Anti-Slavery Society and, though self-conscious about
his lack of education, began writing for the *Liberator,* an aboli-
tionist newspaper. His first published book, *Narrative of the
Life of Frederick Douglass* (1845), made him nationally famous, and he later wrote two more-extended autobiographies, *My Bondage and My Freedom* (1855) and *Life and
Times of Frederick Douglass* (1881).

I left Master Thomas's house, and went to live with Mr. Covey,
on the 1st of January, 1833. I was now, for the first time in my
life, a field hand. In my new employment, I found myself even more
awkward than a country boy appeared to be in a large city. I had
been at my new home but one week before Mr. Covey gave me a
very severe whipping, cutting my back causing the blood to run,
and raising ridges on my flesh as large as my little finger. The details
of this affair are as follows: Mr. Covey sent me, very early in the
morning of one of our coldest days in the month of January, to the
woods, to get a load of wood. He gave me a team of unbroken oxen.
He told me which was the in-hand ox, and which the off-hand one.
He then tied the end of a large rope around the horns of the in-
hand ox, and gave me the other end of it, and told me, if the ox-
en started to run, that I must hold on upon the rope. I had never
driven oxen before, and of course I was very awkward. I, however,
succeeded in getting to the edge of the woods with little difficulty; but I had got a very few rods into the woods, when the oxen
took fright, and started full tilt, carrying the cart against trees,
and over stumps, in the most frightful manner. I expected every

moment that my brains would be dashed out against the trees. After running thus for a considerable distance, they finally upset the
cart, sashing it with great force against a tree, and threw themselves into a dense thicket. How I escaped death, I do not know.
There I was, entirely alone, in a thick wood, in a place new to me.
My cart was upset and shattered, my oxen were entangled among
the young trees, and there was none to help me. After a long spell
of effort, I succeeded in getting my cart righted, my oxen disen-
tangled, and again yoked to the cart. I now proceeded with my
team to the place where I had, the day before, been chopping
wood, and loaded my cart pretty heavily, thinking in this way to
tame my oxen. I then proceeded on my way home. I had now con-
sumed one half of the day. I got out of the woods safely, and now
felt out of danger. I stopped my oxen to open the woods gate; and
just as I did so, before I could get hold of my ox-rope, the oxen
again started, rushed through the gate, catching it between the
wheel and the body of the cart, tearing it to pieces, and coming
within a few inches of crushing me against the gate-post. Thus
twice, in one short day, I escaped death by the merest chance. On
my return, I told Mr. Covey what had happened, and how it happened. He ordered me to return to the woods again immediately.
I did so, and he followed on after me. Just as I got into the woods,
he came up and told me to stop my cart, and that he would teach
me how to trifle away my time, and break gates. He then went
to a large gum-tree, and with his axe cut three large switches, and,
after trimming them up neatly with his pocket-knife, he ordered
me to take off my clothes. I made him no answer, but stood with
my clothes on. He repeated his order. I still made him no answer,
nor did I move to strip myself. Upon this he rushed at me with
the fierceness of a tiger, tore off my clothes, and lashed me till he
had worn out his switches, cutting me so savagely as to leave the
marks visible for a long time after. This whipping was the first of
a number just like it, and for similar offences.

I lived with Mr. Covey one year. During the first six months,
of that year, scarce a week passed without his whipping me. I was
seldom free from a sore back. My awkwardness was almost always his
excuse for whipping me. We were worked fully up to the point of
endurance. Long before day we were up, our horses fed, and by the
first approach of day we were off to the field with our hoes and
ploughing teams. Mr. Covey gave us enough to eat, but scarce time
to eat it. We were often less than five minutes taking our meals.
We were often in the field from the first approach of day till its
last lingering ray had left us; and at saving-fodder time, midnight
often caught us in the field binding blades.

Covey would be out with us. The way he used to stand it, was this. He would spend the most of his afternoons in bed. He would then come out fresh in the evening, ready to urge us on with his words, example, and frequently with the whip. Mr. Covey was one of the few slaveholders who could and did work with his hands. He was a hard-working man. He knew by himself just what a man or a boy could do. There was no deceiving him. His work went on in his absence almost as well as in his presence; and he had the faculty of making us feel that he was ever present with us. This he did by surprising us. He seldom approached the spot where we were at work openly, if he could do it secretly. He always aimed at taking us by surprise. Such was his cunning, that we used to call him, among ourselves, "the snake." When we were at work in the cornfield, he would sometimes crawl on his hands and knees to avoid detection, and all at once he would rise nearly in our midst, and scream out, "Ha, ha! Come, come! Dash on, dash on!" This being his mode of attack, it was never safe to stop a single minute. His comings were like a thief in the night. He appeared to us as being ever at hand. He was under every tree, behind every stump, in every bush, and at every window, on the plantation. He would sometimes mount his horse, as if bound to St. Michael's, a distance of seven miles, and in half an hour afterwards you would see him coiled up in the corner of the wood-fence, watching every motion of the slaves. He would, for this purpose, leave his horse tied up in the woods. Again, he would sometimes walk up to us, and give us orders as though he was upon the point of starting on a long journey, turn his back upon us, and make as though he was going to the house to get ready; and, before he would get half way thither, he would turn short and crawl into a fence-corner, or behind some tree, and there watch us till the going down of the sun.

Mr. Covey's *forte* consisted in his power to deceive. His life was devoted to planning and perpetrating the grossest deceptions. Every thing he possessed in the shape of learning or religion, he made conform to his disposition to deceive. He seemed to think himself equal to deceiving the Almighty. He would make a short prayer in the morning, and a long prayer at night; and, strange as it may seem, few men would at times appear more devotional than he. The exercises of his family devotions were always commenced with singing; and, as he was a very poor singer himself, the duty of raising the hymn generally came upon me. He would read his hymn, and nod at me to commence. I would at times do so; at others, I would not. My non-compliance would almost always produce much confusion. To show himself independent of me, he would start and stag-

ger through with his hymn in the most discordant manner. In this
state of mind, he prayed with more than ordinary spirit. Poor man!
such was his disposition, and success at deceiving, I do verily believe
that he sometimes deceived himself into the solemn belief, that
he was a sincere worshipper of the most high God; and this, too,
at a time when he may be said to have been guilty of compelling
his woman slave to commit the sin of adultery. The facts in the
case are these: Mr. Covey was a poor man; he was just commencing
in life; he was only able to buy one slave; and, shocking as is the
fact, he bought her, as he said, for *a breeder*. This woman was
named Caroline. Mr. Covey bought her from Mr. Thomas Lowe,
about six miles from St. Michael's. She was a large, able-bodied
woman, about twenty years old. She had already given birth to one
child, which proved her to be just what he wanted. After buying
her, he hired a married man of Mr. Samuel Harrison, to live with
him one year; and him he used to fasten up with her every night!
The result was, that, at the end of the year, the miserable woman
gave birth to twins. At this result Mr. Covey seemed to be highly
pleased, both with the man and the wretched woman. Such was
his joy, and that of his wife, that nothing they could do for Caroline during her confinement was too good, or too hard, to be done.
The children were regarded as being quite an addition to his
wealth.

If at any one time of my life more than another, I was made
to drink the bitterest dregs of slavery, that time was during the
first six months of my stay with Mr. Covey. We were worked in
all weathers. It was never too hot or too cold; it could never rain,
blow, hail, or snow, too hard for us to work in the field. Work,
work, work, was scarcely more the order of the day than of the
night. The longest days were too short for him, and the shortest
nights too long for him. I was somewhat unmanageable when I first
went there, but a few months of this discipline tamed me. Mr.
Covey succeeded in breaking me. I was broken in body, soul, and spirit. My natural elasticity was crushed, my intellect languished, the
disposition to read departed, the cheerful spark that lingered
about my eye died; the dark night of slavery closed in upon me; and
behold a man transformed into a brute!

Sunday was my only leisure time. I spent this in a sort of
beast-like stupor, between sleep and wake, under some large tree.
At times I would rise up, a flash of energetic freedom would dart
through my soul, accompanied with a faint beam of hope, that
flickered for a moment, and then vanished. I sank down again,
mourning over my wretched condition. I was sometimes prompted

to take my life, and that of Covey, but was prevented by a combination of hope and fear. My sufferings on this plantation seem now like a dream rather than a stern reality.

Our house stood within a few rods of the Chesapeake Bay, whose broad bosom was ever white with sails from every quarter of the habitable globe. Those beautiful vessels, robed in purest white, so delightful to the eye of freemen, were to me so many shrouded ghosts, to terrify and torment me with thoughts of my wretched condition. I have often, in the deep stillness of a summer's Sabbath, stood all alone upon the lofty banks of that noble bay, and traced, with saddened heart and tearful eye, the countless number of sails moving off to the mighty ocean. The sight of these always affected me powerfully. My thoughts would compel utterance; and there, with no audience but the Almighty, I would pour out my soul's complaint, in my rude way, with an apostrophe to the moving multitude of ships:—

"You are loosed from your moorings, and are free; I am fast in my chains, and am a slave! You move merrily before the gentle gale, and I sadly before the bloody whip! You are freedom's swift-winged angels, that fly round the world; I am confined in bands of iron! O that I were free! O, that I were on one of your gallant decks, and under your protecting wing! Alas! betwixt me and you, the turbid waters roll. Go on, go on. O that I could also go! Could I but swim! If I could fly! O, why was I born a man, of whom to make a brute! The glad ship is gone; she hides in the dim distance. I am left in the hottest hell of unending slavery. O God, save me! God, deliver me! Let me be free! Is there any God? Why am I a slave? I will run away. I will not stand it. Get caught, or get clear, I'll try it. I had as well die with ague as the fever. I have only one life to lose. I had as well be killed running as die standing. Only think of it; one hundred miles straight north, and I am free! Try it? Yes! God helping me, I will. It cannot be that I shall live and die a slave. I will take to the water. This very bay shall yet bear me into freedom. The steamboats steered in a north-east course from North Point. I will do the same; and when I get to the head of the bay, I will turn my canoe adrift, and walk straight through Delaware into Pennsylvania. When I get there, I shall not be required to have a pass; I can travel without being disturbed. Let but the first opportunity offer, and, come what will, I am off. Meanwhile, I will try to bear up under the yoke. I am not the only slave in the world. Why should I fret? I can bear as much as any of them. Besides, I am but a boy, and all boys are bound to some one. It may be that my misery in slavery will only increase my happiness when I get free. There is a better day coming."

Thus I used to think, and thus I used to speak to myself; goaded almost to madness at one moment, and at the next reconciling myself to my wretched lot.

I have already intimated that my condition was much worse, during the first six months of my stay at Mr. Covey's, than in the last six. The circumstances leading to the change in Mr. Covey's course toward me form an epoch in my humble history. You have seen how a man was made a slave; you shall see how a slave was made a man. On one of the hottest days of the month of August, 1833, Bill Smith, William Hughes, a slave named Eli, and myself, were engaged in fanning wheat. Hughes was clearing the fanned wheat from before the fan, Eli was turning, Smith was feeding, and I was carrying wheat to the fan. The work was simple, requiring strength rather than intellect; yet, to one entirely unused to such work, it came very hard. About three o'clock of that day, I broke down; my strength failed me; I was seized with a violent aching of the head, attended with extreme dizziness; I trembled in every limb. Finding what was coming, I nerved myself up, feeling it would never do to stop work. I stood as long as I could stagger to the hopper with grain. When I could stand no longer, I fell, and felt as if held down by an immense weight. The fan of course stopped; every one had his own work to do; and no one could do the work of the other, and have his own go on at the same time.

Mr. Covey was at the house, about one hundred yards from the treading-yard where we were fanning. On hearing the fan stop, he left immediately, and came to the spot where we were. He hastily inquired what the matter was. Bill answered that I was sick, and there was no one to bring wheat to the fan. I had by this time crawled away under the side of the post and rail-fence by which the yard was enclosed, hoping to find relief by getting out of the sun. He then asked where I was. He was told by one of the hands. He came to the spot, and, after looking at me awhile, asked me what was the matter. I told him as well as I could, for I scarce had strength to speak. He then gave me a savage kick in the side, and told me to get up. I tried to do so, but fell back in the attempt. He gave me another kick, and again told me to rise. I again tried, and succeeded in gaining my feet; but, stooping to get the tub with which I was feeding the fan, I again staggered and fell. While down in this situation, Mr. Covey took up the hickory slat with which Hughes had been striking off the half-bushel measure, and with it gave me a heavy blow upon the head, making a large wound, and the blood ran freely; and with this again told me to get up. I made no effort to comply, having now made up my mind to let him do his worst. In a short time after receiving this blow, my head grew better. Mr. Covey had now left me to my fate. At this moment I resolved, for the first time, to go to my master, enter a complaint, and ask his protection. In order to [do] this, I must that afternoon walk seven miles; and this, under the circumstances, was truly a severe undertaking. I was exceedingly feeble; made so as much by the kicks and blows which I received, as by the severe fit of sickness to which I had been subjected. I, however, watched my chance, while Covey was looking in an opposite direction, and started for St. Michael's. I succeeded in getting a considerable distance on my way to the woods, when Covey discovered me, and called after me to come back, threatening what he would do if I did not come. I disregarded both his calls and his threats, and made my way to the woods as fast as my feeble state would allow; and thinking I might be overhauled by him if I kept the road, I walked through the woods, keeping far enough from the road to avoid detection, and near enough to prevent losing my way I had not gone far before my little strength again failed me. I could go no farther. I fell down, and lay for a considerable time. The blood was yet oozing from the wound on my head. For a time I thought I should bleed to death; and think now that I should have done so, but that the blood so matted my hair as to stop the wound. After lying there about three quarters of an hour, I nerved myself up again, and started on my way, through bogs and briers, barefooted and bareheaded, tearing my feet sometimes at nearly every step; and after a journey of about seven miles, occupying some five hours to perform it, I arrived at master's store. I then presented an appearance enough to affect any but a heart of iron. From the crown of my head to my feet, I was covered with blood. My hair was all clotted with dust and blood; my shirt was stiff with blood. My legs and feet were torn in sundry places with briers and thorns, and were also covered with blood. I suppose I looked like a man who had escaped a den of wild beasts, and barely escaped them. In this state I appeared before my master, humbly entreating him to interpose his authority for my protection. I told him all the circumstances as well as I could, and it seemed, as I spoke, at times to affect him. He would then walk the floor, and seek to justify Covey by saying he expected I deserved it. He asked me what I wanted. I told him, to let me get a new home; that as sure as I lived with Mr. Covey again, I should live with but to die with him; that Covey would surely kill me; he was in a fair way for it. Master Thomas ridiculed the idea that there was any danger of Mr. Covey's killing me, and said that he knew Mr. Covey; that he was a good man, and that he could not think of taking me from him; that, should he do so, he would lose the whole year's wages; that I belonged to Mr. Covey for one year, and that I must go back to him, come what might; and that I must not trouble him with any more stories, or that he would himself *get hold of me.* After threatening me thus, he gave me a very large dose of salts, telling me that I might remain in St. Michael's that night, (it being quite late,) but that I must be off back to Mr. Covey's early in the morning; and that if I did not, he would *get hold of me,* which meant that he would whip me. I remained all night, and, according to his orders, I started off to Covey's in the morning, (Saturday morning,) wearied in body and broken in spirit. I got no supper that night, or breakfast that morning. I reached Covey's about nine o'clock; and just as I was getting over the fence that divided Mrs. Kemp's fields from ours, out ran Covey with his cowskin, to give me another whipping. Before he could reach me, I succeeded in getting to the cornfield; and as the corn was very high, it afforded me the means of hiding. He seemed very angry, and searched for me a long time. My behavior was altogether unaccountable. He finally gave up the chase, thinking, I suppose, that I must come home for something to eat; he would give himself no further trouble in looking for me. I spent that day mostly in the woods, having the alternative before me,—to go home and be whipped to death, or stay in the woods and be starved to death. That night, I fell in with Sandy Jenkins, a slave with whom I was somewhat acquainted. Sandy had a free wife who lived about four miles from Mr. Covey's; and it being Saturday, he was on his way to see her. I told him my circumstances, and he very kindly invited me to go home with him. I went home with him, and talked this whole matter over, and got his advice as to what course it was best for me to pursue. I found Sandy an old adviser. He told me, with great solemnity, I must go back to Covey; but that before I went, I must go with him into another part of the woods, where there was a certain *root,* which, if I would take some of it with me, carrying it *always on my right side,* would render it impossible for Mr. Covey, or any other white man, to whip me. He said he had carried it for years; and since he had done so, he had never received a blow, and never expected to while he carried it. I at first rejected the idea, that the simple carrying of a root in my pocket would have any such effect as he had said, and was not disposed to take it; but Sandy impressed the necessity with much earnestness, telling me it could do no harm, if it did no good. To please him, I at length took the root, and, according to his direction, carried it upon my right side. This was Sunday morning. I immediately started for home; and upon entering the yard gate, out came Mr. Covey on his way to meeting. He spoke to me very kindly, made me drive the pigs from a lot near by, and passed on towards the church. Now, this singular conduct of Mr. Covey really made me begin to think that there was something in the *root* which Sandy had given me; and had it been on any other day than Sunday, I could have attributed the conduct to no other cause than the influence of that root; and as it was, I was half inclined to think the *root* to be something more than I at first had taken it to be. All went well till Monday morning. On this morning, the virtue of the *root* was fully tested. Long before daylight, I was called to go and rub, curry, and feed, the horses. I obeyed, and was glad to obey. But whilst thus engaged, whilst in the act of throwing down some blades from the loft, Mr. Covey entered the stable with a long rope; and just as I was half out of the loft, he caught hold of my legs, and was about tying me. As soon as I found what he was up to, I gave a sudden spring, and as I did so, he holding to my legs, I was brought sprawling on the stable floor. Mr. Covey seemed now to think he had me, and could do what he pleased; but at this moment—from whence came the spirit I don't know—I resolved to fight; and, suiting my action to the resolution, I seized Covey hard by the throat; and as I did so, I rose. He held on to me, and I to him. My resistance was so entirely unexpected, that Covey seemed taken all aback. He trembled like a leaf. This gave me assurance, and I held him uneasy, causing the blood to run where I touched him with the ends of my fingers. Mr. Covey soon called out to Hughes for help. Hughes came, and, while Covey held me, attempted to tie my right hand. While he was in the act of doing so, I watched my chance, and gave him a heavy kick close under the ribs. This kick fairly sickened Hughes, so that he left me in the hands of Mr. Covey. This kick had the effect of not only weakening Hughes, but Covey also. When he saw Hughes bending over with pain, his courage quailed. He asked me if I meant to persist in my resistance. I told him I did, come what might; that he had used me like a brute for six months, and that I was determined to be used so no longer. With that, he strove to drag me to a stick that was lying just out of the stable door. He meant to knock me down. But just as he was leaning over to get the stick, I seized him with both hands by his collar, and brought him by a sudden snatch to the ground. By this time, Bill came. Covey called upon him for assistance. Bill wanted to know what he could do. Covey said, "Take hold of him, take hold of him!" Bill said his master hired him out to work, and not to help to whip me; so he left Covey and myself to fight our own battle out. We were at it for nearly two hours. Covey at length let me go, puffing and blowing at a great rate, saying that if I had not resisted, he would not have whipped me half so much.

The truth was, that he had not whipped me at all. I considered him as getting entirely the worst end of the bargain; for he had drawn no blood from me, but I had from him. The whole six months afterwards, that I spent with Mr. Covey, he never laid the weight of his finger upon me in anger. He would occasionally say, he didn't want to get hold of me again. "No," thought I, "you need not; for you will come off worse than you did before."

This battle with Mr. Covey was the turning-point in my career as a slave. It rekindled the few expiring embers of freedom, and revived within me a sense of my own manhood. It recalled the departed self-confidence, and inspired me again with a determination to be free. The gratification afforded by the triumph was a full compensation for whatever else might follow, even death itself. He only can understand the deep satisfaction which I experienced, who has himself repelled by force the bloody arm of slavery. I felt as I never felt before. It was a glorious resurrection, from the tomb of slavery, to the heaven of freedom. My long-crushed spirit rose, cowardice departed, bold defiance took its place; and I now resolved that, however long I might remain a slave in form, the day had passed forever when I could be a slave in fact. I did not hesitate to let it be known of me, that the white man who expected to succeed in whipping, must also succeed in killing me.

From this time I was never again what might be called fairly whipped, though I remained a slave four years afterwards. I had several fights, but was never whipped.

It was for a long time a matter of surprise to me why Mr. Covey did not immediately have me taken by the constable to the whipping-post, and there regularly whipped for the crime of raising my hand against a white man in defence of myself. And the only explanation I can now think of does not entirely satisfy me; but such as it is, I will give it. Mr. Covey enjoyed the most unbounded reputation for being a first-rate overseer and negro-breaker. It was of considerable importance to him. That reputation was at stake; and had he sent me—a boy about sixteen years old—to the public whipping-post, his reputation would have been lost; so, to save his reputation, he suffered me to go unpunished.

when I was a child

LILLIAN SMITH (1897–1966) struggled against cancer from 1953 until her death in 1966; and her writing, both during this period and earlier, is marked by the same quiet courage that characterized her personal life. In her novel *Strange Fruit,* for example, Smith treats interracial love and violence with such honesty that, when the book was published in 1944, efforts were made to suppress it; indeed, many of Smith's neighbors expressed shock that a white southern woman could have imagined such a story. Smith's nonfictional works include *Killers of the Dream* (1949; revised 1961), from which "When I Was a Child" is taken; *The Journey* (1954); *Now Is the Time* (1955), a statement about the importance of implementing the 1954 Supreme Court decision on desegregation; and *Our Faces, Our Words* (1964).

Even its children know that the South is in trouble. No one has to tell them; no words said aloud. To them, it is a vague thing weaving in and out of their play, like a ghost haunting an old graveyard or whispers after the household sleeps—fleeting mystery, vague menace, to which each responds in his own way. Some learn to screen out all except the soft and the soothing; others deny even as they see plainly, and hear. But all know that under quiet words and warmth and laughter, under the slow ease and tender concern about small matters, there is a heavy burden on all of us and as heavy a refusal to confess it. The children know this "trouble" is bigger than they, bigger than their family, bigger than their church, so big that people turn away from its size. They have seen it flash out like lightning and shatter a town's peace, have felt it tear up all they believe in. They have measured its giant strength and they feel weak when they remember.

This haunted childhood belongs to every southerner. Many of us run away from it but we come back like a hurt animal to its wound, or a murderer to the scene of his sin. The human heart

REPRINTED from *Killers of the Dream* by Lillian Smith. By permission of W. W. Norton & Company, Inc. Copyright © 1949, 1961 by Lillian Smith.

dares not stay away too long from that which hurt it most. There is a return journey to anguish that few of us are released from making.

We who were born in the South call this mesh of feeling and memory "loyalty." We think of it sometimes as "love." We identify with the South's trouble as if we, individually, were responsible for all of it. We defend the sins and sorrows of three hundred years as if each sin had been committed by us alone and each sorrow had cut across our heart. We are as hurt at criticism of our region as if our own name were called aloud by the critic. We have known guilt without understanding it, and there is no tie that binds men closer to the past and each other than that.

It is a strange thing, this umbilical cord uncut. In times of ease, we do not feel its pull, but when we are threatened with change, suddenly it draws the whole white South together in a collective fear and fury that wipe our minds clear of reason and we are blocked off from sensible contact with the world we live in.

To keep this resistance strong, wall after wall has been thrown up in the southern mind against criticism from without and within. Imaginations close tight against the hurt of others; a regional armoring takes place to keep out the "enemies" who would make our trouble different—or maybe rid us of it completely. For it is a trouble that we do not want to give up. We are as involved with it as a child who cannot be happy at home and cannot bear to tear himself away, or as a grown-up who has fallen in love with his own disease. We southerners have identified with the long sorrowful past on such deep levels of love and hate and guilt that we do not know how to break old bonds without pulling our lives down. *Change* is the evil word, a shrill clanking that makes us know too well our servitude. *Change* means leaving one's memories, one's sins, one's ancient prison, the room where one was born. How can we do this when we are tied fast!

The white man's burden is his own childhood. Every southerner knows this. Though he may deny it even to himself, yet he drags through life with him the heavy weight of a past that never eases and is rarely understood, of desire never appeased, of dreams that died in his heart.

In this South I was born and now live. Here it was that I began to grow, seeking my way, as do all children, through the honeycomb cells of our life to the bright reality outside. Sometimes it was as if all doors opened inward. . . . Sometimes we children lost even the desire to get outside and tried only to make a comfortable home of the trap of swinging doors that history and religion and a war, man's greed and his guilt had placed us in at birth.

It is not easy to pick out of such a life those strands that
have to do only with color, only with Negro-white relationships,
only with religion or sex, for they are knit of the same fibers that
have gone into the making of the whole fabric, woven into its basic patterns and designs. Religion . . . sex . . . race . . . money . . .
avoidance rites . . . malnutrition . . . dreams—no part of these can
be looked at and clearly seen without looking at the whole of
them. For, as a painter mixes colors and makes of them new colors,
so religion is turned into something different by race, and segregation is colored as much by sex as by skin pigment, and money is no
longer a coin but a lost wish wandering through a man's whole life.

A child's lessons are blended of these strands however dissonant
a design they make. The mother who taught me what I know of
tenderness and love and compassion taught me also the bleak rituals of keeping Negroes in their place. The father who rebuked me
for an air of superiority toward schoolmates from the mill and
rounded out his rebuke by gravely reminding me that "all men are
brothers," trained me in the steel-rigid decorums I must demand of
every colored male. They who so gravely taught me to split my body
from my feelings and both from my "soul," taught me also to split
my conscience from my acts and Christianity from southern tradition.

Neither the Negro nor sex was often discussed at length in our
home. We were given no formal instruction in these difficult matters but we learned our lessons well. We learned the intricate system of taboos, of renunciations and compensations, of manners,
voice modulations, words, feelings, along with our prayers, our toilet habits, and our games. I do not remember how or when, but
by the time I had learned that God is love, that Jesus is His Son
and came to give us more abundant life, that all men are brothers
with a common Father, I also knew that I was better than a Negro, that all black folks have their place and must be kept in it,
that sex has its place and must be kept in it, that a terrifying
disaster would befall the South if ever I treated a Negro as my social equal and as terrifying a disaster would befall my family if ever
I were to have a baby outside of marriage. I had learned that God
so loved the world that He gave His only begotten Son so that
we might have segregated churches in which it was my duty to
worship each Sunday and on Wednesday at evening prayers. I had
learned that white southerners are a hospitable, courteous, tactful
people who treat those of their own group with consideration and
who as carefully segregate from all the richness of life "for their own
good and welfare" thirteen million people whose skin is colored a
little differently from my own.

I knew by the time I was twelve that a member of my family would always shake hands with old Negro friends, would speak gently and graciously to members of the Negro race unless they forgot their place, in which event icy peremptory tones would draw lines beyond which only the desperate would dare take one step. I knew that to use the word "nigger" was unpardonable and no well-bred southerner was quite so crude as to do so; nor would a well-bred southerner call a Negro "mister" or invite him into the living room or eat with him or sit by him in public places.

I knew that my old nurse who had patiently cared for me through long months of illness, who had given me refuge when a little sister took my place as the baby of the family, who comforted me, soothed, fed me, delighted me with her stories and games, let me fall asleep on her deep warm breast, was not worthy of the passionate love I felt for her but must be given instead a half-smiled-at affection similar to that which one feels for one's dog. I knew but I never believed it, that the deep respect I felt for her, the tenderness, the love, was a childish thing which every normal child outgrows, that such love begins with one's toys and is discarded with them, and that somehow—though it seemed impossible to my agonized heart—I too, must outgrow these feelings. I learned to give presents to this woman I loved, instead of esteem and honor. I learned to use a soft voice to oil my words of superiority. I learned to cheapen with tears and sentimental talk of "my old mammy" one of the profound relationships of my life. I learned the bitterest thing a child can learn: that the human relations I valued most were held cheap by the world I lived in.

From the day I was born, I began to learn my lessons. I was put in a rigid frame too intricate, too complex, too twisting to describe here so briefly, but I learned to conform to its slide-rule measurements. I learned that it is possible to be a Christian and a white southerner simultaneously; to be a gentlewoman and an arrogant callous creature in the same moment; to pray at night and ride a Jim Crow car the next morning and to feel comfortable in doing both. I learned to believe in freedom, to glow when the word democracy is used, and to practice slavery from morning to night. I learned it the way all of my southern people learn it: by closing door after door until one's mind and heart and conscience are blocked off from each other and from reality.

I closed the doors. Or perhaps they were closed for me. Then one day they began to open again. Why I had the desire or the strength to open them or what strange accident or circumstance opened them for me would require in the answering an account too long, too particular, too stark to make here. And perhaps I should not have the insight or wisdom that such an analysis would demand of me, nor the will to make it. I know only that the doors opened, a little; that somewhere along that iron corridor we travel from babyhood to maturity, doors swinging inward began to swing outward, showing glimpses of the world beyond, of that clear bright thing we call "reality."

I believe there is one experience in my childhood which pushed these doors open, a little. And I am going to tell it here, although I know well that to excerpt from a life and family background one incident and name it as a "cause" of a change in one's life direction is a distortion and often an irrelevance. The profound hungers of a child and how they are filled have too much to do with the way in which experiences are assimilated to tear an incident out of a life and look at it in isolation. Yet, with these reservations, I shall tell it, not because it was in itself so severe a trauma, but because it became for me a symbol of buried experiences that I did not have access to. It is an incident that has rarely happened to other southern children. In a sense, it is unique. But it was an acting-out, a special private production of a little script that is written on the lives of most southern children before they know words. Though they may not have seen it staged this way, each southerner has had his own dramatization of the theme.

I should like to preface the account by giving a brief glimpse of my family and background, hoping that the reader, entering my home with me, will be able to blend the ragged edges of this isolated experience into a more full life picture and in doing so will see that it is, in a sense, everybody's story.

I was born and reared in a small Deep South town whose population was about equally Negro and white. There were nine of us who grew up freely in a rambling house of many rooms, surrounded by big lawn, back yard, gardens, fields, and barn. It was the kind of home that gathers memories like dust, a place filled with laughter and play and pain and hurt and ghosts and games. We were given such advantages of schooling, music, and art as were available in the South, and our world was not limited to the South, for travel to far places seemed a simple, natural thing to us, and usually there was one of the family in a remote part of the earth.

We knew we were a respected and important family of this small town but beyond this knowledge we gave little thought to status. Our father made money in lumber and naval stores for the excitement of making and losing it—not for what money can buy nor the security which it sometimes gives. I do not remember at any time wanting "to be rich" nor do I remember that thrift and saving were ideals which our parents considered important enough to urge upon us. Always in the family there was an acceptance of risk, a mild delight even in burning bridges, an expectant "what will happen now!" We were not irresponsible; living according to the pleasure principle was by no means our way of life. On the contrary we were trained to think that each of us should do something that would be of genuine usefulness to the world, and the family thought it right to make sacrifices if necessary, to give each child adequate preparation for this life's work. We were also trained to think learning important, and books, but "bad" books our mother burned. We valued music and art and craftsmanship but it was people and their welfare and religion that were the foci around which our lives seemed naturally to move. Above all else, the important thing was what we "planned to do with our lives." That each of us must do something was as inevitable as breathing for we owed a "debt to society which must be paid." This was a family commandment.

While many of our neighbors spent their energies in counting limbs on the family tree and grafting some on now and then to give symmetry to it, or in reliving the old bitter days of Reconstruction licking scars to cure their vague malaise, or in fighting each battle and turn of battle of that Civil War which has haunted the southern conscience so long, my father was pushing his nine children straight into the future. "You have your heritage," he used to say, "some of it good, some not so good; and as far as I know you had the usual number of grandmothers and grandfathers. Yes, there were slaves, far too many of them in the family, but that was your grandfather's mistake, not yours. The past has been lived. It is gone. The future is yours. What are you going to do with it?" Always he asked this question of his children and sometimes one knew it was but an echo of the old question he had spent his life trying to answer for himself. For always the future held my father's dreams; always there, not in the past, did he expect to find what he had spent his life searching for.

We lived the same segregated life as did other southerners but our parents talked in excessively Christian and democratic terms. We were told ten thousand times that status and money are unimportant (though we were well supplied with both); we were told that "all men are brothers," that we are a part of a democracy and must act like democrats. We were told that the teachings of Jesus are real and important and could be practiced if we tried. We were told also that to be "radical" is bad, silly too; and that one must always conform to the "best behavior" of one's community and make it better if one can. We were taught that we were superior not to people but to hate and resentment, and that no member of the Smith family could stoop so low as to have an enemy. No matter what injury was done us, we must not injure ourselves further by retaliating. That was a family commandment too.

We had family prayers once each day. All of us as children read the Bible in its entirety each year. We memorized hundreds of Bible verses and repeated them at breakfast, and said "sentence prayers" around the family table. God was not someone we met on Sunday but a permanent member of our household. It never occurred to me until I was fourteen or fifteen years old that He did not see every act and thought and chalk up the daily score on eternity's tablets.

Despite the strain of living so intimately with God, the nine of us were strong, healthy, energetic youngsters who filled our days with play and sports and music and books and managed to live much of our lives on the careless level at which young lives should be lived. We had our times of profound anxiety of course, for there were hard lessons to be learned about the body and "bad things" to be learned about sex. Sometimes I have wondered how we ever learned them with a mother so shy with words.

She was a wistful creature who loved beautiful things like lace and sunsets and flowers in a vague inarticulate way, and took good care of her children. We always knew this was not her world but one she accepted under duress. Her private world we rarely entered, though the shadow of it lay at times heavily on our hearts.

Our father owned large business interests, employed hundreds of colored and white laborers, paid them the prevailing low wages, worked them the prevailing long hours, built for them mill towns (Negro and white), built for each group a church, saw to it that religion was supplied free, saw to it that a commissary supplied commodities at a high price, and in general managed his affairs much as ten thousand other southern businessmen managed theirs.

Even now, I can hear him chuckling as he told my mother how he won his fight for Prohibition. The high point of the campaign was election afternoon, when he lined up the entire mill force of several hundred (white and black), passed out a shining silver dollar to each one of them, marched them in and voted liquor out of our county. It was a great day in his life. He had won the Big Game, a game he was always playing with himself against all kinds of evil. It did not occur to him to scrutinize the methods he used. Evil was a word written in capitals; the devil was smart; if you wanted to win you outsmarted him. It was as simple as that.

He was a practical, hardheaded, warmhearted, high-spirited

man born during the Civil War, earning his living at twelve, struggling through bitter decades of Reconstruction and post-Reconstruction, through populist movement, through the panic of 1893, the panic of 1907, on into the twentieth century accepting his region as he found it, accepting its morals and its mores as he accepted its climate, with only scorn for those who held grudges against the North or pitied themselves or the South; scheming, dreaming, expanding his business, making and losing money, making friends whom he did not lose, with never a doubt that God was always by his side whispering hunches as to how to pull off successful deals. When he lost, it was his own fault. When he won, God had helped him.

Once while we were kneeling at family prayers the fire siren at the mill sounded the alarm that the mill was on fire. My father did not falter from his prayer. The alarm sounded again and again—which signified that the fire was big. With quiet dignity he continued his talk with God while his children sweated and wriggled and hearts beat out of their chests in excitement. He was talking to God—how could he hurry out of the presence of the Most High to save his mills! When he finished his prayer, he quietly stood up, laid the Bible carefully on the table. Then, and only then, did he show an interest in what was happening in Mill Town. . . . When the telegram was placed in his hands telling of the death of his beloved favorite son, he gathered his children together, knelt down, and in a steady voice which contained no hint of his shattered heart, loyally repeated, "God is our refuge and strength, a very present help in trouble. Therefore will we not fear, though the earth be removed, and though the mountains be carried into the midst of the sea." On his deathbed, he whispered to his old Business Partner in Heaven: "I have fought the fight; I have kept the faith."

Against this backdrop the drama of the South was played out one day in my life:

A little white girl was found in the colored section of our town, living with a Negro family in a broken-down shack. This family had moved in only a few weeks before and little was known of them. One of the ladies in my mother's club, while driving over to her washerwoman's, saw the child swinging on a gate. The shack, as she said, was hardly more than a pigsty and this white child was living with ignorant and dirty and sick-looking colored folks. "They must have kidnapped her," she told her friends. Genuinely shocked, the clubwomen busied themselves in an attempt to do something, for the child was very white indeed. The strange Negroes were sub-

jected to a grueling questioning and finally grew frightened and eva-
sive and refused to talk at all. This only increased the suspicion of
the white group, and the next day the clubwomen, escorted by
the town marshal, took the child from her adopted family despite
their tears.

She was brought to our home. I do not know why my mother
consented to this plan. Perhaps because she loved children and
always showed tenderness and concern for them. It was easy for one
more to fit into our ample household and Janie was soon at home
there. She roomed with me, sat next to me at the table; I found
Bible verses for her to say at breakfast; she wore my clothes, played
with my dolls and followed me around from morning to night. She
was dazed by her new comforts and by the interesting activities of
this big lively family; and I was as happily dazed, for her adoration
was a new thing to me; and as time passed a quick, childish, and
deeply felt bond grew up between us.

But a day came when a telephone message was received from a
colored orphanage. There was a meeting at our home, whispers,
shocked exclamations. All afternoon the ladies went in and out of
our house talking to Mother in tones too low for children to hear.
And as they passed us at play, most of them looked quickly at Janie and quickly looked away again, though a few stopped and stared
at her as if they could not tear their eyes from her face. When my
father came home in the evening Mother closed her door against
our young ears and talked a long time with him. I heard him laugh,
heard Mother say, "But Papa, this is no laughing matter!" And
then they were back in the living room with us and my mother
was pale and my father was saying, "Well, work it out, honey, as
best you can. After all, now that you know, it is pretty simple."

In a little while my mother called my sister and me into her
bedroom and told us that in the morning Janie would return to
Colored Town. She said Janie was to have the dresses the ladies had
given her and a few of my own, and the toys we had shared with
her. She asked me if I would like to give Janie one of my dolls. She
seemed hurried, though Janie was not to leave until next day. She
said, "Why not select it now?" And in dreamlike stiffness I
brought in my dolls and chose one for Janie. And then I found it
possible to say, "Why? Why is she leaving? She likes us, she hardly
knows them. She told me she had been with them only a month."

"Because," Mother said gently, "Janie is a little colored girl."

"But she can't be. She's white!"

"We were mistaken. She is colored."

"But she looks——"

"She is colored. Please don't argue!"

"What does it mean?" I whispered.

"It means," Mother said slowly, "that she has to live in Colored Town with colored people."

"But why? She lived here three weeks and she doesn't belong to them, she told me she didn't."

"She is a little colored girl."

"But you said yourself that she has nice manners. You said that," I persisted.

"Yes, she is a nice child. But a colored child cannot live in our home."

"Why?"

"You know, dear! You have always known that white and colored people do not live together."

"Can she come over to play?"

"No."

"I don't understand."

"I don't either," my young sister quavered.

"You're too young to understand. And don't ask me again, ever again, about this!" Mother's voice was sharp but her face was sad and there was no certainty left there. She hurried out and busied herself in the kitchen and I wandered through that room where I had been born, touching the old familiar things in it, looking at them, trying to find the answer to a question that moaned in my mind like a hurt thing. . . .

And then I went out to Janie, who was waiting, knowing things were happening that concerned her but waiting until they were spoken aloud.

I do not know quite how the words were said but I told her that she was to return in the morning to the little place where she had lived because she was colored and colored children could not live with white children.

"Are you white?" she said.

"I'm white," I replied, "and my sister is white. And you're colored. And white and colored can't live together because my mother says so."

"Why?" Janie whispered.

"Because they can't," I said. But I knew, though I said it firmly, that something was wrong. I knew my father and mother whom I passionately admired had done that which did not fit in with their teachings. I knew they had betrayed something which they held dear. And I was shamed by their failure and frightened, for I felt that they were no longer as powerful as I had thought. There was something Out There that was stronger that they and I could not bear to believe it. I could not confess that my father, who had always solved the family dilemmas easily and with laughter, could not solve this. I knew that my mother who was so good to children did not believe in her heart that she was being good to this child. There was not a word in my mind that said it but my body knew and my glands, and I was filled with anxiety.

But I felt compelled to believe they were right. It was the only way my world could be held together. And, like a slow poison, it began to seep through me: *I was white. She was colored. We must not be together. It was bad to be together. Though you ate with your nurse when you were little, it was bad to eat with any colored person after that. It was bad just as other things were bad that your mother had told you. It was bad that she was to sleep in the room with me that night. It was bad. . . .*

I was suddenly full of guilt. For three weeks I had done things that white children are not supposed to do. And now I knew these things had been wrong.

I went to the piano and began to play, as I had always done when I was in trouble. I tried to play Paderewski's *Minuet* and as I stumbled through it, the little girl came over and sat on the bench with me. Feeling lonely, lost in these deep currents that were sweeping through our house that night, she crept closer and put her arms around me and I shrank away as if my body had been uncovered. I had not said a word, I did not say one, but she knew, and tears slowly rolled down her little white face.. . . .

And then I forgot it. For more than thirty years the experience was wiped out of my memory. But that night, and the weeks it was tied to, worked its way like a splinter, bit by bit down to the hurt places in my memory and festered there. And as I grew older, as more experiences collected around that faithless time, as memories of earlier, more profound hurts crept closer and closer, drawn to that night as if to a magnet, I began to know that people who talked of love and Christianity and democracy did not mean it. That is a hard thing for a child to learn. I still admired my parents, there was so much that was strong and vital and sane and good about them and I never forgot this; I stubbornly believed in their sincerity, as I do to this day, and I loved them. Yet in my heart they were under suspicion. Something was wrong.

Something was wrong with a world that tells you that love is good and people are important and then forces you to deny love and to humiliate people. I knew, though I would not for years confess it aloud, that in trying to shut the Negro race away from us, we have shut ourselves away from so many good, creative, honest, deeply human things in life. I began to understand so slowly at first but more and more clearly as the years passed, that the

warped, distorted frame we have put around every Negro child from
birth is around every white child also. Each is on a different side
of the frame but each is pinioned there. And I knew that what
cruelly shapes and cripples the personality of one is as cruelly shaping
and crippling the personality of the other. I began to see that
though we may, as we acquire new knowledge, live through new
experiences, examine old memories, gain the strength to tear the
frame from us, yet we are stunted and warped and in our lifetime
cannot grow straight again any more than can a tree, put in a
steel-like twisting frame when young, grow tall and straight when
the frame is torn away at maturity.

As I sit here writing, I can almost touch that little town,
so close is the memory of it. There it lies, its main street lined
with great oaks, heavy with matted moss that swings softly even
now as I remember. A little white town rimmed with Negroes,
making a deep shadow on the whiteness. There it lies, broken in
two by one strange idea. Minds broken in two. Hearts broken. Conscience torn from acts. A culture split in a thousand pieces. That
is segregation. I am remembering: a woman in a mental hospital
walking four steps out, four steps in, unable to go further because
she has drawn an invisible line around her small world and is terrified
to take one step beyond it. . . . A man in a Disturbed Ward as-
signing "places" to the other patients and violently insisting that
each stay in his place. . . . A Negro woman saying to me so quietly,
"We cannot ride together on the bus, you know. It is not legal
to be human in Georgia."

Memory, walking the streets of one's childhood . . . of the
town where one was born.

the pheasant hunt

FREDERICK D. WATKINS (1953–   ) wrote the following essay while a student at Denison University. He is a native of West Hartford, Connecticut.

Two men and a boy of ten years followed a black Labrador Retriever named Teyko along the dirt road. Even though the men flanked him, the boy felt very tall, for he was on his first hunting trip with his father. Over his shoulder, emulating his father, the boy carried his new 4-10 gauge double-barreled shotgun. He was very proud of the gun because his father had given it to him on his tenth birthday. Rick had long awaited this hunting trip because he knew how much hunting meant to his father; and Rick wanted to please his dad.

"Dad?" Rick asked.

"Yes, son," his father answered.

"Were you really only six years old the first time your father took you hunting?"

"Yup. But as I told you before, there were different circumstances then. . . ."

"Circumstances?"

"Ah . . . situations . . . things were different then. We lived on a farm and also there were no strict hunting laws as there are today."

"How about you, Dr. Smith?" asked Rick. "How old were you the first time you went hunting?"

The third person, Dr. Smith, was the same age as Rick's father, forty-five. He hadn't said much while the three were walking: he had been watching the air, the tree tops, the underbrush, and the dog all at the same time, looking for birds.

"Oh, I guess . . ." he paused. He took his shotgun from over his shoulder and rested it in the crook of his arm. Then he took a pipe out of his breast pocket and put it into his mouth. He seemed to be relaxing, to be taking a break. "I guess I was about the same age as your father. I lived on a farm also, and my dad liked to hunt very much. He got me interested in it. In the late fall, we'd get all bundled up and go down to the lake to hunt ducks. Hunting ducks is different from hunting pheasant. When you hunt ducks, you sit in an area where the ducks can't see you, and you wait for the ducks to come to you. When they fly over where you are, you shoot one down, and a dog goes to retrieve the duck from the water."

"How come the dog doesn't eat the duck?" asked Rick.

"He's trained not to."

"Oh. Boy, I'd sure like to try duck hunting sometime."

Rick's father spoke up. "It's just like Teyko, Rick. You see, it is Teyko's instinct to point at game birds. That's why we bring him along. He shows us where the bird is, we give him the signal, and he flushes the bird out . . . makes the bird fly. Then after the bird is shot, Teyko will find it and bring it back to us."

"So Teyko will show us where the birds are, huh," thought Rick. "I'll just keep an eye on that dog. I want to get a bird."

About twenty-five yards ahead, Teyko, the black Labrador Retriever, was moving in a quick lateral pace, traveling back and forth across the direction in which the three people were walking. His head was down near the ground so his nose would be sure not to miss the scent of any bird. Occasionally, Teyko would lift his head up, cock his ears back, and look at the hunters as though he was making sure they were following him. His tail was continually wagging.

"One of the nicest things about hunting is watching a good bird dog work," said Dr. Smith.

"I agree," said Rick's dad. "I really enjoy just being outdoors, walking in undeveloped land, admiring the trees and shrubs. . . . It's really great."

That particular day it was great. The autumn air was crisp and clear. The trees were in their most colorful stage of foliage and small animals were scurrying here and there. One could easily tell that winter was coming. The setting was really nice—just the three people, their dog, and nature were all that the world at that time consisted of.

The dirt road which the hunters were following led to a very large field with groves of trees scattered here and there. Dr. Smith removed the pipe from his mouth and returned it to his breast pocket. The men now carried their shotguns with both hands, ready to aim at a moment's notice. Rick decided to do the same, but he'd keep the safety on, just so there would not be any accident.

"We have to be very quiet now," his father told him. "No

more talking. Keep your eyes and ears open, and watch the dog."

"Okay."

In the field, it was hard to see the dog for the grass came up to his haunches. His tail stuck out though, and when he picked his head up, you could see Teyko well.

Rick's heart was pounding. After every step he took, he cringed because he thought he was making too much noise. The grass was very dry, and it was hard to walk on it without making a small crackle.

Time passed. It was midafternoon and there had been no birds. Teyko was still working, and the men were still following him; but there had not been any birds. Rick's arms had long since grown tired of holding the shotgun at the ready, and it was again resting on his shoulder. Rick was growing tired and bored, but he wanted to get a pheasant for his father.

At five o'clock, the trio decided to head home. Teyko was called back. The three started back down the dirt road, with Teyko at the heels of Rick's father. For the dog, the day was over; he had tried his best, there just weren't any birds.

Then Rick happened to look up into the top of a pine tree. There, on a branch about fifty feet above the hunters, was a pheasant.

"Dad!"

"What's the matter?"

"Look!" whispered Rick pointing up.

"A nice one," commented Dr. Smith. "A hen."

Teyko saw the bird also. He started to get excited, but the pheasant seemed to know she was safe from the dog, for she did not move.

"Can I get it, Dad?" asked Rick.

"Not like that," said his father. "We'll make it fly, and then you can try."

Rick's father and Dr. Smith put down their shotguns and began to throw sticks and stones at the bird. But she did not fly, she thought she was safe.

"Come on, Dad. Let me get it please?"

"That bird must be sick," commented Dr. Smith. "She just won't fly." He threw another stick at the pheasant. It hit the bird in the chest just below the head, but she did not move. "What the hell?" He looked at Rick's father and then nodded his head toward the bird.

"Go ahead, Rick," his father said.

A smile came over Rick's face. He aimed the shotgun up at the bird. The bird still did not move. Rick squeezed the trigger just as he had been taught.

Bam!

Everything was silent. The whole world stopped. The thud of the pheasant hitting the ground in front of Rick was the only noise. Teyko went to the pheasant, picked it up in his mouth, brought the bird to Rick's feet, and dropped it. Rick stared at the dead bird on the ground in front of him. Dr. Smith said nothing and Rick's father said nothing. Rick was no longer smiling. A pool of blood formed around the head of the pheasant. Rick could not see the bird because his vision was blurred. He was crying.

Rick never did go duck hunting.

from
an unfinished woman

LILLIAN HELLMAN (1905–   ) is known for dramas that
exhibit skillful craftsmanship and moral force, such plays as:
The Children's Hour (1934), *The Little Foxes* (1939), *Watch
on the Rhine* (1941), and *The Searching Wind* (1945). Having
led a somewhat dramatic life herself, Hellman is also the author of two memoirs, *An Unfinished Woman* (1969), from
which the following excerpt is taken, and *Pentimento: A Book
of Portraits* (1973).

There was a heavy fig tree on the lawn where the house turned the
corner into the side street, and to the front and sides of the fig
tree were three live oaks that hid the fig from my aunts' boardinghouse. I suppose I was eight or nine before I discovered the pleasures of the fig tree, and although I have lived in many houses since
then, including a few I made for myself, I still think of it as my
first and most beloved home.

I learned early, in our strange life of living half in New York and
half in New Orleans, that I made my New Orleans teachers uncomfortable because I was too far ahead of my schoolmates, and my New
York teachers irritable because I was too far behind. But in New
Orleans, I found a solution: I skipped school at least once a week
and often twice, knowing that nobody cared or would report my
absence. On those days I would set out for school done up in polished strapped shoes and a prim hat against what was known as
"the climate," carrying my books and a little basket filled with
delicious stuff my Aunt Jenny and Carrie, the cook, had made for
my school lunch. I would round the corner of the side street, move
on toward St. Charles Avenue, and sit on a bench as if I were waiting for a streetcar until the boarders and the neighbors had gone
to work or settled down for the post-breakfast rest that all
Southern ladies thought necessary. Then I would run back to the

146

fig tree, dodging in and out of bushes to make sure the house had
no dangers for me. The fig tree was heavy, solid, comfortable, and
I had, through time, convinced myself that it wanted me, missed
me when I was absent, and approved all the rigging I had done for
the happy days I spent in its arms: I had made a sling to hold the
school books, a pulley rope for my lunch basket, a hole for the bottle of afternoon cream-soda pop, a fishing pole and a smelly little
bag of elderly bait, a pillow embroidered with a picture of Henry
Clay on a horse that I had stolen from Mrs. Stillman, one of my
aunts' boarders, and a proper nail to hold my dress and shoes to keep
them neat for the return to the house.

It was in that tree that I learned to read, filled with the
passions that can only come to the bookish, grasping, very young,
bewildered by almost all of what I read, sweating in the attempt
to understand a world of adults I fled from in real life but desperately wanted to join in books. (I did not connect the grown men
and women in literature with the grown men and women I saw
around me. They were, to me, another species.)

It was in the fig tree that I learned that anything alive in
water was of enormous excitement to me. True, the water was
gutter water and the fishing could hardly be called that: sometimes the things that swam in New Orleans gutters were not
pretty, but I didn't know what was pretty and I liked them all.
After lunch—the men boarders returned for a large lunch and a
siesta—the street would be safe again, with only the noise from
Carrie and her helpers in the kitchen, and they could be counted
on never to move past the back porch, or the chicken coop. Then
I would come down from my tree to sit on the side street gutter
with my pole and bait. Often I would catch a crab that had wandered in from the Gulf, more often I would catch my favorite, the
crayfish, and sometimes I would, in that safe hour, have at least
six of them for my basket. Then, about 2:30, when house and
street would stir again, I would go back to my tree for another few
hours of reading or dozing or having what I called the ill hour. It
is too long ago for me to know why I thought the hour "ill," but
certainly I did not mean sick. I think I meant an intimation of
sadness, a first recognition that there was so much to understand
that one might never find one's way and the first signs, perhaps,
that for a nature like mine, the way would not be easy. I cannot
be sure that I felt all that then, although I can be sure that it
was in the fig tree, a few years later, that I was first puzzled by
the conflict which would haunt me, harm me, and benefit me the
rest of my life: simply, the stubborn, relentless, driving desire to
be alone as it came into conflict with the desire not to be alone

when I wanted not to be. I already guessed that other people wouldn't allow that, although, as an only child, I pretended for the rest of my life that they would and must allow it to me.

I liked my time in New Orleans much better than I liked our six months apartment life in New York. The life in my aunts' boardinghouse seemed remarkably rich. And what a strange lot my own family was. My aunts Jenny and Hannah were both tall, large women, funny and generous, who coming from a German, cultivated, genteel tradition had found they had to earn a living and earned it without complaint, although Jenny, the prettier and more complex, had frequent outbursts of interesting temper. It was strange, I thought then, that my mother, who so often irritated me, was treated by my aunts as if she were a precious Chinese clay piece from a world they didn't know. And in a sense, that was true: her family was rich, she was small, delicately made and charming—she was a sturdy, brave woman, really, but it took years to teach me that—and because my aunts loved my father very much, they were good to my mother, and protected her from the less wellborn boarders. I don't think they understood—I did, by some kind of child's malice—that my mother enjoyed the boarders and listened to them with the sympathy Jenny couldn't afford. I suppose none of the boarders were of great interest, but I was crazy about what I thought went on behind their doors.

I was conscious that Mr. Stillman, a large, loose, good-looking man, flirted with my mother and sang off key. I knew that a boarder called Collie, a too thin, unhappy looking, no-age man, worked in his uncle's bank and was drunk every night. He was the favorite of the lady boarders, who didn't think he'd live very long. (They were wrong: over twenty years later, on a visit to my retired aunts, I met him in Galatoire's restaurant looking just the same.) And there were two faded, sexy, giggly sisters called Fizzy and Sarah, who pretended to love children and all trees. I once overheard a fight between my mother and father in which she accused him of liking Sarah. I thought that was undignified of my mother and was pleased when my father laughed it off as untrue. He was telling the truth about Sarah: he liked Fizzy, and the day I saw them meet and get into a taxi in front of a restaurant on Jackson Avenue was to stay with me for many years. I was in a black rage, filled with fears I couldn't explain, with pity and contempt for my mother, with an intense desire to follow my father and Fizzy to see whatever it was they might be doing, and to kill them for it. An hour later, I threw myself from the top of the fig tree and broke my nose, although I did not know I had broken a bone and was concerned only with the hideous pain.

I went immediately to Sophronia, who had been my nurse

when I was a small child before we moved, or half moved, to New York. She worked now for people who lived in a large house a street-car ride from ours, and she took care of two little red-haired boys whom I hated with pleasure in my wicked jealousy. Sophronia was the first and most certain love of my life. (Years later, when I was a dangerously rebellious young girl, my father would say that if he had been able to afford Sophronia through the years, I would have been under the only control I ever recognized.) She was a tall, handsome, light tan woman—I still have many pictures of the brooding face—who was for me, as for so many other white Southern children, the one and certain anchor so needed for the young years, so forgotten after that. (It wasn't that way for us: we wrote and met as often as possible until she died when I was in my twenties, and the first salary check I ever earned she returned to me in the form of a gold chain.) The mother of the two red-haired boys didn't like my visits to Sophronia and so I always arrived by the back door.

But Sophronia was not at home on the day of my fall. I sat on her kitchen steps crying and holding my face until the cook sent the upstairs maid to Audubon Park on a search for Sophronia. She came, running, I think for the first time in the majestic movements of her life, waving away the two redheads. She took me to her room and washed my face and prodded my nose and put her hand over my mouth when I screamed. She said we must go immediately to Dr. Fenner, but when I told her that I had thrown myself from the tree, she stopped talking about the doctor, bandaged my face, gave me a pill, put me on her bed and lay down beside me. I told her about my father and Fizzy and fell asleep. When I woke up she said that she'd walk me home. On the way she told me that I must say nothing about Fizzy to anybody ever, and that if my nose still hurt in a few days I was only to say that I had fallen on the street and refuse to answer any questions about how I fell. A block away from my aunts' house we sat down on the steps of the Baptist church. She looked sad and I knew that I had displeased her. I touched her face, which had always been between us a way of saying that I was sorry.

She said, "Don't go through life making trouble for people."

I said, "If I tell you I won't tell about Fizzy, then I won't tell."

She said, "Run home now. Goodbye."

And it was to be goodbye for another year, because I had forgotten that we were to leave for New York two days later, and when I telephoned to tell that to Sophronia the woman she worked for said I wasn't to telephone again. In any case, I soon forgot about Fizzy, and when the bandage came off my nose—it looked

different but not different enough—our New York doctor said that
it would heal by itself, or whatever was the nonsense they believed
in those days about broken bones.

We went back to New Orleans the next year and the years after that until I was sixteen, and they were always the best times
of my life. It was Aunt Hannah who took me each Saturday to the
movies and then to the French Quarter, where we bought smelly
old leather books and she told me how it all had been when she
was a girl: about my grandmother—I remembered her—who had been
a very tall woman with a lined, severe face and a gentle nature;
about my grandfather, dead before I was born, who, in his portrait
over the fireplace, looked too serious and distinguished. They had,
in a middle-class world, evidently been a strange couple, going their
own way with little interest in money or position, loved and respected by their children. "Your grandfather used to say" was a common way to begin a sentence, and although whatever he said had
been law, he had allowed my father and aunts their many eccentri-
cities in a time and place that didn't like eccentrics, and to such
a degree that not one of his children ever knew they weren't like
other people. Hannah, for example, once grew angry—the only time
I ever saw her show any temper—when my mother insisted I finish
my dinner: she rose and hit the table, and told my mother and the
startled boarders that when she was twelve years old she had decided she didn't ever want to eat with people again and so she had
taken to sitting on the steps of the front porch and my grandmother, with no comment, had for two years brought her dinner on
a tray, and so what was wrong with one dinner I didn't feel like
sitting through?

I think both Hannah and Jenny were virgins, but if they were,
there were no signs of spinsterhood. They were nice about married
people, they were generous to children, and sex was something to
have fun about. Jenny had been the consultant to many neighborhood young ladies before their marriage night, or the night of their
first lover. One of these girls, a rich ninny, Jenny found irritating
and unpleasant. When I was sixteen I came across the two of them
in earnest conference on the lawn, and later Jenny told me that
the girl had come to consult her about how to avoid pregnancy.

"What did you tell her?"

"I told her to have a glass of ice water right before the sacred
act and three sips during it."

When we had finished laughing, I said, "But she'll get pregnant."

"He's marrying her for money, he'll leave her when he gets it.
This way at least maybe she'll have a few babies for herself."

And four years later, when I wrote my aunts that I was going
to be married, I had back a telegram: FORGET ABOUT THE GLASS OF
ICE WATER TIMES HAVE CHANGED.

I think I learned to laugh in that house and to knit and em-
broider and sew a straight seam and to cook. Each Sunday it was
my job to clean the crayfish for the wonderful bisque, and it was
Jenny and Carrie, the cook, who taught me to make turtle soup,
and how to kill a chicken without ladylike complaints about the
horror of dealing death, and how to pluck and cook the wild ducks
that were hawked on our street every Sunday morning. I was
taught, also, that if you gave, you did it without piety and didn't
boast about it. It had been one of my grandfather's laws, in the
days when my father and aunts were children, that no poor person
who asked for anything was ever to be refused, and his children
fulfilled the injunction. New Orleans was a city of many poor
people, particularly black people, and the boardinghouse kitchen after the house dinner was, on most nights, a mighty pleasant place:
there would often be as many as eight or ten people, black and
white, almost always very old or very young, who sat at the table
on the kitchen porch while Carrie ordered the kitchen maids and
me to bring the steaming platters and the coffeepots.

It was on such a night that I first saw Leah, a light tan girl
of about fifteen with red hair and freckles, a flat, ugly face, and
a big stomach. I suppose I was about fourteen years old that night,
but I remember her very well because she stared at me through her
hungry eating. She came again about a week later, and this time
Carrie herself took the girl aside and whispered to her, but I don't
think the girl answered her because Carrie shrugged and moved away.
The next morning, Hannah, who always rose at six to help Jenny
before she went to her own office job, screamed outside my bedroom
window. Leaning out, I saw Hannah pointing underneath the house
and saying softly, "Come out of there."

Slowly the tan-red girl crawled out. Hannah said, "You must
not stay under there. It's very wet. Come inside, child, and dry
yourself out." From that day on Leah lived somewhere in the house,
and a few months later had her baby in the City Hospital. The
baby was put out for adoption on Sophronia's advice with a little
purse of money from my mother. I never knew what Leah did in the
house, because when she helped with the dishes Carrie lost her
temper, and when she tried making beds Jenny asked her not to,
and once when she was raking leaves for the gardener he yelled, "You
ain't in your proper head," so in the end, she took to following me
around.

I was, they told me, turning into a handful. Mrs. Stillman

said I was wild, Mr. Stillman said that I would, of course, bring pain
to my mother and father, and Fizzy said I was just plain disgusting
mean. It had been a bad month for me. I had, one night, fallen
asleep in the fig tree and, coming down in the morning, refused to
tell my mother where I had been. James Denery the Third had hit
me very hard in a tug-of-war and I had waited until the next day
to hit him over the head with a porcelain coffeepot and then his
mother complained to my mother. I had also refused to go back to
dancing class.

And I was now spending most of my time with a group from
an orphanage down the block. I guess the orphan group was no more
attractive than any other, but to be an orphan seemed to me desirable and a self-made piece of independence. In any case, the or-
phans were more interesting to me than my schoolmates, and if
they played rougher they complained less. Frances, a dark beauty of
my age, queened it over the others because her father had been
killed by the Mafia. Miriam, small and wiry, regularly stole my al-
lowance from the red purse my aunt had given me, and the one time
I protested she beat me up. Louis Calda was religious and spoke to
me about it. Pancho was dark, sad, and, to me, a poet, because
once he said, "Yo te amo." I could not sleep a full night after this
declaration, and it set up in me forever after both sympathy and
irritability with the first sexual stirrings of little girls, so masked,
so complex, so foolish as compared with the sex of little boys. It
was Louis Calda who took Pancho and me to a Catholic Mass that
could have made me a fourteen-year-old convert. But Louis explained that he did not think me worthy, and Pancho, to stop
my tears, cut off a piece of his hair with a knife, gave it to me
as a gift from royalty, and then shoved me into the gutter. I
don't know why I thought this an act of affection, but I did, and
went home to open the back of a new wristwatch my father had
given me for my birthday and to put the lock of hair in the back.
A day later when the watch stopped, my father insisted I give it
to him immediately, declaring that the jeweler was unreliable.

It was that night that I disappeared, and that night that
Fizzy said I was disgusting mean, and Mr. Stillman said I would forever pain my mother and father, and my father turned on both of
them and said he would handle his family affairs himself without
comments from strangers. But he said it too late. He had come
home very angry with me: the jeweler, after my father's complaints
about his unreliability, had found the lock of hair in the back of
the watch. What started out to be a mild reproof on my father's
part soon turned angry when I wouldn't explain about the hair.
(My father was often angry when I was most like him.) He was so
angry that he forgot that he was attacking me in front of the

Stillmans, my old rival Fizzy, and the delighted Mrs. Dreyfus, a new, rich boarder who only that afternoon had complained about my bad manners. My mother left the room when my father grew angry with me. Hannah, passing through, put up her hand as if to stop my father and then, frightened of the look he gave her, went out to the porch. I sat on the couch, astonished at the pain in my head. I tried to get up from the couch, but one ankle turned and I sat down again, knowing for the first time the rampage that could be caused in me by anger. The room began to have other forms, the people were no longer men and women, my head was not my own. I told myself that my head had gone somewhere and I have little memory of anything after my Aunt Jenny came into the room and said to my father, "Don't you remember?" I have never known what she meant, but I knew that soon after I was moving up the stair-case, that I slipped and fell a few steps, that when I woke up hours later in my bed, I found a piece of angel cake—an old love, an old custom—left by my mother on my pillow. The headache was worse and I vomited out of the window. Then I dressed, took my red purse, and walked a long way down St. Charles Avenue. A St. Charles Avenue mansion had on its back lawn a famous doll's-house, an elaborate copy of the mansion itself, built years before for the small daughter of the house. As I passed this showpiece, I saw a po-liceman and moved swiftly back to the doll palace and crawled in-side. If I had known about the fantasies of the frightened, that ridiculous small house would not have been so terrible for me. I was surrounded by ornate, carved reproductions of the mansion furni-ture, scaled for children, bisque figurines in miniature, a working toilet seat of gold leaf in suitable size, small draperies of damask with a sign that said "From the damask of Marie Antoinette," a miniature samovar with small bronze cups, and a tiny Madame Récam-ier couch on which I spent the night, my legs on the floor. I must have slept, because I woke from a nightmare and knocked over a bisque figurine. The noise frightened me, and since it was now al-most light, in one of those lovely mist mornings of late spring when every flower in New Orleans seems to melt and mix with the air, I crawled out. Most of that day I spent walking, although I had a long session in the ladies' room of the railroad station. I had four dollars and two bits, but that wasn't much when you meant it to last forever and when you knew it would not be easy for a fourteen-year-old girl to find work in a city where too many people knew her. Three times I stood in line at the railroad ticket win-dows to ask where I could go for four dollars, but each time the question seemed too dangerous and I knew no other way of asking it.

Toward evening, I moved to the French Quarter, feeling sad

and envious as people went home to dinner. I bought a few Tootsie
Rolls and a half loaf of bread and went to the St. Louis Cathedral
in Jackson Square. (It was that night that I composed the prayer
that was to become, in the next five years, an obsession, mumbled
over and over through the days and nights: "God forgive me, Papa
forgive me, Mama forgive me, Sophronia, Jenny, Hannah, and all
others, through this time and that time, in life and in death."
When I was nineteen, my father, who had made several attempts
through the years to find out what my lip movements meant as
I repeated the prayer, said, "How much would you take to stop
that? Name it and you've got it." I suppose I was sick of the nonsense by that time because I said, "A leather coat and a feather
fan," and the next day he bought them for me.) After my loaf of
bread, I went looking for a bottle of soda pop and discovered, for
the first time, the whorehouse section around Bourbon Street.
The women were ranged in the doorways of the cribs, making the
first early evening offers to sailors, who were the only men in the
streets. I wanted to stick around and see how things like that
worked, but the second or third time I circled the block, one of
the girls called out to me. I couldn't understand the words, but
the voice was angry enough to make me run toward the French
Market.

The Market was empty except for two old men. One of them
called to me as I went past, and I turned to see that he had
opened his pants and was shaking what my circle called "his thing."
I flew across the street into the coffee stand, forgetting that the
owner had known me since I was a small child when my Aunt Jenny
would rest from her marketing tour with a cup of fine, strong coffee.

He said, in the patois, *"Que faites, ma 'fant? Je suis fermé."*

I said, *"Rien.* My *tante attend*—Could I have a doughnut?"

He brought me two doughnuts, saying one was *lagniappe,* but
I took my doughnuts outside when he said, *"Mais où est vo' tante
à c' heure?"*

I fell asleep with my doughnuts behind a shrub in Jackson
Square. The night was damp and hot and through the sleep there
were many voices and, much later, there was music from somewhere
near the river. When all sounds had ended, I woke, turned my head,
and knew I was being watched. Two rats were sitting a few feet
from me. I urinated on my dress, crawled backwards to stand up,
screamed as I ran up the steps of St. Louis Cathedral and pounded
on the doors. I don't know when I stopped screaming or how I got
to the railroad station, but I stood against the wall trying to
tear off my dress and only knew I was doing it when two women

stopped to stare at me. I began to have cramps in my stomach of a kind I had never known before. I went into the ladies' room and sat bent in a chair, whimpering with pain. After a while the cramps stopped, but I had an intimation, when I looked into the mirror, of something happening to me: my face was blotched, and there seemed to be circles and twirls I had never seen before, the straight blonde hair was damp with sweat, and a paste of green from the shrub had made lines on my jaw. I had gotten older.

Sometime during that early morning I half washed my dress, threw away my pants, put cold water on my hair. Later in the morning a cleaning woman appeared, and after a while began to ask questions that frightened me. When she put down her mop and went out of the room, I ran out of the station. I walked, I guess, for many hours, but when I saw a man on Canal Street who worked in Hannah's office, I realized that the sections of New Orleans that were known to me were dangerous for me.

Years before, when I was a small child, Sophronia and I would go to pick up, or try on, pretty embroidered dresses that were made for me by a colored dressmaker called Bibettera. A block up from Bibettera's there had been a large ruin of a house with a sign, ROOMS—CLEAN—CHEAP, and cheerful people seemed always to be moving in and out of the house. The door of the house was painted a bright pink. I liked that and would discuss with Sophronia why we didn't live in a house with a pink door.

Bibettera was long since dead, so I knew I was safe in this Negro neighborhood. I went up and down the block several times, praying that things would work and I could take my cramps to bed. I knocked on the pink door. It was answered immediately by a small young man.

I said, "Hello." He said nothing.

I said, "I would like to rent a room, please."

He closed the door but I waited, thinking he had gone to get the lady of the house. After a long time, a middle-aged woman put her head out of a second-floor window and said, "What you at?"

I said, "I would like to rent a room, please. My mama is a widow and has gone to work across the river. She gave me money and said to come here until she called for me."

"Who your mama?"

"Er. My mama."

"What you at? Speak out."

"I told you. I have money . . ." But as I tried to open my purse, the voice grew angry.

"This is a nigger house. Get you off. *Vite.*"

I said, in a whisper, "I know. I'm part nigger."

The small young man opened the front door. He was laughing. "You part mischief. Get the hell out of here."

I said, "Please"—and then, "I'm related to Sophronia Mason. She told me to come. Ask her."

Sophronia and her family were respected figures in New Orleans Negro circles, and because I had some vague memory of her stately bow to somebody as she passed this house, I believed they knew her. If they told her about me I would be in trouble, but phones were not usual then in poor neighborhoods, and I had no other place to go.

The woman opened the door. Slowly I went into the hall.

I said, "I won't stay long. I have four dollars and Sophronia will give more if . . ."

The woman pointed up the stairs. She opened the door of a small room. "Washbasin place down the hall. Toilet place behind the kitchen. Two-fifty and no fuss, no bother."

I said, "Yes ma'am, yes ma'am," but as she started to close the door, the young man appeared.

"Where your bag?"

"Bag?"

"Nobody put up here without no bag."

"Oh. You mean the bag with my clothes? It's at the station. I'll go and get it later . . ." I stopped because I knew I was about to say I'm sick, I'm in pain, I'm frightened.

He said, "I say you lie. I say you trouble. I say you get out."

I said, "And I say you shut up."

Years later, I was to understand why the command worked, and to be sorry that it did, but that day I was very happy when he turned and closed the door. I was asleep within minutes.

Toward evening, I went down the stairs, saw nobody, walked a few blocks and bought myself an oyster loaf. But the first bite made me feel sick, so I took my loaf back to the house. This time, as I climbed the steps, there were three women in the parlor, and they stopped talking when they saw me. I went back to sleep immediately, dizzy and nauseated.

I woke to a high, hot sun and my father standing at the foot of the bed staring at the oyster loaf.

He said, "Get up now and get dressed."

I was crying as I said, "Thank you, Papa, but I can't."

From the hall, Sophronia said, "Get along up now. *Vite.* The morning is late."

My father left the room. I dressed and came into the hall carrying my oyster loaf. Sophronia was standing at the head of the stairs. She pointed out, meaning my father was on the street.

I said, "He humiliated me. He did. I won't . . ."

She said, "Get you going or I will never see you whenever again."

I ran past her to the street. I stood with my father until Sophronia joined us, and then we walked slowly, without speaking, to the streetcar line. Sophronia bowed to us, but she refused my father's hand when he attempted to help her into the car. I ran to the car meaning to ask her to take me with her, but the car moved and she raised her hand as if to stop me. My father and I walked again for a long time.

He pointed to a trash can sitting in front of a house. "Please put that oyster loaf in the can."

At Vanalli's restaurant, he took my arm. "Hungry?"

I said, "No, thank you, Papa."

But we went through the door. It was, in those days, a New Orleans custom to have an early black coffee, go to the office, and after a few hours have a large breakfast at a restaurant. Vanalli's was crowded, the headwaiter was so sorry, but after my father took him aside, a very small table was put up for us—too small for my large father, who was accommodating himself to it in a manner most unlike him.

He said, "Jack, my rumpled daughter would like cold crayfish, a nice piece of pompano, a separate bowl of Béarnise sauce, don't ask me why, French fried potatoes . . ."

I said, "Thank you, Papa, but I am not hungry. I don't want to be here."

My father waved the waiter away and we sat in silence until the crayfish came. My hand reached out instinctively and then drew back.

My father said, "Your mother and I have had an awful time."

I said, "I'm sorry about that. But I don't want to go home, Papa."

He said, angrily, "Yes, you do. But you want me to apologize first. I do apologize but you should not have made me say it."

After a while I mumbled, "God forgive me, Papa forgive me, Mama forgive me, Sophronia, Jenny, Hannah . . ."

"Eat your crayfish."

I ate everything he had ordered and then a small steak. I suppose I had been mumbling throughout my breakfast.

My father said, "You're talking to yourself. I can't hear you. What are you saying?"

"God forgive me, Papa forgive me, Mama forgive me, Sophronia, Jenny . . ."

My father said, "Where do we start your training as the first Jewish nun on Prytania Street?"

When I finished laughing, I liked him again. I said, "Papa, I'll tell you a secret. I've had very bad cramps and I am beginning to bleed. I'm changing life."

He stared at me for a while. Then he said, "Well, it's not the way it's usually described, but it's accurate, I guess. Let's go home now to your mother."

We were never, as long as my mother and father lived, to mention that time again. But it was of great importance to them and I've thought about it all my life. From that day on I knew my power over my parents. That was not to be too important: I was ashamed of it and did not abuse it too much. But I found out something more useful and more dangerous: if you are willing to take the punishment, you are halfway through the battle. That the issue may be trivial, the battle ugly, is another point.

AFTERWORD

In *Gandhi's Truth,* a remarkable biography of India's most famous leader, Erik Erikson writes at some length about "the Event" in Gandhi's life. This event, as Erikson describes it, was Gandhi's discovery, during a labor dispute, of the style of leadership that was to profoundly influence India's movement toward independence. Probably none of us can realistically expect to have the kind of powerful impact on history that Gandhi did, but all of us can hope to make important discoveries about ourselves and our world as a result of singularly important experiences in our lives. In "When I Was a Child," for example, Lillian Smith tells of an experience that came to have intense meaning for her, as she tried to understand her childhood in a small southern town. She does not claim that the experience changed the direction of her life, but rather that it stands for a number of experiences that did make a very important difference.

When Frederick Douglass wrote his first autobiography, he included a number of events that had influenced his escape from slavery. He emphasized particularly an experience that occurred four years before his escape: his refusal to be punished by his master. As Douglass looked back on it from the vantage point of freedom, this event suggested a transformation so great that religious language could be used to describe it: "It was a glorious resurrection, from the tomb of slavery, to the heaven of freedom." (Since he remained a slave "in form" for another four years, it is clear that Douglass is referring here to a change in his sense of himself.)

Douglass was probably about sixteen years old when the crucial event occurred. Few adults, let alone sixteen-year-olds, have experienced such radical transformation, but most of us can recall experiences that have changed our minds, taught us something, somehow made a difference in our beliefs or attitudes. Rick Watkins, as a college freshman, recalled such an experience in "The Pheasant Hunt." Watkins had been reading Ernest Hemingway's *In Our Time* when he wrote "The Pheasant Hunt," and his essay shows the influence of Hemingway's terse, controlled style. It is an effective piece of writing, partly because of the careful attention to the details of the hunt and the unobtrusive control. One unusual characteristic of the essay is Watkins's use of the third person in references to himself. This technique, which Norman Mailer employs in *The Armies of the Night* (see page 80), gives the description of the hunt a tone of detachment that Watkins might not have achieved had he used the first person.

The account of running away from home written by Lillian Hellman makes use of precisely evoked memories from her early childhood and considerable description of New Orleans. But the essay focuses on an event that taught Hellman something about her own strength and independence. Much of the material in the first half of the selection prepares us to understand the significance of Hellman's act of rebellion against the adult world.

Suggested writing assignment

Describe as fully as you can an event that seemed to make a difference in your life. The most dramatic choices may not be the best ones. The death of a friend or relative, for instance, clearly fits the assignment; but such experiences are very difficult to describe coherently, partly because they require substantial treatment of the relationship that has been broken. Without that kind of background material, such an essay can seem sentimental. The range of other possible topics is very wide. I have received first-rate essays on such topics as the following: a first solo flight, the removal of orthodontic braces, a mud-sliding experience, participation in an important track meet, a fellow student's decision to leave college, a crisis at summer camp, a deer hunt, a swimming accident, a religious experience at summer camp, an encounter with residents of a small town in Russia, a decision to play hookey, a visit to a nursing home, and a visit to Manhattan. It is interesting to write an essay of this kind in both the first and third persons as a way of discovering the advantages of the two perspectives.

five: the self and others

the hidden wound

WENDELL BERRY (1934–   ), a teacher and organic farmer in his native Kentucky, is a writer of poetry, fiction, and essays—most of which suggest his strong interest in the environment. His literary works include the novels *Nathan Coulter* (1961) and *A Place On Earth* (1967) and such poetry volumes as *The Broken Ground* (1965), *Openings* (1968), *Findings* (1969), *Farming: A Handbook* (1970), and *The Country of Marriage* (1973). In addition, Berry is the author of several collections of essays, namely *The Long-Legged House* (1969); *The Hidden Wound* (1971), from which the following character sketch is taken; and *A Continuous Harmony* (1972).

I believe it was when I was three years old that Nick Watkins, a black man, came to work for my Grandfather Berry. I don't remember when he came, which is to say that I don't remember not knowing him. When I was older and Nick and I would reminisce about the beginnings of our friendship, he used to laugh and tell me that when he first came I would follow him around calling him Tommy. Tommy was the hand who had lived there just before Nick. It was one of those conversations that are repeated ritually between friends. I would ask Nick to tell how it had been when he first came, and he would always tell that about me calling him Tommy, and he would laugh. At the age of eight or nine the story was very important to me because it meant that Nick and I had known each other since way back, and were old buddies.

I have no idea of Nick's age when I first knew him. He must have been in his late fifties, and he worked for us until his death in, I believe, 1945—a period of about eight years. During that time one of my two or three chief ambitions was to be with him. With my brother or by myself, I dogged his steps. So faithful a follower, and so young and self-important and venturesome, as I was, I must have been a trial to him. But he never ran out of patience.

From something philosophical and serene in that patience, and from a few things he said to me, I know that Nick had worked hard ever since his childhood. He told me that when he was a small boy he had worked for a harsh white woman, a widow or a spinster. When he milked, the cow would often kick the bucket over, and he would have to carry it back to the house empty, and the white woman would whip him. He had worked for hard bosses. Like thousands of others of his race he had lived from childhood with the knowledge that his fate was to do the hardest of work for the smallest of wages, and that there was no hope of living any other way.

White people thought of Nick as "a good nigger," and within the terms of that designation he had lived his life. But in my memory of him, and I think in fact, he was possessed of a considerable dignity. I think this was because there was a very conscious peace and faithfulness that he had made between himself and his lot. When there was work to be done, he did it dependably and steadily and well, and thus escaped the indignity of being bossed. I do not remember seeing him servile or obsequious. My grandfather, within the bounds of the racial bias, thought highly of him. He admired him particularly, I remember, as a teamster, and was always pointing him out to me as an example: "Look a yonder how old Nick sets up to drive his mules. Look how he takes hold of the lines. Remember that, and you'll know something."

In the eight or so years that Nick lived on the place, he and my grandfather spent hundreds and hundreds of work days together. When Nick first came there my grandfather was already in his seventies. Beyond puttering around and "seeing to things," which he did compulsively as long as he could stand up, he had come to the end of his working time. But despite the fact that my father had quietly begun to make many of the decisions in the running of the farm, and had assumed perhaps most of the real worries of running it, the old man still thought of himself as the sovereign ruler there, and it could be a costly mistake to attempt to deal with him on the assumption that he wasn't. He still got up at daylight as he always had, and when Nick and the other men on the place went to work he would be with them, on horseback, following the mule teams to the field. He rode a big bay mare named Rose; he would continue to ride her past the time when he could get into the saddle by himself. Through the long summer days he would stay with Nick, sitting and watching and talking, reminiscing, or riding behind him as he drove the rounds of a pasture on a mowing machine. When there was work that he could do, he would be into it until he tired out, and then he would invent an errand so he could get away with dignity.

Given Nick's steadiness at work, I don't think my grandfather stayed with him to boss him. I think he stayed so close because he couldn't stand not to be into what was going on, and because he needed the company of men of his own kind, working men. I have the clearest memory of the two of them passing again and again in the slowly shortening rounds of a big pasture, Nick driving a team of good black mules hitched to a mowing machine, my grandfather on the mare always only two or three steps behind the cutter bar. I don't know where I am in the memory, perhaps watching from the shade of some bush in a fencerow. In the bright hot sun of the summer day they pass out of sight and the whole landscape falls quiet. And then I hear the chuckling of the machine again, and then I see the mules' ears and my grandfather's hat appear over the top of the ridge, and they all come back into sight and pass around again. Within the steady monotonous racket of the machine, they keep a long silence, rich, it seems to me, with the deep camaraderie of men who have known hard work all their lives. Though their long labor in barns and fields had been spent in radically different states of mind, with radically different expectations, it was a common ground and a bond between them—never by men of their different colors, in that time and place, to be openly acknowledged or spoken of. Nick drives on and on into the day, deep in his silence, erect, alert and solemn faced with the patience that has kept with him through thousands of such days before, the elemental reassurance that dinnertime will come, and then quitting time, supper and rest. Behind him as the day lengthens, my grandfather dozes on the mare; when he sways in the saddle the mare steps under him, keeping him upright. Nick would claim that the mare did this out of a conscious sense of responsibility, and maybe she did.

On those days I know that Nick lived in constant fear that the mare too would doze and step over the cutter bar, and would be cut and would throw her rider before the mules could be stopped. Despite my grandfather's unshakable devotion to the idea that he was still in charge of things, it was clearly Nick who bore the great responsibility of those days. Because of childishness or whatever, the old man absolutely refused to accept the limits of age. He was fiercely headstrong in everything, and so was constantly on the verge of doing some damage to himself. I can see Nick working along, pretending not to watch him, but watching him all the same out the corner of his eye, and then hustling anxiously to the rescue: "Whoa, boss. Whoa. Wait, boss." When he had my brother and me, and maybe another boy or two, to look after as well, Nick must have been driven well nigh out of his mind, but he never showed it.

When they were in the mowing or other such work, Nick and my grandfather were hard to associate with. Of course we could get on horseback ourselves and ride along behind the old man's mare, but it was impossible to talk and was consequently boring. But there was other work, such as fencing or the handwork in the crops, that allowed the possibility of conversation, and whenever we could we got into that—in everybody's way, whether we played or tried to help, often getting scolded, often aware when we were not being scolded that we were being stoically put up with, but occasionally getting the delicious sense that we were being kindly indulged and catered to for all our sakes, or the deeply justifying sense that we were being of use.

I remember one fine day we spent with Nick and our grandfather, cutting a young sassafras thicket that had grown up on the back of the place. Nick would fell the little trees with his ax, cutting them off about waist high, so that when they sprouted the cattle would browse off the foliage and so finally kill them. We would pile the trees high on the sled, my brother and I would lie on the mass of springy branches, in the spiced sweetness of that foliage, among the pretty leaves and berries, and Nick would drive us down the hill to unload the sled in a wash that our grandfather was trying to heal.

That was quiet slow work, good for talk. At such times the four of us would often go through a conversation about taking care of Nick when he got old. I don't remember how this conversation would start. Perhaps Nick would bring the subject up out of some anxiety he had about it. But our grandfather would say, "Don't you worry, Nick. These boys'll take care of you."

And one of us would say, "Yessir, Nick, we sure will."

And our grandfather would shake his head in sober emphasis and say, "By God, they'll do it!"

Usually, then, there would follow an elaborately detailed fantasy in which Nick would live through a long carefree old age, with good foxhounds and time to hunt, looked after by my brother and me who by then would have grown up to be lawyers or farmers.

Another place we used to talk was in the barn. Usually this would be on a rainy day, or in the late evening after work. Nick and the old man would sit in the big doorway on upturned buckets, gazing out into the lot. They would talk about old times. Or we would all talk about horses, and our grandfather would go through his fantasy of buying six good colts for my brother and me to break and train. Or we would go through the fantasy of Nick's old age.

Or our grandfather would get into a recurrent fantasy all his own about buying a machine, which was his word for automobile. According to the fantasy, he would buy a good new machine, and Nick would drive it, and they would go to town and to "Louisville" and maybe other places. The intriguing thing about this plan was that it was based on the old man's reasoning that since Nick was a fine teamster he was therefore a fine automobile driver. Which Nick wasn't; he couldn't drive an automobile at all. But as long as Nick lived, our grandfather clung to that dream of buying a good car. Under the spell of his own talk about it, he always believed that he was right on the verge of doing it.

We also talked about the war that was being fought "across the waters." The two men were deeply impressed with the magnitude of the war and with the ominous new weapons that were being used in it. I remember sitting there in the barn door one day and hearing our grandfather say to Nick: "They got cannons now that'll shoot clean across the water. Good God Amighty!" I suppose he meant the English Channel, but I thought then that he meant the ocean. It was one of the ways the war and modern times became immediate to my imagination.

A place I especially liked to be with Nick was at the woodpile. At his house and at my grandparents' the cooking was still done on wood ranges, and Nick had to keep both kitchens supplied with stove wood. The logs would be laid up in a sawbuck and sawed to the proper lengths with a crosscut saw, and then the sawed lengths would be split on the chopping block with an ax. It was a daily thing throughout the year, but more wood was needed of course in the winter than in the summer. When I was around I would often help Nick with the sawing, and then sit up on the sawbuck to watch while he did the chopping, and then I would help him carry the wood in to the woodbox in the kitchen. Those times I would carry on long conversations, mostly by myself; Nick, who needed his breath for the work, would reply in grunts and monosyllables.

Summer and winter he wore two pairs of pants, usually an old pair of dress pants with a belt under a pair of bib overalls, swearing they kept him cool in hot weather and warm in cold. Like my grandfather, he often wore an old pair of leather puttees, or he would have his pants legs tied snugly above his shoe tops with a piece of twine. As I remember he wore felt hats that were stained and sweaty and shaped to his character. He had a sober open dignified face and gentle manners, quick to smile and to laugh. His teeth were amber stained from chewing tobacco. His hands were as hard as leather; one of my hopes was someday to have hands as hard as his. He seemed instinctively to be a capable handler of stock. He could talk untiringly of good saddle horses and good work teams that he had known. He was an incurable fox hunter and was never without a hound or two. I think he found it easy to be solitary and quiet.

I heard my grandfather say to him one day: "Nick, you're the first darkie I ever saw who didn't sing while he worked."

But there were times, I knew, when Nick did sing. It was only one little snatch of a song that he sang. When the two of us would go on horseback to the store or to see about some stock— Nick on my grandfather's mare, I on a pony—and we had finished our errand and started home, Nick would often sing: "Get along home, home, Cindy, get along home!" And he would laugh.

"Sing it again," I would say.

And he would sing it again.

notes of a native son

JAMES BALDWIN (1924–   ), even among those who do not like his fiction, is widely acknowledged to be one of the finest essayists of the twentieth century. One source of his extraordinary literary power seems to be his ability to probe the complexity of his own selfhood with such honesty and courage that he ultimately gets beyond the self. As critic Alfred Kazin has suggested, "the great thing about [Baldwin's] essays is that the form allows him to work out from all the conflicts raging in *him,* so that finally the 'I,' the 'James Baldwin' who is so sassy and despairing and bright, manages, without losing his authority as the central speaker, to show us all the different people hidden in him, all the voices from whom the 'I' alone can speak" (*Contemporaries,* Little, Brown, 1962, p. 254).

Baldwin's fiction includes *Go Tell It on the Mountain* (1953); *Giovanni's Room* (1958); *Another Country* (1962); *Going to Meet the Man* (1966), an unfairly neglected collection of short stories; *Tell Me How Long the Train's Been Gone* (1966); and *If Beale Street Could Talk* (1974). In addition to *Notes of a Native Son* (1955), from which the following essay is taken, Baldwin has published three other collections of essays: *Nobody Knows My Name (1960); The Fire Next Time* (1963); and *No Name in the Street* (1972).

On the 29th of July, in 1943, my father died. On the same day, a few hours later, his last child was born. Over a month before this, while all our energies were concentrated in waiting for these events, there had been, in Detroit, one of the bloodiest race riots of the century. A few hours after my father's funeral, while he lay in state in the undertaker's chapel, a race riot broke out in Harlem. On the morning of the 3rd of August, we drove my father to the graveyard through a wilderness of smashed plate glass.

The day of my father's funeral had also been my nineteenth birthday. As we drove him to the graveyard, the spoils of injustice, anarchy, discontent, and hatred were all around us. It seemed to me that God himself had devised, to mark my father's end, the most sustained and brutally dissonant of codas. And it seemed to me, too, that the violence which rose all about us as my father left the world had been devised as a corrective for the pride of his eldest son. I had declined to believe in that apocalypse which had been central to my father's vision; very well, life seemed to be saying, here is something that will certainly pass for an apocalypse until the real thing comes along. I had inclined to be contemptuous of my father for the conditions of his life, for the conditions of our lives. When his life had ended I began to wonder about that life and also, in a new way, to be apprehensive about my own.

I had not known my father very well. We had got on badly, partly because we shared, in our different fashions, the vice of stubborn pride. When he was dead I realized that I had hardly ever spoken to him. When he had been dead a long time I began to wish I had. It seems to be typical of life in America, where opportunities, real and fancied, are thicker than anywhere else on the globe, that the second generation has no time to talk to the first. No one, including my father, seems to have known exactly how old he was, but his mother had been born during slavery. He was of the first generation of free men. He, along with thousands of other Negroes, came North after 1919 and I was part of that generation which had never seen the landscape of what Negroes sometimes call the Old Country.

He had been born in New Orleans and had been a quite young man there during the time that Louis Armstrong, a boy, was running errands for the dives and honky-tonks of what was always presented to me as one of the most wicked of cities—to this day, whenever I think of New Orleans, I also helplessly think of Sodom and Gomorrah. My father never mentioned Louis Armstrong, except to forbid us to play his records; but there was a picture of him on our wall for a long time. One of my father's strong-willed female relatives had placed it there and forbade my father to take it down. He never did, but he eventually maneuvered her out of the house and when, some years later, she was in trouble and near death, he refused to do anything to help her.

He was, I think, very handsome. I gather this from photographs and from my own memories of him, dressed in his Sunday best and on his way to preach a sermon somewhere, when I was little. Handsome, proud, and ingrown, "like a toe-nail," somebody said. But he looked to me, as I grew older, like pictures I had seen of African tribal chieftains: he really should have been naked, with war-paint on and barbaric mementos, standing among spears. He could be chilling in the pulpit and indescribably cruel in his personal life and he was certainly the most bitter man I have ever met; yet it must be said that there was something else in him, buried in him, which lent him his tremendous power and, even, a rather crushing charm. It had something to do with his blackness, I think—he was very black—with his blackness and his beauty, and with the fact that he knew that he was black but did not know that he was beautiful. He claimed to be proud of his blackness but it had also been the cause of much humiliation and it had fixed bleak boundaries to his life. He was not a young man when we were growing up and he had already suffered many kinds of ruin; in his outrageously demanding and protective way he loved his children, who were black like him and menaced, like him; and all these things sometimes showed in his face when he tried, never to my knowledge with any success, to establish contact with any of us. When he took one of his children on his knee to play, the child always became fretful and began to cry; when he tried to help one of us with our homework the absolutely unabating tension which emanated from him caused our minds and our tongues to become paralyzed, so that he, scarcely knowing why, flew into a rage and the child, not knowing why, was punished. If it ever entered his head to bring a surprise home for his children, it was, almost unfailingly, the wrong surprise and even the big watermelons he often brought home on his back in the summertime led to the most appalling scenes. I do not remember, in all those years, that one of his children was ever glad to see him come home. From what I was able to gather of his early life, it seemed that this inability to establish contact with other people had always marked him and had been one of the things which had driven him out of New Orleans. There was something in him, therefore, groping and tentative, which was never expressed and which was buried with him. One saw it most clearly when he was facing new people and hoping to impress them. But he never did, not for long. We went from church to smaller and more improbable church, he found himself in less and less demand as a minister, and by the time he died none of his friends had come to see him for a long time. He had lived and died in an intolerable bitterness of spirit and it frightened me, as we drove him to the graveyard through those unquiet, ruined streets, to see how powerful and overflowing this bitterness could be and to realize that this bitterness now was mine.

When he died I had been away from home for a little over a year. In that year I had had time to become aware of the meaning of all my father's bitter warnings, had discovered the secret of his proudly pursed lips and rigid carriage: I had discovered the weight of

white people in the world. I saw that this had been for my ances-
tors and now would be for me an awful thing to live with and that
the bitterness which had helped to kill my father could also kill
me.

He had been ill a long time—in the mind, as we now realized,
reliving instances of his fantastic intransigence in the new light of
his affliction and endeavoring to feel a sorrow for him which never,
quite, came true. We had not known that he was being eaten up
by paranoia, and the discovery that his cruelty, to our bodies and
our minds, had been one of the symptoms of his illness was not,
then, enough to enable us to forgive him. The younger children
felt, quite simply, relief that he would not be coming home anymore. My mother's observation that it was he, after all, who had
kept them alive all these years meant nothing because the problems of keeping children alive are not real for children. The older
children felt, with my father gone, that they could invite their
friends to the house without fear that their friends would be in-
sulted or, as had sometimes happened with me, being told that
their friends were in league with the devil and intended to rob our
family of everything we owned. (I didn't fail to wonder, and it
made me hate him, what on earth we owned that anybody else
would want.)

His illness was beyond all hope of healing before one realized
that he was ill. He had always been so strange and had lived, like
a prophet, in such unimaginably close communion with the Lord
that his long silences which were punctuated by moans and hallelu-
jahs and snatches of old songs while he sat at the living-room window never seemed odd to us. It was not until he refused to eat
because, he said, his family was trying to poison him that my
mother was forced to accept as a fact what had, until then, been
only an unwilling suspicion. When he was committed, it was discovered that he had tuberculosis and, as it turned out, the disease
of his mind allowed the disease of his body to destroy him. For the
doctors could not force him to eat, either, and, though he was fed
intravenously, it was clear from the beginning that there was no
hope for him.

In my mind's eye I could see him, sitting at the window,
locked up in his terrors; hating and fearing every living soul including his children who had betrayed him, too, by reaching towards
the world which had despised him. There were nine of us. I began
to wonder what it could have felt like for such a man to have had
nine children whom he could barely feed. He used to make little
jokes about our poverty, which never, of course, seemed very funny
to us; they could not have seemed very funny to him, either, or

else our all too feeble response to them would never have caused such rages. He spent great energy and achieved, to our chagrin, no small amount of success in keeping us away from the people who surrounded us, people who had all-night rent parties to which we listened when we should have been sleeping, people who cursed and drank and flashed razor blades on Lenox Avenue. He could not understand why, if they had so much energy to spare, they could not use it to make their lives better. He treated almost everybody on our block with a most uncharitable asperity and neither they, nor, of course, their children were slow to reciprocate.

The only white people who came to our house were welfare workers and bill collectors. It was almost always my mother who dealt with them, for my father's temper, which was at the mercy of his pride, was never to be trusted. It was clear that he felt their very presence in his home to be a violation: this was conveyed by his carriage, almost ludicrously stiff, and by his voice, harsh and vindictively polite. When I was around nine or ten I wrote a play which was directed by a young, white schoolteacher, a woman, who then took an interest in me, and gave me books to read and, in order to corroborate my theatrical bent, decided to take me to see what she somewhat tactlessly referred to as "real" plays. Theatergoing was forbidden in our house, but, with the really cruel intuitiveness of a child, I suspected that the color of this woman's skin would carry the day for me. When, at school, she suggested taking me to the theater, I did not, as I might have done if she had been a Negro, find a way of discouraging her, but agreed that she should pick me up at my house one evening. I then, very cleverly, left all the rest to my mother, who suggested to my father, as I knew she would, that it would not be very nice to let such a kind woman make the trip for nothing. Also, since it was a schoolteacher, I imagine that my mother countered the idea of sin with the idea of "education," which word, even with my father, carried a kind of bitter weight.

Before the teacher came my father took me aside to ask *why* she was coming, what *interest* she could possibly have in our house, in a boy like me. I said I didn't know but I, too, suggested that it had something to do with education. And I understood that my father was waiting for me to say something—I didn't quite know what; perhaps that I wanted his protection against this teacher and her "education." I said none of these things and the teacher came and we went out. It was clear, during the brief interview in our living room, that my father was agreeing very much against his will and that he would have refused permission if he had dared. The fact that he did not dare caused me to despise him: I had no way of knowing that he was facing in that living room a wholly unprecedented and frightening situation.

Later, when my father had been laid off from his job, this woman became very important to us. She was really a very sweet and generous woman and went to a great deal of trouble to be of help to us, particularly during one awful winter. My mother called her by the highest name she knew: she said she was a "christian." My father could scarcely disagree but during the four or five years of our relatively close association he never trusted her and was always trying to surprise in her open, Midwestern face the genuine, cunningly hidden, and hideous motivation. In later years, particularly when it began to be clear that this "education" of mine was going to lead me to perdition, he became more explicit and warned me that my white friends in high school were not really my friends and that I would see, when I was older, how white people would do anything to keep a Negro down. Some of them could be nice, he admitted, but none of them were to be trusted and most of them were not even nice. The best thing was to have as little to do with them as possible. I did not feel this way and I was certain, in my innocence, that I never would.

But the year which preceded my father's death had made a great change in my life. I had been living in New Jersey, working in defense plants, working and living among southerners, white and black. I knew about the south, of course, and about how southerners treated Negroes and how they expected them to behave, but it had never entered my mind that anyone would look at me and expect *me* to behave that way. I learned in New Jersey that to be a Negro meant, precisely, that one was never looked at but was simply at the mercy of the reflexes the color of one's skin caused in other people. I acted in New Jersey as I had always acted, that is as though I thought a great deal of myself—I had to *act* that way—with results that were, simply, unbelievable. I had scarcely arrived before I had earned the enmity, which was extraordinarily ingenious, of all my superiors and nearly all my co-workers. In the beginning, to make matters worse, I simply did not know what was happening. I did not know what I had done, and I shortly began to wonder what *anyone* could possibly do, to bring about such unanimous, active, and unbearably vocal hostility. I knew about jim-crow but I had never experienced it. I went to the same self-service restaurant three times and stood with all the Princeton boys before the counter, waiting for a hamburger and coffee; it was always an extraordinarily long time before anything was set before me; but it was not until the fourth visit that I learned that, in fact, nothing had ever been set before me: I had simply picked something up. Negroes were not served there, I was told, and they had been waiting for me to realize that I was always the only Negro present. Once I was told this, I determined to go there all the time. But now they were ready for me and, though some dreadful scenes were subsequently enacted in that restaurant, I never ate there again.

It was the same story all over New Jersey, in bars, bowling alleys, diners, places to live. I was always being forced to leave, silently, or with mutual imprecations. I very shortly became notorious and children giggled behind me when I passed and their elders whispered or shouted—they really believed that I was mad. And it did begin to work on my mind, of course; I began to be afraid to go anywhere and to compensate for this I went places to which I really should not have gone and where, God knows, I had no desire to be. My reputation in town naturally enhanced my reputation at work and my working day became one long series of acrobatics designed to keep me out of trouble. I cannot say that these acrobatics succeeded. It began to seem that the machinery of the organization I worked for was turning over, day and night, with but one aim: to eject me. I was fired once, and contrived, with the aid of a friend from New York, to get back on the payroll; was fired again, and bounced back again. It took a while to fire me for the third time, but the third time took. There were no loopholes anywhere. There was not even any way of getting back inside the gates.

That year in New Jersey lives in my mind as though it were the year during which, having an unsuspected predilection for it, I first contracted some dread, chronic disease, the unfailing symptom of which is a kind of blind fever, a pounding in the skull and fire in the bowels. Once this disease is contracted, one can never be really carefree again, for the fever, without an instant's warning, can recur at any moment. It can wreck more important things than race relations. There is not a Negro alive who does not have this rage in his blood—one has the choice, merely, of living with it consciously or surrendering to it. As for me, this fever has recurred in me, and does, and will until the day I die.

My last night in New Jersey, a white friend from New York took me to the nearest big town, Trenton, to go to the movies and have a few drinks. As it turned out, he also saved me from, at the very least, a violent whipping. Almost every detail of that night stands out very clearly in my memory. I even remember the name of the movie we saw because its title impressed me as being so patly ironical. It was a movie about the German occupation of France, starring Maureen O'Hara and Charles Laughton and called *This Land Is Mine.* I remember the name of the diner we walked into when the movie ended: it was the "American Diner." When we walked in the counterman asked what we wanted and I remember answering with the casual sharpness which had become my habit: "We want a hamburger and a cup of coffee, what do you think we want?" I do not know why, after a year of such rebuffs, I so completely failed to anticipate his answer, which was, of course, "We don't serve Negroes here." This reply failed to discompose me, at least for the moment. I made some sardonic comment about the name of the diner and we walked out into the streets.

This was the time of what was called the "brown-out," when the lights in all American cities were very dim. When we re-entered the streets something happened to me which had the force of an optical illusion, or a nightmare. The streets were very crowded and I was facing north. People were moving in every direction but it seemed to me, in that instant, that all of the people I could see, and many more than that, were moving toward me, against me, and that everyone was white. I remember how their faces gleamed. And I felt, like a physical sensation, a *click* at the nape of my neck as though some interior string connecting my head to my body had been cut. I began to walk. I heard my friend call after me, but I ignored him. Heaven only knows what was going on in his mind, but he had the good sense not to touch me—I don't know what would have happened if he had—and to keep me in sight. I don't know what was going on in my mind, either; I certainly had no conscious plan. I wanted to do something to crush these white faces, which were crushing me. I walked for perhaps a block or two until I came to an enormous, glittering, and fashionable restaurant in which I knew not even the intercession of the Virgin would cause me to be served. I pushed through the doors and took the first vacant seat I saw, at a table for two, and waited.

I do not know how long I waited and I rather wonder, until today, what I could possibly have looked like. Whatever I looked like, I frightened the waitress who shortly appeared, and the moment she appeared all of my fury flowed towards her. I hated her for her white face, and for her great, astounded, frightened eyes. I felt that if she found a black man so frightening I would make her fright worth-while.

She did not ask me what I wanted, but repeated, as though she had learned it somewhere, "We don't serve Negroes here." She did not say it with the blunt, derisive hostility to which I had grown so accustomed, but, rather, with a note of apology in her voice, and fear. This made me colder and more murderous than ever. I felt I had to do something with my hands. I wanted her to come close enough for me to get her neck between my hands.

So I pretended not to have understood her, hoping to draw

her closer. And she did step a very short step closer, with her pencil poised incongruously over her pad, and repeated the formula:
". . . don't serve Negroes here."

Somehow, with the repetition of that phrase, which was
already ringing in my head like a thousand bells of a nightmare, I
realized that she would never come any closer and that I would
have to strike from a distance. There was nothing on the table
but an ordinary water-mug half full of water, and I picked this up
and hurled it with all my strength at her. She ducked and it
missed her and shattered against the mirror behind the bar. And,
with that sound, my frozen blood abruptly thawed, I returned from
wherever I had been, I *saw*, for the first time, the restaurant, the
people with their mouths open, already, as it seemed to me, rising
as one man, and I realized what I had done, and where I was, and
I was frightened. I rose and began running for the door. A round,
potbellied man grabbed me by the nape of the neck just as I reached the
doors and began to beat me about the face. I kicked him and got loose
and ran into the streets. My friend whispered, *"Run!"* and I ran.

My friend stayed outside the restaurant long enough to misdir-
ect my pursuers and the police, who arrived, he told me, at once.
I do not know what I said to him when he came to my room that
night. I could not have said much. I felt, in the oddest, most awful way, that I had somehow betrayed him. I lived it over and over
and over again, the way one relives an automobile accident after it
has happened and one finds oneself alone and safe. I could not get
over two facts, both equally difficult for the imagination to grasp,
and one was that I could have been murdered. But the other was
that I had been ready to commit murder. I saw nothing very clearly
but I did see this: that my life, my *real* life, was in danger, and
not from anything other people might do but from the hatred I
carried in my own heart.

II

I had returned home around the second week in June—in great
haste because it seemed that my father's death and my mother's
confinement were both but a matter of hours. In the case of my
mother, it soon became clear that she had simply made a miscalcu-
lation. This had always been her tendency and I don't believe that
a single one of us arrived in the world, or has since arrived anywhere
else, on time. But none of us dawdled so intolerably about the
business of being born as did my baby sister. We sometimes amused
ourselves, during those endless, stifling weeks, by picturing the baby
sitting within in the safe, warm dark, bitterly regretting the ne-

cessity of becoming a part of our chaos and stubbornly putting it off as long as possible. I understood her perfectly and congratulated her on showing such good sense so soon. Death, however, sat as purposefully at my father's bedside as life stirred within my mother's womb and it was harder to understand why he so lingered in that long shadow. It seemed that he had bent, and for a long time, too, all of his energies towards dying. Now death was ready for him but my father held back.

All of Harlem, indeed, seemed to be infected by waiting. I had never before known it to be so violently still. Racial tensions throughout this country were exacerbated during the early years of the war, partly because the labor market brought together hundreds of thousands of ill-prepared people and partly because Negro soldiers, regardless of where they were born, received their military training in the south. What happened in defense plants and army camps had repercussions, naturally, in every Negro ghetto. The situation in Harlem had grown bad enough for clergymen, policemen, educators, politicians, and social workers to assert in one breath that there was no "crime wave" and to offer, in the very next breath, suggestions as to how to combat it. These suggestions always seemed to involve playgrounds, despite the fact that racial skirmishes were occurring in the playgrounds, too. Playground or not, crime wave or not, the Harlem police force had been augmented in March, and the unrest grew—perhaps, in fact, partly as a result of the ghetto's instinctive hatred of policemen. Perhaps the most revealing news item, out of the steady parade of reports of muggings, stabbings, shootings, assaults, gang wars, and accusations of police brutality, is the item concerning six Negro girls who set upon a white girl in the subway because, as they all too accurately put it, she was stepping on their toes. Indeed she was, all over the nation.

I had never before been so aware of policemen, on foot, on horseback, on corners, everywhere, always two by two. Nor had I ever been so aware of small knots of people. They were on stoops and on corners and in doorways, and what was striking about them, I think, was that they did not seem to be talking. Never, when I passed these groups, did the usual sound of a curse or a laugh ring out and neither did there seem to be any hum of gossip. There was certainly, on the other hand, occurring between them communication extraordinarily intense. Another thing that was striking was the unexpected diversity of the people who made up these groups. Usually, for example, one would see a group of sharpies standing on the street corner, jiving the passing chicks; or a group of older men, usually, for some reason, in the vicinity of a barber shop, discussing

baseball scores, or the numbers, or making rather chilling observations about women they had known. Women, in a general way,
tended to be seen less often together—unless they were church
women, or very young girls, or prostitutes met together for an unprofessional instant. But that summer I saw the strangest combi-
nations: large, respectable, churchly matrons standing on the
stoops or the corners with their hair tied up, together with a girl
in sleazy satin whose face bore the marks of gin and the razor, or
heavy-set, abrupt, non-nonsense older men, in company with the
most disreputable and fanatical "race" men, or these same "race"
men with the sharpies, or these sharpies with the churchly women.
Seventh Day Adventists and Methodists and Spiritualists seemed
to be hobnobbing with Holyrollers and they were all, alike, entangled with the most flagrant disbelievers; something heavy in
their stance seemed to indicate that they had all, incredibly, seen
a common vision, and on each face there seemed to be the same
strange, bitter shadow.

The churchly women and the matter-of-fact, no-nonsense men
had children in the Army. The sleazy girls they talked to had lovers
there, the sharpies and the "race" men had friends and brothers
there. It would have demanded an unquestioning patriotism, happily as uncommon in this country as it is undesirable, for these
people not to have been disturbed by the bitter letters they received, by the newspaper stories they read, not to have been enraged by the posters, then to be found all over New York, which
described the Japanese as "yellow-bellied Japs." It was only the
"race" men, to be sure, who spoke ceaselessly of being revenged—how
this vengeance was to be exacted was not clear—for the indignities
and dangers suffered by Negro boys in uniform; but everybody felt a
directionless, hopeless bitterness, as well as that panic which can
scarcely be suppressed when one knows that a human being one loves
is beyond one's reach, and in danger. This helplessness and this
gnawing uneasiness does something, at length, to even the tough-
est mind. Perhaps the best way to sum all this up is to say that
the people I knew felt, mainly, a peculiar kind of relief when they
knew that their boys were being shipped out of the south, to do
battle overseas. It was, perhaps, like feeling that the most dangerous part of a dangerous journey had been passed and that now, even
if death should come, it would come with honor and without the
complicity of their countrymen. Such a death would be, in short,
a fact with which one could hope to live.

It was on the 28th of July, which I believe was a Wednesday,
that I visited my father for the first time during his illness and
for the last time in his life. The moment I saw him I knew why

I had put off this visit so long. I had told my mother that I did not want to see him because I hated him. But this was not true. It was only that I *had* hated him and I wanted to hold on to this hatred. I did not want to look on him as a ruin: it was not a ruin I had hated. I imagine that one of the reasons people cling to their hates so stubbornly is because they sense, once hate is gone, that they will be forced to deal with pain.

We traveled out to him, his older sister and myself, to what seemed to be the very end of a very Long Island. It was hot and dusty and we wrangled, my aunt and I, all the way out, over the fact that I had recently begun to smoke and, as she said, to give myself airs. But I knew that she wrangled with me because she could not bear to face the fact of her brother's dying. Neither could I endure the reality of her despair, her unstated bafflement as to what had happened to her brother's life, and her own. So we wrangled and I smoked and from time to time she fell into a heavy reverie. Covertly, I watched her face, which was the face of an old woman; it had fallen in, the eyes were sunken and lightless; soon she would be dying, too.

In my childhood—it had not been so long ago—I had thought her beautiful. She had been quick-witted and quick-moving and very generous with all the children and each of her visits had been an event. At one time one of my brothers and myself had thought of running away to live with her. Now she could no longer produce out of her handbag some unexpected and yet familiar delight. She made me feel pity and revulsion and fear. It was awful to realize that she no longer caused me to feel affection. The closer we came to the hospital the more querulous she became and at the same time, naturally, grew more dependent on me. Between pity and guilt and fear I began to feel that there was another me trapped in my skull like a jack-in-the-box who might escape my control at any moment and fill the air with screaming.

She began to cry the moment we entered the room and she saw him lying there, all shriveled and still, like a little black monkey. The great, gleaming apparatus which fed him and would have compelled him to be still even if he had been able to move brought to mind, not beneficence, but torture; the tubes entering his arm made me think of pictures I had seen when a child, of Gulliver, tied down by the pygmies on that island. My aunt wept and wept, there was a whistling sound in my father's throat; nothing was said; he could not speak. I wanted to take his hand, to say something. But I do not know what I could have said, even if he could have heard me. He was not really in that room with us, he had at last really embarked on his journey; and though my aunt told

me that he said he was going to meet Jesus, I did not hear anything except that whistling in his throat. The doctor came back
and we left, into that unbearable train again, and home. In the
morning came the telegram saying that he was dead. Then the
house was suddenly full of relatives, friends, hysteria, and confusion
and I quickly left my mother and the children to the care of those
impressive women, who, in Negro communities at least, automati-
cally appear at times of bereavement armed with lotions, proverbs,
and patience, and an ability to cook. I went downtown. By the
time I returned, later the same day, my mother had been carried
to the hospital and the baby had been born.

III

For my father's funeral I had nothing black to wear and this
posed a nagging problem all day long. It was one of those problems,
simple, or impossible of solution, to which the mind insanely clings
in order to avoid the mind's real trouble. I spent most of that day
at the downtown apartment of a girl I knew, celebrating my birthday with whiskey and wondering what to wear that night. When
planning a birthday celebration one naturally does not expect that
it will be up against competition from a funeral and this girl had
anticipated taking me out that night, for a big dinner and a
night club afterwards. Sometime during the course of that long day
we decided that we would go out anyway, when my father's funeral
service was over. I imagine I decided it, since, as the funeral hour
approached, it became clearer and clearer to me that I would not
know what to do with myself when it was over. The girl, stifling
her very lively concern as to the possible effects of the whiskey on
one of my father's chief mourners, concentrated on being concilia-
tory and practically helpful. She found a black shirt for me somewhere and ironed it and, dressed in the darkest pants and jacket
I owned, and slightly drunk, I made my way to my father's funeral.

The chapel was full, but not packed, and very quiet. There
were, mainly, my father's relatives, and his children, and here and
there I saw faces I had not seen since childhood, the faces of my
father's one-time friends. They were very dark and solemn now,
seeming somehow to suggest that they had known all along that
something like this would happen. Chief among the mourners was
my aunt, who had quarreled with my father all his life; by which
I do not mean to suggest that her mourning was insincere or that
she had not loved him. I suppose that she was one of the few
people in the world who had, and their incessant quarreling proved
precisely the strength of the tie that bound them. The only

other person in the world, as far as I knew, whose relationship to my father rivaled my aunt's in depth was my mother, who was not there.

It seemed to me, of course, that it was a very long funeral. But it was, if anything, a rather shorter funeral than most, nor, since there were no overwhelming, uncontrollable expressions of grief, could it be called—if I dare to use the word—successful. The minister who preached my father's funeral sermon was one of the few my father had still been seeing as he neared his end. He presented to us in his sermon a man whom none of us had ever seen—a man thoughtful, patient, and forbearing, a Christian inspiration to all who knew him, and a model for his children. And no doubt the children, in their disturbed and guilty state, were almost ready to believe this; he had been remote enough to be anything and, anyway, the shock of the incontrovertible, that it was really our father lying up there in that casket, prepared the mind for anything. His sister moaned and this grief-stricken moaning was taken as corroboration. The other faces held a dark, non-committal thoughtfulness. This was not the man they had known, but they had scarcely expected to be confronted with *him;* this was, in a sense deeper than questions of fact, the man they had not known, and the man they had not known may have been the real one. The real man, whoever he had been, had suffered and now he was dead: this was all that was sure and all that mattered now. Every man in the chapel hoped that when his hour came he, too, would be eulogized, which is to say forgiven, and that all of his lapses, greeds, errors, and strayings from the truth would be invested with coherence and looked upon with charity. This was perhaps the last thing human beings could give each other and it was what they demanded, after all, of the Lord. Only the Lord saw the midnight tears, only He was present when one of His children, moaning and wringing hands, paced up and down the room. When one slapped one's child in anger the recoil in the heart reverberated through heaven and became part of the pain of the universe. And when the children were hungry and sullen and distrustful and one watched them, daily, growing wilder, and further away, and running headlong into danger, it was the Lord who knew what the charged heart endured as the strap was laid to the backside; the Lord alone who knew what one *would* have said if one had had, like the Lord, the gift of the living word. It was the Lord who knew of the impossibility every parent in that room faced: how to prepare the child for the day when the child would be despised and how to *create* in the child—by what means?—a stronger antidote to this poison than one had found for oneself. The avenues, side streets, bars, bil-

liard halls, hospitals, police stations, and even the playgrounds of
Harlem—not to mention the houses of correction, the jails, and
the morgue—testified to the potency of the poison while remaining silent as to the efficacy of whatever antidote, irresistibly raising
the question of whether or not such an antidote existed; raising,
which was worse, the question of whether or not an antidote
was desirable; perhaps poison should be fought with poison. With
these several schisms in the mind and with more terrors in the
heart than could be named, it was better not to judge the man
who had gone down under an impossible burden. It was better to
remember: *Thou knowest this man's fall; but thou knowest not his
wrassling.*

While the preacher talked and I watched the children—years
of changing their diapers, scrubbing them, slapping them, taking
them to school, and scolding them had had the perhaps inevitable
result of making me love them, though I am not sure I knew this
then—my mind was busily breaking out with a rash of disconnected
impressions. Snatches of popular songs, indecent jokes, bits of books
I had read, movie sequences, faces, voices, political issues—I
thought I was going mad; all these impressions suspended, as it
were, in the solution of the faint nausea produced in me by the
heat and liquor. For a moment I had the impression that my alco-
holic breath, inefficiently disguised with chewing gum, filled the
entire chapel. Then someone began singing one of my father's favorite songs and, abruptly, I was with him, sitting on his knee, in the
hot, enormous, crowded church which was the first church we attended. It was the Abyssinia Baptist Church on 138th Street.
We had not gone there long. With this image, a host of others
came. I had forgotten, in the rage of my growing up, how proud my
father had been of me when I was little. Apparently, I had had a
voice and my father had liked to show me off before the members
of the church. I had forgotten what he had looked like when he
was pleased but now I remembered that he had always been grinning
with pleasure when my solos ended. I even remembered certain expressions on his face when he teased my mother—had he loved her?
I would never know. And when had it all begun to change? For now
it seemed that he had not always been cruel. I remembered being
taken for a haircut and scraping my knee on the footrest of the
barber's chair and I remembered my father's face as he soothed my
crying and applied the stinging iodine. Then I remembered our
fights, fights which had been of the worst possible kind because my
technique had been silence.

I remembered the one time in all our life together when we
had really spoken to each other.

It was on a Sunday and it must have been shortly before I left home. We were walking, just the two of us, in our usual silence, to or from church. I was in high school and had been doing a lot of writing and I was, at about this time, the editor of the high school magazine. But I had also been a Young Minister and had been preaching from the pulpit. Lately, I had been taking fewer engagements and preached as rarely as possible. It was said in the church, quite truthfully, that I was "cooling off."

My father asked me abruptly, "You'd rather write than preach, wouldn't you?"

I was astonished at his question—because it was a real question. I answered, "Yes."

That was all we said. It was awful to remember that that was all we had *ever* said.

The casket now was opened and the mourners were being led up the aisle to look for the last time on the deceased. The assumption was that the family was too overcome with grief to be allowed to make this journey alone and I watched while my aunt was led to the casket and, muffled in black, and shaking, led back to her seat. I disapproved of forcing the children to look on their dead father, considering that the shock of his death, or, more truthfully, the shock of death as a reality, was already a little more than a child could bear, but my judgment in this matter had been overruled and there they were, bewildered and frightened and very small, being led, one by one, to the casket. But there is also something very gallant about children at such moments. It has something to do with their silence and gravity and with the fact that one cannot help them. Their legs, somehow, seem *exposed,* so that it is at once incredible and terribly clear that their legs are all they have to hold them up.

I had not wanted to go to the casket myself and I certainly had not wished to be led there, but there was no way of avoiding either of these forms. One of the deacons led me up and I looked on my father's face. I cannot say that it looked like him at all. His blackness had been equivocated by powder and there was no suggestion in that casket of what his power had or could have been. He was simply an old man dead, and it was hard to believe that he had ever given anyone either joy or pain. Yet, his life filled that room. Further up the avenue his wife was holding his newborn child. Life and death so close together, and love and hatred, and right and wrong, said something to me which I did not want to hear concerning man, concerning the life of man.

After the funeral, while I was downtown desperately celebrating my birthday, a Negro soldier, in the lobby of the Hotel Braddock, got into a fight with a white policeman over a Negro girl. Negro girls, white policemen, in or out of uniform, and Negro males—in or out of uniform—were part of the furniture of the lobby of the Hotel Braddock and this was certainly not the first time such an incident had occurred. It was destined, however, to receive an unprecedented publicity, for the fight between the policeman and the soldier ended with the shooting of the soldier. Rumor, flowing immediately to the streets outside, stated that the soldier had been shot in the back, an instantaneous and revealing invention, and that the soldier had died protecting a Negro woman. The facts were somewhat different—for example, the soldier had not been shot in the back, and was not dead, and the girl seems to have been as dubious a symbol of womanhood as her white counterpart in Georgia usually is, but no one was interested in the facts. They preferred the invention because this invention expressed and corroborated their hates and fears so perfectly. It is just as well to remember that people are always doing this. Perhaps many of those legends, including Christianity, to which the world clings began their conquest of the world with just some such concerted surrender to distortion. The effect, in Harlem, of this particular legend was like the effect of a lit match in a tin of gasoline. The mob gathered before the doors of the Hotel Braddock simply began to swell and to spread in every direction, and Harlem exploded.

The mob did not cross the ghetto lines. It would have been easy, for example, to have gone over Morningside Park on the west side or to have crossed the Grand Central railroad tracks at 125th Street on the east side, to wreak havoc in white neighborhoods. The mob seems to have been mainly interested in something more potent and real than the white face, that is, in white power, and the principal damage done during the riot of the summer of 1943 was to white business establishments in Harlem. It might have been a far bloodier story, of course, if, at the hour the riot began, these establishments had still been open. From the Hotel Braddock the mob fanned out, east and west along 125th Street, and for the entire length of Lenox, Seventh, and Eighth avenues. Along each of these avenues, and along each major side street—116th, 125th, 135th, and so on—bars, stores, pawnshops, restaurants, even little luncheonettes had been smashed open and entered and looted—looted, it might be added, with more haste than efficiency. The shelves really looked as though a bomb had struck them. Cans of beans and soup and dog food, along with toilet paper, corn flakes, sardines, and milk tumbled every which way, and abandoned cash registers and cases of beer leaned crazily out of the splintered

windows and were strewn along the avenues. Sheets, blankets, and
clothing of every description formed a kind of path, as though
people had dropped them while running. I truly had not realized
that Harlem *had* so many stores until I saw them all smashed open;
the first time the word *wealth* ever entered my mind in relation
to Harlem was when I saw it scattered in the streets. But one's
first, incongruous impression of plenty was countered immediately
by an impression of waste. None of this was doing anybody any good.
It would have been better to have left the plate glass as it had
been and the goods lying in the stores.

It would have been better, but it would also have been intolerable, for Harlem had needed something to smash. To smash something is the ghetto's chronic need. Most of the time it is the
members of the ghetto who smash each other, and themselves. But
as long as the ghetto walls are standing there will always come a
moment when these outlets do not work. That summer, for example, it was not enough to get into a fight on Lenox Avenue, or
curse out one's cronies in the barber shops. If ever, indeed, the violence which fills Harlem's churches, pool halls, and bars erupts outward in a more direct fashion, Harlem and its citizens are likely to
vanish in an apocalyptic flood. That this is not likely to happen
is due to a great many reasons, most hidden and powerful among
them the Negro's real relation to the white American. This relation prohibits, simply, anything as uncomplicated and satisfactory
as pure hatred. In order really to hate white people, one has to
blot so much out of the mind—and the heart—that this hatred
itself becomes an exhausting and self-destructive pose. But this
does not mean, on the other hand, that love comes easily: the
white world is too powerful, too complacent, too ready with gra-
tuitous humiliation, and, above all, too ignorant and too innocent for that. One is absolutely forced to make perpetual qualifications and one's own reactions are always canceling each other out.
It is this, really, which has driven so many people mad, both white
and black. One is always in the position of having to decide between amputation and gangrene. Amputation is swift but time
may prove that the amputation was not necessary—or one may
delay the amputation too long. Gangrene is slow, but it is impossible to be sure that one is reading one's symptoms right. The idea
of going through life as a cripple is more than one can bear, and
equally unbearable is the risk of swelling up slowly, in agony, with
poison. And the trouble, finally, is that the risks are real even if
the choices do not exist.

"But as for me and my house," my father had said, "we will
serve the Lord." I wondered, as we drove him to his resting place,

what this line had meant for him. I had heard him preach it many times. I had preached it once myself, proudly giving it an interpretation different from my father's. Now the whole thing came back to me, as though my father and I were on our way to Sunday school and I were memorizing the golden text: *And if it seem evil unto you to serve the Lord, choose you this day whom you will serve; whether the gods which your fathers served that were on the other side of the flood, or the gods of the Amorites, in whose land ye dwell: but as for me and my house, we will serve the Lord.* I suspected in these familiar lines a meaning which had never been there for me before. All of my father's texts and songs, which I had decided were meaningless, were arranged before me at his death like empty bottles, waiting to hold the meaning which life would give them for me. This was his legacy: nothing is ever escaped. That bleakly memorable morning I hated the unbelievable streets and the Negroes and whites who had, equally, made them that way. But I knew that it was folly, as my father would have said, this bitterness was folly. It was necessary to hold on to the things that mattered. The dead man mattered, the new life mattered; blackness and whiteness did not matter; to believe that they did was to acquiesce in one's own destruction. Hatred, which could destroy so much, never failed to destroy the man who hated and this was an immutable law.

It began to seem that one would have to hold in the mind forever two ideas which seemed to be in opposition. The first idea was acceptance, the acceptance, totally without rancor, of life as it is, and men as they are: in the light of this idea, it goes without saying that injustice is a commonplace. But this did not mean that one could be complacent, for the second idea was of equal power: that one must never, in one's own life, accept these injustices as commonplace but must fight them with all one's strength. This fight begins, however, in the heart and it now had been laid to my charge to keep my own heart free of hatred and despair. This intimation made my heart heavy and, now that my father was irrecoverable, I wished that he had been beside me so that I could have searched his face for the answers which only the future would give me now.

Alek Therien
the woodchopper

HENRY DAVID THOREAU

Who should come to my lodge this morning but a true Homeric or Paphlagonian man,—he had so suitable and poetic a name that I am sorry I cannot print it here,—a Canadian, a woodchopper and post-maker, who can hole fifty posts in a day, who made his last supper on a woodchuck which his dog caught. He, too, has heard of Homer, and, "if it were not for books," would "not know what to do rainy days," though perhaps he has not read one wholly through for many rainy seasons. Some priest who could pronounce the Greek itself taught him to read his verse in the Testament in his native parish far away; and now I must translate to him, while he holds the book, Achilles' reproof to Patroclus for his sad countenance.—"Why are you in tears, Patroclus, like a young girl?"—

> Or have you alone heard some news from Phthia?
> They say that Menoetius lives yet, son of Actor,
> And Peleus lives, son of Aeacus, among the Myrmidons,
> Either of whom having died, we should greatly grieve.

He says, "That's good." He has a great bundle of white oak bark under his arm for a sick man, gathered this Sunday morning. "I suppose there's no harm in going after such a thing to-day," says he. To him Homer was a great writer, though what his writing was about he did not know. A more simple and natural man it would be hard to find. Vice and disease, which cast such a sombre moral hue over the world, seemed to have hardly any existence for him. He was about twenty-eight years old, and had left Canada and his father's house a dozen years before to work in the States, and earn money to buy a farm with at last, perhaps in his native country. He was cast in the coarsest mould; a stout but sluggish body, yet gracefully carried, with a thick sunburnt neck, dark bushy hair, and dull sleepy blue eyes, which were occasionally lit up with expression.

He wore a flat gray cloth cap, a dingy wool-colored greatcoat, and cowhide boots. He was a great consumer of meat, usually carrying his dinner to his work a couple of miles past my house,—for he chopped all summer,—in a tin pail; cold meats, often cold wood-chucks, and coffee in a stone bottle which dangled by a string from his belt; and sometimes he offered me a drink. He came along to get to his work, such as Yankees exhibit. He wasn't a-going to hurt himself. He didn't care if he only earned his board. Frequently he would leave his dinner in the bushes, when his dog had caught a woodchuck by the way, and go back a mile and a half to dress it and leave it in the cellar of the house where he boarded, after deli-berating first for half an hour whether he could not sink it in the pond safely till nightfall,—loving to dwell long upon these themes. He would say, as he went by in the morning, "How thick the pi-geons are! If working every day were not my trade, I could get all the meat I should want by hunting,—pigeons, woodchucks, rab-bits, partridges,—by gosh! I could get all I should want for a week in one day."

He was a skilful chopper, and indulged in some flourishes and or-naments in his art. He cut his trees level and close to the ground, that the sprouts which came up afterward might be more vigorous and a sled might slide over the stumps; and instead of leaving a whole tree to support his corded wood, he would pare it away to a slender stake or splinter which you could break off with your hand at last.

He interested me because he was so quiet and solitary and so happy withal; a well of good humor and contentment which over-flowed at his eyes. His mirth was without alloy. Sometimes I saw him at his work in the woods, felling trees, and he would greet me with a laugh of inexpressible satisfaction, and a salutation in Cana-dian French, though he spoke English as well. When I approached him he would suspend his work, and with half-suppressed mirth lie along the trunk of a pine which he had felled, and, peeling off the inner bark, roll it up into a ball and chew it while he laughed and talked. Such an exuberance of animal spirits had he that he some-times tumbled down and rolled on the ground with laughter at anything which made him think and tickled him. Looking round upon the trees he would exclaim,—"By George! I can enjoy myself well enough here chopping; I want no better sport." Sometimes, when at leisure, he amused himself all day in the woods with a pocket pistol, firing salutes to himself at regular intervals as he walked. In the winter he had a fire by which at noon he warmed his coffee in a kettle; and as he sat on a log to eat his dinner the chickadees would sometimes come round and alight on his arm and peck at the potato in his fingers; and he said that he "liked to have the little *fellers* about him."

In him the animal man chiefly was developed. In physical endurance and contentment he was cousin to the pine and the rock. I asked him once if he was not sometimes tired at night, after working all day; and he answered, with a sincere and serious look, "Gorrappit, I never was tired in my life." But the intellectual and what is called spiritual man in him were slumbering as in an infant. He had been instructed only in that innocent and ineffectual way in which the Catholic priests teach the aborigines, by which the pupil is never educated to the degree of consciousness, but only to the degree of trust and reverence, and a child is not made a man, but kept a child. When Nature made him, she gave him a strong body and contentment for his portion, and propped him on every side with reverence and reliance, that he might live out his three-score years and ten a child. He was so genuine and unsophisticated that no introduction would serve to introduce him, more than if you introduced a woodchuck to your neighbor. He had got to find him out as you did. He would not play any part. Men paid him wages for work, and so helped to feed and clothe him; but he never exchanged opinions with them. He was so simply and naturally humble—if he can be called humble who never aspires—that humility was no distinct quality in him, nor could he conceive of it. Wiser men were demigods to him. If you told him that such a one was coming, he did as if he thought that anything so grand would expect nothing of himself, but take all the responsibility on itself, and let him be forgotten still. He never heard the sound of praise. He particularly reverenced the writer and the preacher. Their performances were miracles. When I told him that I wrote considerably, he thought for a long time that it was merely the handwriting which I meant, for he could write a remarkably good hand himself. I sometimes found the name of his native parish handsomely written in the snow by the highway, with the proper French accent, and knew that he had passed. I asked him if he ever wished to write his thoughts. He said that he had read and written letters for those who could not, but he never tried to write thoughts,—no, he could not, he could not tell what to put first, it would kill him, and then there was spelling to be attended to at the same time!

I heard that a distinguished wise man and reformer asked him if he did not want the world to be changed; but he answered with a chuckle of surprise in his Canadian accent, not knowing that the question had ever been entertained before, "No, I like it well enough." It would have suggested many things to a philosopher to have dealings with him. To a stranger he appeared to know nothing of things in general; yet I sometimes saw in him a man whom I had not seen before, and I did not know whether he was as wise as Shakespeare or as simply ignorant as a child, whether to suspect him of a fine poetic consciousness or of stupidity. A townsman told me that when he met him sauntering through the village in his small close-fitting cap, and whistling to himself, he reminded him of a prince in disguise.

His only books were an almanac and an arithmetic, in which last he was considerably expert. The former was a sort of cyclopaedia to him, which he supposed to contain an abstract of human knowledge, as indeed it does to a considerable extent. I loved to sound him on the various reforms of the day, and he never failed to look at them in the most simple and practical light. He had never heard of such things before. Could he do without factories? I asked. He had worn the homemade Vermont gray, he said, and that was good. Could he dispense with tea and coffee? Did this country afford any beverage beside water? He had soaked hemlock leaves in water and drank it, and thought that was better than water in warm weather. When I asked him if he could do without money, he showed the convenience of money in such a way as to suggest and coincide with the most philosophical accounts of the origin of this institution, and the very derivation of the word *pecunia*. If an ox were his property, and he wished to get needles and thread at the store, he thought it would be inconvenient and impossible soon to go on mortgaging some portion of the creature each time to that amount. He could defend many institutions better than any philosopher, because, in describing them as they concerned him, he gave the true reason for their prevalence, and speculation had not suggested to him any other. At another time, hearing Plato's definition of a man,—a biped without feathers,—and that one exhibited a cock plucked and called it Plato's man, he thought it an important difference that the *knees* bent the wrong way. He would sometimes exclaim, "How I love to talk! By George, I could talk all day!" I asked him once, when I had not seen him for many months, if he had got a new idea this summer. "Good Lord," said he, "a man that has to work as I do, if he does not forget the ideas he has had, he will do well. May be the man you hoe with is inclined to race; then, by gorry, your mind must be there; you think of weeds." He would sometimes ask me first on such occasions, if I had made any improvement. One winter day I asked him if he was always satisfied with himself, wishing to suggest a substitute within him for the priest without, and some higher motive for living. "Satisfied!" said he; "some men are satisfied with one thing, and some with another. One man, perhaps, if he has got enough, will be satisfied to sit all day with his back to the fire and his belly to the table, by George!" Yet I never, by any manoeuvring, could get him to take the spiritual view of things; the highest that he appeared to conceive of was a simple expediency, such as you might expect an animal to appreciate; and this, practically, is true of most men. If I suggested any improvement in his mode of life, he merely answered, without expressing any regret, that it was too late. Yet he thoroughly believed in honesty and the like virtues.

There was a certain positive originality, however slight, to be detected in him, and I occasionally observed that he was thinking for himself and expressing his own opinion, a phenomenon so rare that I would any day walk ten miles to observe it, and it amounted to the re-origination of many of the institutions of society. Though he hesitated, and perhaps failed to express himself distinctly, he always had a presentable thought behind. Yet his thinking was so primitive and immersed in his animal life, that, though more promising than a merely learned man's, it rarely ripened to anything which can be reported. He suggested that there might be men of genius in the lowest grades of life, however permanently humble and illiterate, who take their own view always, or do not pretend to see at all; who are as bottomless even as Walden Pond was thought to be, though they may be dark . . .

a Christmas memory

TRUMAN CAPOTE (1924–   ) is most widely known as the author of *In Cold Blood* (1966), a meticulous and imaginative rendering of an actual murder case. Described by Capote as a "non-fiction novel," the book demonstrates two features of his literary style: a very careful attention to the details and speech patterns of everyday life, and a nightmarish land-scape of dark imagining. Capote's other works include *Other Voices, Other Rooms* (1948); *Tree of Night* (1949), a collec-tion of short stories; *The Grass Harp* (1953); and *Breakfast at Tiffany's* (1958), from which the following autobiographical story is taken.

Imagine a morning in late November. A coming of winter morning more than twenty years ago. Consider the kitchen of a spreading old house in a country town. A great black stove is its main fea-ture; but there is also a big round table and a fireplace with two rocking chairs placed in front of it. Just today the fireplace com-menced its seasonal roar.

A woman with shorn white hair is standing at the kitchen window. She is wearing tennis shoes and a shapeless gray sweater over a summery calico dress. She is small and sprightly, like a ban-tam hen; but, due to a long youthful illness, her shoulders are piti-fully hunched. Her face is remarkable—not unlike Lincoln's, craggy like that, and tinted by sun and wind; but it is delicate too, finely boned, and her eyes are sherry-colored and timid. "Oh my," she exclaims, her breath smoking the windowpane, "it's fruitcake weather!"

The person to whom she is speaking is myself. I am seven; she is sixty-something. We are cousins, very distant ones, and we have lived together—well, as long as I can remember. Other people inhab-it the house, relatives; and though they have power over us, and frequently make us cry, we are not, on the whole, too much aware of them. We are each other's best friend. She calls me Buddy, in memory of a boy who was formerly her best friend. The other Buddy died in the 1880s, when she was still a child. She is still a child.

"I knew it before I got out of bed," she says, turning away from the window with a purposeful excitement in her eyes. "The courthouse bell sounded so cold and clear. And there were no birds singing; they've gone to warmer country, yes indeed. Oh, Buddy, stop stuffing biscuit and fetch our buggy. Help me find my hat. We've thirty cakes to bake."

It's always the same: a morning arrives in November, and my friend, as though officially inaugurating the Christmas time of year that exhilarates her imagination and fuels the blaze of her heart, announces: "It's fruitcake weather! Fetch our buggy. Help me find my hat."

The hat is found, a straw cartwheel corsaged with velvet roses out-of-doors has faded: it once belonged to a more fashionable relative. Together, we guide our buggy, a dilapidated baby carriage, out to the garden and into a grove of pecan trees. The buggy is mine; that is, it was bought for me when I was born. It is made of wicker, rather unraveled, and the wheels wobble like a drunkard's legs. But it is a faithful object; springtimes, we take it to the woods and fill it with flowers, herbs, wild fern for our porch pots; in the summer, we pile it with picnic paraphernalia and sugar-cane fishing poles and roll it down to the edge of a creek; it has its winter uses, too: as a truck for hauling firewood from the yard to the kitchen, as a warm bed for Queenie, our tough little orange and white rat terrier who has survived distemper and two rattlesnake bites. Queenie is trotting beside it now.

Three hours later we are back in the kitchen hulling a heaping buggyload of windfall pecans. Our backs hurt from gathering them: how hard they were to find (the main crop having been shaken off the trees and sold by the orchard's owners, who are not us) among the concealing leaves, the frosted, deceiving grass. Caarackle! A cheery crunch, scraps of miniature thunder sound as the shells collapse and the golden mound of sweet oily ivory meat mounts in the milk-glass bowl. Queenie begs to taste, and now and again my friend sneaks her a mite, though insisting we deprive ourselves. "We mustn't, Buddy. If we start, we won't stop. And there's scarcely enough as there is. For thirty cakes." The kitchen is growing dark. Dusk turns the window into a mirror: our reflections mingle with the rising moon as we work by the fireside in the firelight. At last, when the moon is quite high, we toss the final hull into the fire and, with joined sighs, watch it catch flame. The buggy is empty, the bowl is brimful.

We eat our supper (cold biscuits, bacon, blackberry jam) and discuss tomorrow. Tomorrow the kind of work I like best begins: buying. Cherries and citron, ginger and vanilla and canned Hawaiian pineapple, rinds and raisins and walnuts and whiskey and oh, so much flour, butter, so many eggs, spices, flavorings: why, we'll need a pony to pull the buggy home.

But before these purchases can be made, there is the question of money. Neither of us has any. Except for skinflint sums persons in the house occasionally provide (a dime is considered very big money); or what we earn ourselves from various activities: holding rummage sales, selling buckets of hand-picked blackberries, jars of homemade jam and apple jelly and peach preserves, rounding up flowers for funerals and weddings. Once we won seventy-ninth prize, five dollars, in a national football contest. Not that we know a fool thing about football. It's just that we enter any contest we hear about: at the moment our hopes are centered on the fifty-thousand-dollar Grand Prize being offered to name a new brand of coffee (we suggested "A.M."; and, after some hesitation, for my friend thought it perhaps sacrilegious, the slogan "A.M.! Amen!"). To tell the truth, our only *really* profitable enterprise was the Fun and Freak Museum we conducted in a back-yard woodshed two summers ago. The Fun was a stereopticon with slide views of Washington and New York lent us by a relative who had been to those places (she was furious when she discovered why we'd borrowed it); the Freak was a three-legged biddy chicken hatched by one of our own hens. Everybody hereabouts wanted to see that biddy: we charged grownups a nickel, kids two cents. And took in a good twenty dollars before the museum shut down due to the decease of the main attraction.

But one way and another we do each year accumulate Christmas savings, a Fruitcake Fund. These moneys we keep hidden in an ancient bead purse under a loose board under the floor under a chamber pot under my friend's bed. The purse is seldom removed from this safe location except to make a deposit, or, as happens every Saturday, a withdrawal; for on Saturdays I am allowed ten cents to go to the picture show. My friend has never been to a picture show, nor does she intend to: "I'd rather hear you tell the story, Buddy. That way I can imagine it more. Besides, a person my age shouldn't squander their eyes. When the Lord comes, let me see him clear." In addition to never having seen a movie, she has never: eaten in a restaurant, traveled more than five miles from home, received or sent a telegram, read anything except funny papers and the Bible, worn cosmetics, cursed, wished someone harm, told a lie on purpose, let a hungry dog go hungry. Here are a few things she has done, does do: killed with a hoe the biggest rattlesnake ever seen in this county (sixteen rattles), dip snuff (secretly), tame hummingbirds (just try it) till they balance on her finger, tell ghost stories (we both believe in ghosts) so tingling they chill you in July, talk to herself, take walks in the rain, grow the prettiest japonicas in town, know the recipe for every sort of old-time Indian cure, including a magical wart-remover.

Now, with supper finished, we retire to the room in a faraway part of the house where my friend sleeps in a scrap-quilt-covered iron bed painted rose pink, her favorite color. Silently, wallowing in the pleasures of conspiracy, we take the bead purse from its secret place and spill its contents on the scrap quilt. Dollar bills, tightly rolled and green as May buds. Somber fifty-cent pieces, heavy enough to weight a dead man's eyes. Lovely dimes, the liveliest coin, the one that really jingles. Nickels and quarters, worn smooth as creek pebbles. But mostly a hateful heap of bitter-odored pennies. Last summer others in the house contracted to pay us a penny for every twenty-five flies we killed. Oh, the carnage of August: the flies that flew to heaven! Yet it was not work in which we took pride. And, as we sit counting pennies, it is as though we were back tabulating dead flies. Neither of us has a head for figures; we count slowly, lose track, start again. According to her calculations, we have $12.73. According to mine, exactly $13. "I do hope you're wrong, Buddy. We can't mess around with thirteen. The cakes will fall. Or put somebody in the cemetery. Why, I wouldn't dream of getting out of bed on the thirteenth." This is true: she always spends thirteenths in bed. So, to be on the safe side, we subtract a penny and toss it out the window. Of the ingredients that go into our fruitcakes, whiskey is the most expensive, as well as the hardest to obtain: State laws forbid its sale. But everybody knows you can buy a bottle from Mr. Haha Jones. And the next day, having completed our more prosaic shopping, we set out for Mr. Haha's business address, a "sinful" (to quote public opinion) fish-fry and dancing café down by the river. We've been there before, and on the same errand; but in previous years our dealings have been with Haha's wife, an iodine-dark Indian woman with brassy peroxided hair and a dead-tired disposition. Actually, we've never laid eyes on her husband, though we've heard that he's an Indian too. A giant with razor scars across his cheeks. They call him Haha because he's so gloomy, a man who never laughs. As we approach his café (a large log cabin festooned inside and out with chains of garish-gay naked light bulbs and standing by the river's muddy edge under the shade of river trees where moss drifts through the branches like gray mist) our steps slow down. Even Queenie stops prancing and sticks close by. People have been murdered in Haha's café. Cut to pieces. Hit on the head. There's a case coming up in court next month. Naturally these goings-on happen at night when the colored lights cast crazy patterns and the victrola wails. In the daytime Haha's is shabby and deserted. I knock at the door, Queenie barks, my friend calls: "Mrs. Haha, ma'am? Anyone to home?"

Footsteps. The door opens. Our hearts overturn. It's Mr. Haha Jones himself! And he *is* a giant; he *does* have scars; he *doesn't* smile. No, he glowers at us through Satan-tilted eyes and demands to know: "What you want with Haha?"

For a moment we are too paralyzed to tell. Presently my friend half-finds her voice, a whispery voice at best: "If you please, Mr. Haha, we'd like a quart of your finest whiskey."

His eyes tilt more. Would you believe it? Haha is smiling! Laughing, too. "Which one of you is a drinkin' man?"

"It's for making fruitcakes, Mr. Haha. Cooking."

This sobers him. He frowns. "That's no way to waste good whiskey." Nevertheless, he retreats into the shadowed café and seconds later appears carrying a bottle of daisy yellow unlabeled liquor. He demonstrates its sparkle in the sunlight and says: "Two dollars."

We pay him with nickels and dimes and pennies. Suddenly, jangling the coins in his hand like a fistful of dice, his face softens. "Tell you what," he proposes, pouring the money back into the purse, "just send me one of them fruitcakes instead."

"Well," my friend remarks on our way home, "there's a lovely man. We'll put an extra cup of raisins in *his* cake."

The black stove, stoked with coal and firewood, glows like a lighted pumpkin. Eggbeaters whirl, spoons spin round in bowls of butter and sugar, vanilla sweetens the air, ginger spices it; melting, nose-tingling odors saturate the kitchen, suffuse the house, drift out to the world on puffs of chimney smoke. In four days our work is done. Thirty-one cakes, dampened with whiskey, bask on window sills and shelves.

Who are they for?

Friends. Not necessarily neighbor friends: indeed, the larger share are intended for persons we've met maybe once, perhaps not at all. People who've struck our fancy. Like President Roosevelt. Like the Reverend and Mrs. J. C. Lucey, Baptist missionaries to Borneo who lectured here last winter. Or the little knife grinder who comes through town twice a year. Or Abner Packer, the driver of the six o'clock bus from Mobile, who exchanges waves with us every day as he passes in a dust-cloud whoosh. Or the young Wistons, a California couple whose car one afternoon broke down outside the house and who spent a pleasant hour chatting with us on the porch (young Mr. Wiston snapped our picture, the only one we've ever had taken). Is it because my friend is shy with everyone *except* strangers that these strangers, and merest acquaintances, seem to us our truest friends? I think yes. Also, the scrapbooks we keep of thank-you's on White House stationery, time-to-time communications from California and Borneo, the knife grinder's penny post cards, make us feel connected to eventful worlds beyond the kitchen with its view of a sky that stops.

Now a nude December fig branch grates against the window. The kitchen is empty, the cakes are gone; yesterday we carted the last of them to the post office, where the cost of stamps turned our purse inside out. We're broke. That rather depresses me, but my friend insists on celebrating—with two inches of whiskey left in Haha's bottle. Queenie has a spoonful in a bowl of coffee (she likes her coffee chicory-flavored and strong). The rest we divide between a pair of jelly glasses. We're both quite awed at the prospect of drinking straight whiskey; the taste of it brings screwed-up expressions and sour shudders. But by and by we begin to sing, the two of us singing different songs simultaneously. I don't know the words to mine, just: *Come on along, come on along, to the dark-town strutters' ball.* But I can dance: that's what I mean to be, a tap dancer in the movies. My dancing shadow rollicks on the walls; our voices rock the chinaware; we giggle: as if unseen hands were tickling us. Queenie rolls on her back, her paws plow the air, something like a grin stretches her black lips. Inside myself, I feel warm and sparky as those crumbling logs, carefree as the wind in the chimney. My friend waltzes round the stove, the hem of her poor calico skirt pinched between her fingers as though it were a party dress: *Show me the way to go home,* she sings, her tennis shoes squeaking on the floor. *Show me the way to go home.*

Enter: two relatives. Very angry. Potent with eyes that scold, tongues that scald. Listen to what they have to say, the words tumbling together into a wrathful tune: "A child of seven! whiskey on his breath! are you out of your mind? feeding a child of seven! must be loony! road to ruination! remember Cousin Kate? Uncle Charlie? Uncle Charlie's brother-in-law? shame! scandal! humiliation! kneel, pray, beg the Lord!"

Queenie sneaks under the stove. My friend gazes at her shoes, her chin quivers, she lifts her skirt and blows her nose and runs to her room. Long after the town has gone to sleep and the house is silent except for the chimings of clocks and the sputter of fading fires, she is weeping into a pillow already as wet as a widow's handkerchief.

"Don't cry," I say, sitting at the bottom of her bed and shivering despite my flannel nightgown that smells of last winter's cough syrup, "don't cry," I beg, teasing her toes, tickling her feet, "you're too old for that."

"It's because," she hiccups, "I *am* too old. Old and funny."

"Not funny. Fun. More fun than anybody. Listen. If you don't stop crying you'll be so tired tomorrow we can't go cut a tree."

She straightens up. Queenie jumps on the bed (where Queenie is not allowed) to lick her cheeks. "I know where we'll find real pretty trees, Buddy. And holly, too. With berries big as your eyes. It's way off in the woods. Farther than we've ever been. Papa used to bring us Christmas trees from there: carry them on his shoulder. That's fifty years ago. Well, now: I can't wait for morning."

Morning. Frozen rime lusters the grass; the sun, round as orange and orange as hot-weather moons, balances on the horizon, burnishes the silvered winter woods. A wild turkey calls. A renegade hog grunts in the undergrowth. Soon, by the edge of knee-deep, rapid-running water, we have to abandon the buggy. Queenie wades the stream first, paddles across barking complaints at the swiftness of the current, the pneumonia-making coldness of it. We follow, holding our shoes and equipment (a hatchet, a burlap sack) above our heads. A mile more: of chastising thorns, burs and briers that catch at our clothes; of rusty pine needles brilliant with gaudy fungus and molted feathers. Here, there, a flash, a flutter, an ecstasy of shrillings remind us that not all the birds have flown south. Always, the path unwinds through lemony sun pools and pitch vine tunnels. Another creek to cross: a disturbed armada of speckled trout froths the water round us, and frogs the size of plates practice belly flops; beaver workmen are building a dam. On the farther shore, Queenie shakes herself and trembles. My friend shivers, too: not with cold but enthusiasm. One of her hat's ragged roses sheds a petal as she lifts her head and inhales the pine-heavy air. "We're almost there; can you smell it, Buddy?" she says, as though we were approaching an ocean.

And, indeed, it is a kind of ocean. Scented acres of holiday trees, prickly-leafed holly. Red berries shiny as Chinese bells: black crows swoop upon them screaming. Having stuffed our burlap sacks with enough greenery and crimson to garland a dozen windows, we set about choosing a tree. "It should be," muses my friend, "twice as tall as a boy. So a boy can't steal the star." The one we pick is twice as tall as me. A brave handsome brute that survives thirty hatchet strokes before it keels with a creaking rending cry. Lugging it like a kill, we commence the long trek out. Every few yards we abandon the struggle, sit down and pant. But we have the strength of triumphant huntsmen; that and the tree's virile, icy perfume revive us, goad us on. Many compliments accompany our sunset return along the red clay road to town; but my friend is sly and noncommittal when passers-by praise the treasure perched in our buggy: what a fine tree and where did it come from? "Yonder-ways," she murmurs vaguely. Once a car stops and the rich mill own-er's lazy wife leans out and whines: "Giveya two-bits cash for that ol tree." Ordinarily my friend is afraid of saying no; but on this oc-casion she promptly shakes her head: "We wouldn't take a dollar." The mill owner's wife persists. "A dollar, my foot! Fifty cents. That's my last offer. Goodness, woman, you can get another one." In answer, my friend gently reflects: "I doubt it. There's never two of anything."

Home: Queenie slumps by the fire and sleeps till tomorrow, snoring loud as a human.

A trunk in the attic contains: a shoebox of ermine tails (off the opera cape of a curious lady who once rented a room in the house), coils of frazzled tinsel gone gold with age, one silver star, a brief rope of dilapidated, undoubtedly dangerous candy-like light bulbs. Excellent decorations, as far as they go, which isn't far enough: my friend wants our tree to blaze "like a Baptist window," droop with weighty snows of ornament. But we can't afford the made-in-Japan splendors at the five-and-dime. So we do what we've always done: sit for days at the kitchen table with scissors and crayons and stacks of colored paper. I make sketches and my friend cuts them out: lots of cats, fish too (because they're easy to draw), some apples, some watermelons, a few winged angels devised from saved-up sheets of Hershey-bar tin foil. We use safety pins to attach these creations to the tree; as a final touch, we sprinkle the branches with shredded cotton (picked in August for this pur-pose). My friend, surveying the effect, clasps her hands together. "Now honest, Buddy. Doesn't it look good enough to eat?" Queen-ie tries to eat an angel.

After weaving and ribboning holly wreaths for all the front windows, our next project is the fashioning of family gifts. Tie-dye scarves for the ladies, for the men a home-brewed lemon and licorice and aspirin syrup to be taken "at the first Symptoms of a Cold and after Hunting." But when it comes time for making each other's gift, my friend and I separate to work secretly. I would like to buy her a pearl-handled knife, a radio, a whole pound of chocolate-covered cherries (we tasted some once, and she always swears: "I could live on them, Buddy, Lord yes I could—and that's not taking His name in vain"). Instead, I am building her a kite. She would like to give me a bicycle (she's said so on several million occasions: "If only I could, Buddy. It's bad enough in life to do without something *you* want; but confound it, what gets my goat is not being able to give somebody something you want *them* to have. Only one of these days I will, Buddy. Locate you a bike. Don't ask how. Steal it, maybe"). Instead, I'm fairly certain that she is building me a kite—the same as last year, and the year before: the year before that we exchanged slingshots. All of which is fine by me. For we are champion kite-fliers who study the wind like sailors; my friend, more accomplished than I, can get a kite aloft when there isn't enough breeze to carry clouds.

Christmas Eve afternoon we scrape together a nickel and go to the butcher's to buy Queenie's traditional gift, a good gnawable beef bone. The bone, wrapped in funny paper, is placed high in the tree near the silver star. Queenie knows it's there. She squats at the foot of the tree staring up in a trance of greed: when bedtime arrives she refuses to budge. Her excitement is equaled by my own. I kick the covers and turn my pillow as though it were a scorching summer's night. Somewhere a rooster crows: falsely, for the sun is still on the other side of the world.

"Buddy, are you awake?" It is my friend, calling from her room, which is next to mine; and an instant later she is sitting on my bed holding a candle. "Well, I can't sleep a hoot," she declares. "My mind's jumping like a jack rabbit. Buddy, do you think Mrs. Roosevelt will serve our cake at dinner?" We huddle in the bed, and she squeezes my hand I-love-you. "Seems like your hand used to be so much smaller. I guess I hate to see you grow up. When you're grown up, will we still be friends?" I say always. "But I feel so bad, Buddy. I wanted so bad to give you a bike. I tried to sell my cameo Papa gave me, Buddy—" she hesitates, as though embarrassed—"I made you another kite." Then I confess that I made her one, too; and we laugh. The candle burns too short to hold. Out it goes, exposing the starlight, the stars spinning at the window like a visible caroling that slowly, slowly daybreak silences. Possibly we doze; but the beginnings of dawn splash us like cold water: we're up, wide-eyed and wandering while we wait for others to waken. Quite deliberately my friend drops a kettle on the kitchen floor. I tap-dance in front of closed doors. One by one the household emerges, looking as though they'd like to kill us both; but it's Christmas, so they can't. First, a gorgeous breakfast: just everything you can imagine— from flapjacks and fried squirrel to hominy grits and honey-in-the-comb. Which puts everyone in a good humor except my friend and I. Frankly, we're so impatient to get at the presents we can't eat a mouthful.

Well, I'm disappointed. Who wouldn't be? With socks, a Sunday school shirt, some handkerchiefs, a hand-me-down sweater and a year's subscription to a religious magazine for children. *The Little Shepherd.* It makes me boil. It really does.

My friend has a better haul. A sack of Satsumas, that's her best present. She is proudest, however, of a white wool shawl knitted by her married sister. But she *says* her favorite gift is the kite I built her. And it *is* very beautiful; though not as beautiful as the one she made me, which is blue and scattered with gold and green Good Conduct stars; moreover, my name is painted on it, "Buddy."

"Buddy, the wind is blowing."

The wind is blowing, and nothing will do till we've run to a pasture below the house where Queenie has scooted to bury her bone (and where, a winter hence, Queenie will be buried, too.) There, plunging through the healthy waist-high grass, we unreel our kites, feel them twitching at the string like sly fish as they swim into the wind. Satisfied, sun-warmed, we sprawl in the grass and peel Satsumas and watch our kites cavort. Soon I forget the socks and hand-me-down sweater. I'm as happy as if we'd already won the fifty-thousand-dollar Grand Prize in that coffee-naming contest.

"My, how foolish I am!" my friend cries, suddenly alert, like a woman remembering too late she has biscuits in the oven. "You know what I've always thought?" she asks in a tone of discovery, and not smiling at me but a point beyond. "I've always thought a body would have to be sick and dying before they saw the Lord. And I imagined that when He came it would be like looking at the Baptist window; pretty as colored glass with the sun pouring through, such a shine you don't know it's getting dark. And it's been a comfort: to think of that shine taking away all the spooky feeling. But I'll wager it never happens. I'll wager at the very end a body realizes the Lord has already shown Himself. That things as they are"—her hand circles in a gesture that gathers clouds and kites and grass and Queenie pawing earth over her bone—"just what they've always been, was seeing Him. As for me, I could leave the world with today in my eyes."

This is our last Christmas together.

Life separates us. Those who Know Best decide that I belong in a military school. And so follows a miserable succession of bugle-blowing prisons, grim reveille-ridden summer camps. I have a new home too. But it doesn't count. Home is where my friend is, and there I never go.

And there she remains, puttering around the kitchen. Alone with Queenie. Then alone. ("Buddy dear," she writes in her wild hard-to-read script, "yesterday Jim Macy's horse kicked Queenie bad.

Be thankful she didn't feel much. I wrapped her in a Fine Linen sheet and rode her in the buggy down to Simpson's pasture where she can be with all her Bones . . ."). For a few Novembers she continues to bake her fruitcakes single-handed; not as many, but some: and, of course, she always sends me "the best of the batch." Also, in every letter she encloses a dime wadded in toilet paper: "See a picture show and write me the story." But gradually in her letters she tends to confuse me with her other friend, the Buddy who died in the 1880's; more and more thirteenths are not the only days she stays in bed: a morning arrives in November, a leafless birdless coming of winter morning, when she cannot rouse herself to exclaim: "Oh my, it's fruitcake weather!"

And when that happens, I know it. A message saying so merely confirms a piece of news some secret vein had already received, severing from me an irreplaceable part of myself, letting it loose like a kite on a broken string. That is why, walking across a school campus on this particular December morning, I keep searching the sky. As if I expected to see, rather like hearts, a lost pair of kites hurrying toward heaven.

AFTERWORD

Introducing two people you know well can prove to be a strange experience. Even if you make it obvious that you hope they will become friends, they may remain quite distant. In addition, the chances are good that after they have come to know each other, one of them will someday say to you, "X is nothing like the person you led me to expect." People are mysterious beings, and it is very difficult to sum up one of them in a full-scale biography, let alone a few words. But of course we do it every day; indeed, it is difficult to imagine an extended conversation that does not include some characterization.

There is something about committing a *person* to paper, however, that makes the process seem especially difficult. Perhaps we sense that human beings are too complex ever to be captured in words. As an undergraduate, I devised a short story about the life of an injured logger I had met one summer in Oakridge, Oregon. The following summer I showed my story to a biologist who also knew the injured man. "That's not Joe," he said, and I could tell he was a little angry that I had missed his sense of the man. He was unable to tell me what was wrong with the characterization, however; it just *wasn't Joe*. After a while I came to view his anger as a compliment. The character in my story must have been quite fully developed if its distortions of Joe were so subtle they eluded description. But in any case, the process of trying to capture in words something of the logger's humanity was an important learning experience for me. To write thoughtfully about another human being is to engage in a process of discovery.

Wendell Berry's treatment of Nick Watkins admits a good deal of uncertainty about Nick's character. Berry is careful to show that he is reconstructing a picture of this man from childhood memories, and he acknowledges occasional uncertainties. "I have the clearest memory of the two of them," he says of his grandfather and Nick,

> passing again and again in the slowly shortening rounds of a big pasture, Nick driving a team of good black mules hitched to a mowing machine, my grandfather on the mare always only two or three steps behind the cutter bar. I don't know where I am in the memory, perhaps watching from the shade of some bush in a fence-row.

Far from diminishing our confidence in his account, Berry's admission that he forgets his own place in this memory helps to establish his candor. Part of what makes this sketch of Nick Watkins so convincing is the sense it gives of the ultimate mystery of a man whose life appeared so very simple. Berry implies that as a child he probably knew Nick more fully than others around them did, but even with his openness in the young Berry's presence, Nick was not fully accessible.

There is an interesting paradox involved in "life writing," a phrase sometimes used to describe both biography and autobiography. Because our daily experience makes us feel that others cannot be fully known, we tend to be suspicious of writing that claims to tell all there is to know about a human being. If a character appears too neatly understood, too simply bad or good, or strong or weak, he will seem more like an idea than a person. An effective piece of life writing must, however, do more than say a character is complex or mysterious. It must demonstrate that complexity indirectly, by means of anecdotes, dialogue, comparison, or other techniques the writer is able to use effectively.

James Baldwin's "Notes of a Native Son" uses one such indirect method of characterization. By describing his own experience of racism when he worked in New Jersey defense plants early in the Second World War, Baldwin suggests the source of the terrifying bitterness he saw in his father. His subtle portrait of this man begins with a reference to his death and then, almost shockingly, presents him as he appeared to his children—angry, brutal, distant, and unloved. Next we follow Baldwin through the nightmare of his own experience in New Jersey, an experience which helped him to understand his father. The essay returns, finally, to the father's death, the funeral, and Baldwin's continuing effort to understand his own heritage as he finds it embodied in his father's life. The structure of this long essay is an important part of its power.

Henry Thoreau's sketch of the woodchopper, Alek Therien, is quite different from Baldwin's treatment of his father. Therien was just an acquaintance of Thoreau's, a man who interested Thoreau partly because he seemed so unlike Thoreau himself. It seems clear that Thoreau interviewed Therien much as a reporter might question a celebrity he intended to write about in an article. We can tell from the journal entries in Chapter One that Thoreau puzzled over Therien's character for several years. Like Baldwin and Berry, he makes it clear that, though he offers a rich variety of descriptive detail, conversation, analysis, and stories about the woodchopper, he never "mastered" his subject, never came to know fully the person he describes. Again, structure is important as Thoreau moves from the details of Therien's life style to a discussion of his way of thinking.

Truman Capote's recollection of Miss Sook Faulk might easily have become embarrassingly sentimental, for it is obvious that Capote has strong affection for the memory of this child-woman who was his distant cousin and closest friend. That such sentimentality does not characterize "A Christmas Memory" is due primarily to its humor, authentic dialogue, and careful attention to detail. For example, in describing the drinking episode with which the two friends celebrate their successful fruitcake baking, Capote gives us precise pictures of the glasses from which they drink, their expressions as the whiskey goes down, the shadows on the walls, Queenie's rolling drunk, and most especially, his friend: "My friend waltzes round the stove, the hem of her poor calico skirt pinched between her fingers as though it were a party dress: *Show me the way to go home,* she sings, her tennis shoes squeaking on the floor. *Show me the way to go home.*"

Suggested writing assignments

1. Write a character sketch of someone who interests you but whom you do not know very well when you begin the essay—a local politician, a fellow student, an athlete. Your subject should be someone who is willing to spare time for an interview. Senior citizens who are willing to reflect on their life stories can be ideal subjects for an essay of this kind. If your subject is a public figure, library research can be used as a substitute for direct interviewing.

   An essay of this sort should preserve some sense of the *process* by which it was developed. This does not mean that you must include every question you asked or every source you consulted. But the essay should explain, however indirectly, why you chose this person from among the countless possibilities. And since you are unlikely to know a person completely on the basis of one or two interviews or a bit of library research, your essay should probably convey something of the tentative, searching mood that runs through Thoreau's description of the woodchopper.

2. Write an essay that describes a person who has had some significance in your life. When you choose your subject, remember that the obvious choice—a close relative, for instance—may be the most risky; it is difficult to write well about someone whose life continues to impinge directly on your own. Though his portrait of his father in "Notes of a Native Son" is masterful, it seems unlikely that Baldwin could have written it while he was living in his father's household; their relationship was too painful and confusing then, as Baldwin explains in the essay. Thus it may not be easy to find an appropriate subject for this essay. If the person you describe is too important to you, you may have difficulty writing in a controlled, specific way; if your subject is of very little importance to you, your detachment may make it difficult for you to write an interesting essay.

six: art as experience

living with music

RALPH ELLISON (1914–   ) is the author of *Invisible Man* (1952), which, in a poll of two hundred writers, editors, and critics conducted in 1965 by the *New York Herald Tribune,* was voted the most distinguished novel published in the preceding twenty years. For as many years now the literary public has awaited Ellison's next novel, but thus far only short preliminaries to such a work have appeared, published mainly in literary journals. Ellison's major publication during this period has been *Shadow and Act* (1964), a distinguished collection of largely autobiographical essays, from which "Living with Music" is taken. In his introduction to this collection, Ellison says of its essays: "At best they are an embodiment of a conscious attempt to confront, to peer into, the shadow of my past and to remind myself of the complex resources for imaginative creation which are my heritage."

In those days it was either live with music or die with noise, and we chose rather desperately to live. In the process our apartment— what with its booby-trappings of audio equipment, wires, discs and tapes—came to resemble the Collier mansion, but that was later. First there was the neighborhood, assorted drunks and a singer.

We were living at the time in a tiny ground-floor-rear apartment in which I was also trying to write. I say "trying" advisedly. To our right, separated by a thin wall, was a small restaurant with a juke box the size of the Roxy. To our left, a night-employed swing enthusiast who took his lullaby music so loud that every morning promptly at nine Basie's brasses started blasting my typewriter off its stand. Our living room looked out across a small back yard to a rough stone wall to an apartment building which, towering above, caught every passing thoroughfare sound and rifled it straight down to me. There were also howling cats and barking dogs, none capable of music worth living with, so we'll pass them by.

But the court behind the wall, which on the far side came knee-high to a short Iroquois, was a forum for various singing and/ or preaching drunks who wandered back from the corner bar. From these you sometimes heard a fair barbershop style "Bill Bailey," free-wheeling versions of "The Bastard King of England," the saga of Uncle Bud, or a deeply felt rendition of Leroy Carr's "How Long Blues." The preaching drunks took on any topic that came to mind: current events, the fate of the long-sunk *Titanic* or the relative merits of the Giants and the Dodgers. Naturally there was great argument and occasional fighting—none of it fatal but all of it loud.

I shouldn't complain, however, for these were rather entertaining drunks, who like the birds appeared in the spring and left with the first fall cold. A more dedicated fellow was there all the time, day and night, come rain, come shine. Up on the corner lived a drunk of legend, a true phenomenon, who could surely have qualified as the king of all the world's winos—not excluding the French. He was neither poetic like the others nor ambitious like the singer (to whom we'll presently come) but his drinking bouts were truly awe-inspiring and he was not without his sensitivity. In the throes of his passion he would shout to the whole wide world one concise command, "Shut up!" Which was disconcerting enough to all who heard (except, perhaps, the singer), but such were the labyrinthine acoustics of courtyards and areaways that he seemed to direct his command at me. The writer's block which this produced is indescribable. On one heroic occasion he yelled his obsessive command without one interruption longer than necessary to take another drink (and with no appreciable loss of volume, penetration or authority) for three long summer days and nights, and shortly afterwards he died. Just how many lines of agitated prose he cost me I'll never know, but in all that chaos of sound I sympathized with his obsession, for I, too, hungered and thirsted for quiet. Nor did he inspire me to a painful identification, and for that I was thankful. Identification, after all, involved feelings of guilt and responsibility, and since I could hardly hear my own typewriter keys I felt in no way accountable for his condition. We were simply fellow victims of the madding crowd. May he rest in peace.

No, these more involved feelings were aroused by a more intimate source of noise, one that got beneath the skin and worked into the very structure of one's consciousness—like the "fate" motif in Beethoven's Fifth or the knocking-at-the-gates scene in *Macbeth.* For at the top of our pyramid of noise there was a singer who lived directly above us; you might say we had a singer in our ceiling.

Now, I had learned from the jazz musicians I had known as a

boy in Oklahoma City something of the discipline and devotion to his art required of the artist. Hence I knew something of what the singer faced. These jazzmen, many of them now world-famous, lived for and with music intensely. Their driving motivation was neither money nor fame, but the will to achieve the most eloquent expression of idea-emotions through the technical mastery of their instruments (which, incidentally, some of them wore as a priest wears the cross) and the give and take, the subtle rhythmical shaping and blending of idea, tone and imagination demanded of group improvisation. The delicate balance struck between strong individual personality and the group during those early jam sessions was a marvel of social organization. I had learned too that the end of all this discipline and technical mastery was the desire to express an affirmative way of life through its musical tradition and that this tradition insisted that each artist achieve his creativity within its frame. He must learn the best of the past, and add to it his personal vision. Life could be harsh, loud and wrong if it wished, but they lived it fully, and when they expressed their attitude toward the world it was with a fluid style that reduced the chaos of living to form.

The objectives of these jazzmen were not at all those of the singer on our ceiling, but though a purist committed to the mastery of the *bel canto* style, German *lieder*, modern French art songs and a few American slave songs sung as if *bel canto*, she was intensely devoted to her art. From morning to night she vocalized, regardless of the condition of her voice, the weather or my screaming nerves. There were times when her notes, sifting through her floor and my ceiling, bouncing down the walls and ricocheting off the building in the rear, whistled like tenpenny nails, buzzed like a saw, wheezed like the asthma of a Hercules, trumpeted like an enraged African elephant—and the squeaky pedal of her piano rested plumb center above my typing chair. After a year of non-co-operation from the neighbor on my left I became desperate enough to cool down the hot blast of his phonograph by calling the cops, but the singer presented a serious ethical problem: Could I, an aspiring artist, complain against the hard work and devotion to craft of another aspiring artist?

Then there was my sense of guilt. Each time I prepared to shatter the ceiling in protest I was restrained by the knowledge that I, too, during my boyhood, had tried to master a musical instrument and to the great distress of my neighbors—perhaps even greater than that which I now suffered. For while our singer was concerned basically with a single tradition and style, I had been caught actively between two: that of the Negro folk music, both sacred and profane, slave song and jazz, and that of Western classical music. It was most confusing; the folk tradition demanded that I play what I heard and felt around me, while those who were seeking to teach the classical tradition in the schools insisted that I play strictly according to the book and express that which I was *supposed* to feel. This sometimes led to heated clashes of wills. Once during a third-grade music appreciation class a friend of mine insisted that it was a large green snake he saw swimming down a quiet brook instead of the snowy bird the teacher felt that Saint-Saens' *Carnival of the Animals* should evoke. The rest of us sat there and lied like little black, brown and yellow Trojans about that swan, but our stalwart classmate held firm to his snake. In the end he got himself spanked and reduced the teacher to tears, but truth, reality and our environment were redeemed. For we were all familiar with snakes, while a swan was simply something the Ugly Duckling of the story grew up to be. Fortunately some of us grew up with a genuine appreciation of classical music *despite* such teaching methods. But as an inspiring trumpeter I was to wallow in sin for years before being awakened to guilt by our singer.

Caught mid-rage between my two traditions, where one attitude often clashed with the other and one technique of playing was by the other opposed, I caused whole blocks of people to suffer.

Indeed, I terrorized a good part of an entire city section. During summer vacation I blew sustained tones out of the window for hours, usually starting—especially on Sunday mornings—before breakfast. I sputtered whole days through M. Arban's (he's the great authority on the instrument) double- and triple-tonguing exercises—with an effect like that of a jackass hiccupping off a big meal of briars. During school-term mornings I practiced a truly exhibitionist "Reveille" before leaving for school, and in the evening I generously gave the ever-listening world a long, slow version of "Taps," ineptly played but throbbing with what I in my adolescent vagueness felt was a romantic sadness. For it was farewell to day and a love song to life and a peace-be-with-you to all the dead and dying.

On hot summer afternoons I tormented the ears of all not blessedly deaf with limitations of the latest hot solos of Hot Lips Paige (then a local hero), the leaping right hand of Earl "Fatha" Hines, or the rowdy poetic flights of Louis Armstrong. Naturally I rehearsed also such school-band standbys as the *Light Cavalry* Overture, Sousa's "Stars and Stripes Forever," the *William Tell* Overture, and "Tiger Rag." (Not even an after-school job as office boy to a dentist could stop my efforts. Frequently, by way of encouraging my development in the proper cultural direction, the dentist asked me proudly to render Schubert's *Serenade* for some poor devil with his jaw propped open in the dental chair. When the drill got going, or the forceps bit deep, I blew real strong.)

Sometimes, inspired by the even then considerable virtuosity of the late Charlie Christian (who during our school days played marvelous riffs on a cigar box banjo), I'd give whole summer afternoons and the evening hours after heavy suppers of black-eyed peas and turnip greens, cracklin' bread and buttermilk, lemonade and sweet potato cobbler, to practicing hard-driving blues. Such food oversupplied me with bursting energy, and from listening to Ma Rainey, Ida Cox and Clara Smith, who made regular appearances in our town. I knew exactly how I wanted my horn to sound. But in the effort to make it do so (I was no embryo Joe Smith or Tricky Sam Nanton) I sustained the curses of both Christian and infidel— along with the encouragement of those more sympathetic citizens who understood the profound satisfaction to be found in expressing oneself in the blues.

Despite those who complained and cried to heaven for Gabriel to blow a chorus so heavenly sweet and so hellishly hot that I'd forever put down my horn, there were more tolerant ones who were willing to pay in present pain for future pride.

For who knew what skinny kid with his chops wrapped around a trumpet mouthpiece and a faraway look in his eyes might become the next Armstrong? Yes, and send you, at some big dance a few years hence, into an ecstasy of rhythm and memory and brassy affirmation of the goodness of being alive and part of the community? Someone had to; for it was part of the group tradition—though that was not how they said it.

"Let that boy blow," they'd say to the protesting ones. "He's got to talk baby talk on that thing before he can preach on it. Next thing you know he's liable to be up there with Duke Ellington. Sure, plenty Oklahoma boys are up there with the big bands. Son, let's hear you try those "Trouble in Mind Blues." Now try and make it sound like ole Ida Cox sings it."

And I'd draw in my breath and do Miss Cox great violence.

Thus the crimes and aspirations of my youth. It had been years since I had played the trumpet or irritated a single ear with other than the spoken or written word, but as far as my singing neighbor was concerned I had to hold my peace. I was forced to listen, and in listening I soon became involved to the point of identification. If she sang badly I'd hear my own futility in the windy sound; if well, I'd stare at my typewriter and despair that I should ever make my prose so sing. She left me neither night nor day, this singer on our ceiling, and as my writing languished I became more and more upset. Thus one desperate morning I decided that since I seemed doomed to live within a shrieking chaos I might as well contribute my share; perhaps if I fought noise with noise I'd attain some small peace. Then a miracle: I turned on my radio (an old Philco AM set connected to a small Pilot FM tuner) and I heard the words

> Art thou troubled?
> Music will calm thee . . .

I stopped as though struck by the voice of an angel. It was Kathleen Ferrier, that loveliest of singers, giving voice to the aria from Handel's *Rodelinda*. The voice was so completely expressive of words and music that I accepted it without question—what lover of the vocal art could resist her?

Yet it was ironic, for after giving up my trumpet for the typewriter I had avoided too close a contact with the very art which she recommended as balm. For I had started music early and lived with it daily, and when I broke I tried to break clean. Now in this magical moment all the old love, the old fascination with music superbly rendered, flooded back. When she finished I realized that with such music in my own apartment, the chaotic sounds from without and above had sunk, if not into silence, then well below the level where they mattered. Here was a way out. If I was to live and write in that apartment, it would be only through the grace of music. I had tuned in a Ferrier recital, and when it ended I rushed out for several of her records, certain that now deliverance was mine.

But not yet. Between the hi-fi record and the ear, I learned, there was a new electronic world. In that realization our apartment was well on its way toward becoming an audio booby trap. It was 1949 and I rushed to the Audio Fair. I have, I confess, as much gadget-resistance as the next American of my age, weight and slight income; but little did I dream of the test to which it would be put. I had hardly entered the fair before I heard David Sarser's and Mel Sprinkle's Musician's Amplifier, took a look at its schematic and, recalling a boyhood acquaintance with such matters, decided that I could build one. I did, several times before it measured within specifications. And still our system was lacking. Fortunately my wife shared my passion for music, so we went on to buy, piece by piece, a fine speaker system, a first-rate AM-FM tuner, a transcription turntable and a speaker cabinet. I built half a dozen or more preamplifiers and record compensators before finding a commercial one that satisfied my ear, and, finally, we acquired an arm, a magnetic cartridge and—glory of the house—a tape recorder. All this plunge into electronics, mind you, had as its simple end the enjoyment of recorded music as it was intended to be heard. I was obsessed with the idea of reproducing sound with such fidelity that even when using music as a defense behind which I could write, it would reach the unconscious levels of the mind with the least distortion. And it didn't come easily. There were wires and pieces of equipment all over the tiny apartment (I became a compulsive experimenter) and it was worth your life to move about without first taking careful bearings. Once we were almost crushed in our sleep by the tape machine, for which there was space only on a shelf at the head of our bed. But it was worth it.

For now when we played a recording on our system even the drunks on the wall could recognize its quality. I'm ashamed to admit, however, that I did not always restrict its use to the demands of pleasure or defense. Indeed, with such marvels of science at my control I lost my humility. My ethical consideration for the singer up above shriveled like a plant in too much sunlight. For instead of soothing, music seemed to release the beast in me. Now when jarred from my writer's reveries by some especially enthusiastic flourish of our singer, I'd rush to my music system with blood in my eyes and burst a few decibels in her direction. If she defied me with a few more pounds of pressure against her diaphragm, then a war of decibels was declared.

If, let us say, she were singing "Depuis le Jour" from Louise, I'd put on a tape of Bidu Sayão performing the same aria, and let the rafters ring. If it was some song by Mahler, I'd match her spitefully with Marian Anderson or Kathleen Ferrier; if she offended with something from Der Rosenkavalier, I'd attack her flank with Lotte Lehmann. If she brought me up from my desk with art songs by Ravel or Rachmaninoff, I'd defend myself with Maggie Teyte or Jennie Tourel. If she polished a spiritual to a meaningless artiness I'd play Bessie Smith to remind her of the earth out of which we came. Once in a while I'd forget completely that I was supposed to be a gentleman and blast her with Strauss' Zarathustra, Bartok's Concerto for Orchestra, Ellington's "Flaming Sword," the famous crescendo from The Pines of Rome, or Satchmo scatting, "I'll be Glad When You're Dead" (you rascal you!). Oh, I was living with music with a sweet vengeance.

One might think that all this would have made me her most hated enemy, but not at all. When I met her on the stoop a few weeks after my rebellion, expecting her fully to slap my face, she astonished me by complimenting our music system. She even questioned me concerning the artists I had used against her. After that, on days when the acoustics were right, she'd stop singing until the piece was finished and then applaud—not always, I guessed, without a justifiable touch of sarcasm. And although I was not getting on with my writing, the unfairness of this business bore in upon me. Aware that I could not have withstood a similar comparison with literary artists of like caliber, I grew remorseful. I also came to admire the singer's courage and control, for she was neither intimidated into silence nor goaded into undisciplined screaming; she perservered, she marked the phrasing of the great singers I sent her way, she improved her style.

Better still, she vocalized more softly, and I, in turn, used music less and less as a weapon and more for its magic with mood and memory. After a while a simple twirl of the volume control up a few decibels and down again would bring a live-and-let-live reduction of her volume. We have long since moved from that apartment and that most interesting neighborhood and now the floors and walls of our present apartment are adequately thick and there is even a closet large enough to house the audio system; the only wire visible is that leading from the closet to the corner speaker system. Still we are indebted to the singer and the old environment for forcing us to discover one of the most deeply satisfying aspects of our living. Perhaps the enjoyment of music is always suffused with past experience; for me, at least, this is true.

It seems a long way and a long time from the glorious days of Oklahoma jazz dances, the jam sessions at Halley Richardson's place on Deep Second, from the phonographs shouting the blues in the back alleys I knew as a delivery boy, and from the days when watermelon men with voices like mellow bugles shouted their wares in time with the rhythm of their horses' hoofs and farther still from the washerwomen singing slave songs as they stirred sooty tubs in sunny yards; and a long time, too, from those intense, conflicting days when the school music program of Oklahoma City was tuning our earthy young ears to classical accents—with music appreciation classes and free musical instruments and basic instruction for any child who cared to learn and uniforms for all who made the band. There was a mistaken notion on the part of the some of the teachers that classical music had nothing to do with the rhythms, relaxed or hectic, of daily living, and that one should crook the little finger when listening to such refined strains. And the blues and the spirituals—jazz—? they would have destroyed them and scattered the pieces. Nevertheless, we learned some of it all, for in the United States when traditions are juxtaposed they tend, regardless of what we do to prevent it, irresistibly to merge. Thus musically at least each child in our town was an heir of all ages.

One learns by moving from the familiar to the unfamiliar, and while it might sound incongruous at first, the step from the spirituality of the spirituals to that of the Beethoven of the symphonies or the Bach of the chorales is not as vast as it seems. Nor is the romanticism of a Brahms or Chopin completely unrelated to that of Louis Armstrong. Those who know their native culture and love it unchauvinistically are never lost when encountering the unfamiliar.

Living with music today we find Mozart and Ellington, Kirsten Flagstad and Chippie Hill, William L. Dawson and Carl Orff all forming part of our regular fare. For all exalt life in rhythm and melody; all add to its significance. Perhaps in the swift change of American society in which the meanings of one's origin are so quickly lost, one of the chief values of living with music lies in its power to give us an orientation in time. In doing so, it gives significance to all those indefinable aspects of experience which nevertheless help to make us what we are. In the swift whirl of time music is a constant, reminding us of what we were and of that toward which we aspired. Art thou troubled? Music will not only calm, it will ennoble thee.

homage to El Loco

NORMAN MAILER

The mind returns to the comedy and the religious dedication of the bullfight. Late afternoons of color—hues of lavender, silver, pink, orange silk and gold in the *traje de luces*—now begin to play in one's mind against the small sharp impact on the eyes of horse-balls falling like eggs between the frightened legs of the horse, and the flanks of the bull glistening with the sheen of a dark wet wood. And the blood. The bullfight always gets back to the blood. It pours in gouts down the forequarters of the bull, it wells from the hump of his *morrillo*, and moves in waves of bright red along the muscles of his chest and the heaving of his sides. If he has been killed poorly and the sword goes through his lung, then the animal dies in vomitings of blood. If the matador is working close to the animal, the suit of lights becomes stained—the dark bloodstain is honorable, it is also steeped in horror. Should the taste of your favorite herb come from the death of some rare love, so the life of the bright red blood of an animal river pouring forth becomes some other life as it darkens down to the melancholy hues of an old dried blood which speaks in some lost primitive tongue about the mysteries of death, color, and corruption. The dried blood reminds you of the sordid glory of the bullfight, its hint of the Renaissance when noble figures stated their presence as they paraded through the marketplace and passed by cripples with stumps for legs, a stump for a tongue, and the lewdest grin of the day. Yes, the spectrum of the bullfight goes from courage to gangrene.

In Mexico, the hour before the fight is always the best hour of the week. It would be memorable not to sound like Hemingway, but in fact you would get happy the night before just thinking of that hour next day. Outside the Plaza Mexico, cheap cafés open only on Sunday, and huge as beer gardens, filled with the public (us tourists, hoodlums, pimps, pickpurses and molls, Mexican

REPRINTED by permission of the author and the author's agents, Scott Meredith Literary Agency, 580 Fifth Avenue, New York, New York 10036.

variety—which is to say the whores and headdresses and hindquar-
ters not to be seen elsewhere on earth, for their hair rose vertically
twelve inches from the head, and their posteriors projected horizontally twelve inches back into that space the rest of the whore
had just marched through). The mariachis were out with their romantic haunting caterwauling of guitar, violin, songs of carnival
and trumpet, their song told of hearts which were true and hearts
which were broken, and the wail of the broken heart went right
into the trumpet until there were times when drunk the right
way on tequila or Mexican rum, it was perhaps the best sound heard
this side of Miles Davis. You hear a hint of all that in the Tijuana
Brass.

   You see, my friends, the wild hour was approaching. The horrors
of the week in Mexico were coming to term. Indeed, no week in
Mexico is without its horrors for every last Mexican alive—it is a
city and a country where the bones of the dead seem to give the
smell of their char to every desert wind and auto exhaust and frying
tortilla. The mournfulness of unrequited injustice hangs a shroud
across the centuries. Every Mexican is gloomy until the instant he
becomes happy, and then he is a maniac. He howls, he whistles,
smoke of murder passes off his pores, he bullies, he beseeches friendship, he is a clown, a brigand, a tragic figure suddenly merry. The
intellectuals and the technicians of Mexico abominate their national character because it is always in the way. It puts the cracks
in the plaster of new buildings, it forgets to cement the tiles, it
leaves rags in the new pipes of new office buildings and forgets to
put the gas cap back on the tank. So the intellectuals and the
technicians hate the bullfight as well. You cannot meet a socialist
in Mexico who approves of the running of the bulls. They are trying
to turn Mexico into a modern country, and thus the same war goes
on there that goes on in three-quarters of the world—battlefront
is the new highways to the suburbs, and the corporation's office
buildings, the walls of hospital white, and the myopic sheets of
glass. In Mexico, like everywhere else, it is getting harder and harder
to breathe in a mood through the pores of the city because more
and more of the city is being covered with corporation architecture, with surgical dressing. To the vampires and banshees and dried
blood on the curses of the cactus in the desert is added the horror
of the new technology in an old murder-ridden land. And four
o'clock on Sunday is the beginning of release for some of the horrors
of the week. If many come close to feeling the truth only by telling a lie, so Mexicans come close to love by watching the flow of
blood on an animal's flanks and the certain death of the bull before
the bravery and/or humiliation of the bullfighter.

I could never have understood it if someone tried to explain ahead of time, and in fact, I came to love the bullfight long before I comprehended the first thing about why I did. That was very much to the good. There are not too many experiences a radical American intellectual could encounter in those days (when the youngest generation was called the silent generation) which invaded his sure sense of his own intellectual categories. I did not like the first bullfights I saw, the formality of the ritual bored me, the fights appeared poor (indeed they were) and the human content of the spectacle came out atrocious. Narcissistic matadors, vain when they made a move, pouting like a girl stood up on Saturday night when the crowd turned on them, clumsy at killing, and the crowd, brutal to a man. In the Plaza Mexico, the Indians in the cheap seats buy a paper cup of beer and when they are done drinking, the walk to the W.C. is *miles* away, and besides they are usually feeling sullen, so they urinate in their paper cup and hurl it down in a cascade of harvest gold, Indian piss. If you are an American escorting an American girl who has blond hair, and you have tickets in *Sol,* you buy your girl a cheap sombrero at the gate, for otherwise she will be a prime target of attention. Indeed, you do well not to sit near an American escorting a blond whose head is uncovered, for the aim of a drunken Indian is no better than you when your aim is drunk. So no surprise if one's early detestation of the bullfight was fortified in kidney brew, Azteca.

Members of a minority group are always ready to take punishment, however, and I was damned if I was going to be excluded from still another cult. So I persisted in going to bullfights, and they were a series of lousy bullfights, and then the third or fourth time I got religion. It was a windy afternoon, with threats of rain, and now and then again ten minutes of rain, poisonous black clouds overhead, the chill gloom of a black sky on Sundays in Mexico, and the particular torero (whose name I could not recall for anything) was a clod. He had a nasty build. Little spindly legs, too big a chest, a butt which was broad and stolid, real peasant ass, and a vulgar worried face with a gold tooth. He was engaged with an ugly bull who kept chopping at the muleta with his horns, and occasionally the bull would catch the muleta and fling it in the air and trample it and wonder why the object was either dead or not dead, the bull smelling a hint of his own blood (or the blood of some cousin) on the blood of the muleta, and the crowd would hoot, and the torero would go over to his sword handler at the barrera, and shake his head and come out with a new muleta, and the bull would chop, and the wind would zig the muleta out of control, and then the matador would drop it and scamper back to

the barrera, and the crowd would jeer and piss would fly in yellow
arcs of rainbow through the rain all the way down from the cheap
seats, and the whores would make farting sounds with their spoiled
knowledgeable mouths, while the aficionados would roll their eyes,
and the sound of Mexican laughter, that operative definition of
the echo of total disgust, would shake along like jelly-gasoline
through the crowd.

I got a look at the bullfighter who was the center of all this.
He was not a man I could feel something for. He had a cheap pimp's
face and a dull, thoroughgoing vanity. His face, however, was now
in despair. There was something going on for him more humiliating
than humiliation—as if his life were going to take a turn into
something more dreadful than anything it had encountered until
now. He was in trouble. The dead dull fight he was giving was going
to be death for certain hopes in his psyche. Somehow it was going
to be more final than the average dead dull fight to which he was
obviously all too accustomed. I was watching the despair of a profoundly mediocre man.

Well, he finally gave up any attempt to pass the bull, and he
worked the animal forward with jerks of his muleta to left and
right, a competent rather than a beautiful technique at best, and
even to my untutored eye he was a mechanic at this, and more
whistles, and then desperation all over that vain incompetent
pimp's face, he profiled with his sword, and got it halfway in, and
the animal took a few steps to one side and the other and fell over
quickly.

The art of killing is the last skill you learn to judge in
bullfighting, and the kill on this rainy afternoon left me less impressed than the crowd. Their jeers were replaced by applause (later
I learned the crowd would always applaud a kill in the lung—all audiences are Broadway audiences) and the approbation continued
sufficiently for the torero to take a tour of the ring. He got no
ears, he certainly didn't deserve them, but he had his tour and he
was happy, and in his happiness there was something suddenly likable about him, and I sensed that I was passing through some interesting emotions since I had felt contempt for a stranger and then
a secret and most unsocialistic desire to see this type I did not
like humiliated a little further, and then in turn I was quietly but
most certainly overcome by his last-minute success sufficiently to
find myself liking a kind of man I had never considered near to
human before. So this bad bullfight in the rain had given a drop
of humanity to a very dry area of my heart, and now I knew a little
more and had something to think about which was no longer altogether in category.

We have presented the beginning of a history then—no, say it better—the origin of an addiction. For a drug's first appeal is always existential—our sense of life (once it is made alert by the sensation of its absence) is thereupon so full of need as the desire for a breath of air. The sense of life comes alive in the happy days when the addict first encounters his drug. But all histories of addiction are the same—particularly in the beginning. They fall into the larger category of the history of a passion. So I will spare each and every one of us the titles of the books I read on the running of the bulls, save to mention the climactic purchase of a three-volume set in leather for fifty 1954 dollars (now doubtless in value one hundred) of *Los Toros* by Cossío. Since it was entirely in Spanish, a language I read with about as much ease and pleasure as Very Old English, *Los Toros* remains in my library as a cornerstone of my largest mental department—*The Bureau of Abandoned Projects:* I was going to write *the* novel about bullfight, dig!

Nor will I reminisce about the great bullfighters I saw, of the majesties of Arruza and the *machismo* of Procuna, the liquidities of Silverio and the solemnity of César Girón, no, we will not micturate the last of such memory to tell a later generation about El Ranchero and Ortiz of the Orticina, and Angel Peralta the Rejoneador, nor of Manolete, for he was dead long before I could with confidence distinguish a bull from a heifer or a steer, and no more can I talk of Luis Miguel and Antonio, for neither of them have I seen in a fight, so that all I know of Ordóñez is his reputation, and of Dominguín his style, for I caught his work in a movie once and it was not work the way he made it look. No, enough of these qualifications for *afición.* The fact is that I do not dwell on Arruza and Procuna and Silverio and Girón and Peralta and Ranchero because I did not see them that often and in fact most of them I saw but once. I was always in Mexico in the summer, you see, and the summer is the *temporada de novillos,* which is to say it is the time when the *novilladas* are held, which is to say it is the time of the novices.

Now the fellow who is pushing up this preface for you is a great lover of the bullfight—make on it no mistake. For a great bullfight he would give up just about any other athletic or religious spectacle—the World Series in a minute, a pro football championship, a mass at the Vatican, perhaps even a great heavyweight championship—which, kids, is really saying it. No love like the love for four in the afternoon at the Plaza Mexico. Yet all the great matadors he saw were seen only at special festivals when they fought very small bulls for charity. The novillada is, after all, the time of the novilleros, and a novillero is a bullfighter approximately equal in rank to a Golden Gloves fighter. A very good novillero is like a very good Golden Gloves finalist. The Sugar Ray Robinsons and the Rocky Marcianos of the bullfighting world were glimpsed by me only when they came out of retirement long enough to give the equivalent of a snappy two-round exhibition. My love of bullfighting, and my experience of it as a spectator, was founded then by watching novilleros week after week over two separate summers in Mexico City. So I know as much about bullfighting as a man would know about boxing if he read a lot and heard a lot about great fighters and saw a few movies of them and one or two exhibitions, and also had the intense, if partial, fortune to follow two Golden Gloves tournaments all the way and to follow them with some lively if not always dependable instinct for discerning what was good and what was not so good in the talent before him.

After a while I got good at seeing the flaws and virtues in novilleros, and in fact I began to see so much of their character in their style, and began to learn so much about style by comprehending their character (for nearly everything good or bad about a novice bullfighter is revealed at a great rate) that I began to take the same furious interest and partisanship in the triumph of one style over another that is usually reserved for literary matters (is Philip Roth better than John Updike?—you know) or what indeed average Americans and some not so average might take over political figures. To watch a bullfighter have an undeserved triumph on Sunday afternoon when you detest his style is not the worst preparation for listening to Everett Dirksen nominate Barry Goldwater or hearing Lyndon Johnson give a lecture on TV about Amurrican commitments to the free universe. Everything bad and Godawful about the style of life got into the style of bullfighters, as well as everything light, delightful, honorable and good.

At any rate, about the time I knew a lot about bullfighting, or as much as you could know watching nothing but novilleros week after week, I fell in love with a bullfighter. I never even met this bullfighter, I rush to tell you. I would not have wanted to meet him. Meeting him could only have spoiled the perfection of my love, so pure was my affection. And his name—not one in a thousand of you out there, dear general readers, can have heard of him— his name was El Loco. El Loco, the Crazy One. It is not a term of endearment in Mexico, where half the populace is crazy. To amplify the power of nomenclature, El Loco came from the provinces, he was God's own hick, and his real name was Amado Ramírez, which is like being a boy from Hicksville, Georgia, with a name like Beloved Remington. Yet there was a time when I thought Beloved Remington, which is to say Amado Ramírez, would become the greatest bullfighter in the whole world, and there were critics in Mexico City hoary with *afición* who held the same opinion (if not always in print). He came up one summer a dozen years ago like a rocket, but a rocket with one tube hot and one tube wet and he spun in circles all over the bullfighting world of Mexico City all through the summer and fall.

But we must tell more of what it is like to watch novilleros. You see, novice bullfighters fight bulls who are called *novillos*, and these bulls are a year younger and two to four hundred pounds lighter than the big fighting bulls up around a thousand pounds which matadors must face. So they are less dangerous. They can still kill a man, but not often does that happen—they are more likely to pound and stomp and wound and bruise a novillero than to catch him and play him in the air and stab him up high on the horns the way a terrible full-grown fighting bull can do. In consequence, the analogy to the Golden Gloves is imperfect, for a talented novillero can at his best look as exciting as, or more exciting than, a talented matador—the novice's beast is smaller and less dangerous, so his lack of experience is compensated for by his relative comfort—he is in less danger of getting killed. (Indeed, to watch a consummate matador like Carlos Arruza work with a new young bull is like watching Norman Mailer box with his three-year-old son—absolute mastery is in the air.)

Novilleros possess another virtue. Nobody can contest their *afición*. For every novillero who has a manager, and a rich man to house and feed him, and influential critics to bring him along on the sweet of a bribe or two, there are a hundred devoted all but unknown novilleros who hitch from *poblado* to *poblado* on back dirt roads for the hint of a chance to fight at some fiesta so small the results are not even phoned to Mexico City. Some of these kids spend years in the provinces living on nothing, half-starved in the desire to spend a life fighting bulls and they will fight anything—bulls who are overweight, calves who are under the legal limit, beasts who have fought before and so are sophisticated and dangerous. These provincial novilleros get hurt badly by wounds which show no blood, deep bruises in the liver and kidney from the flat of a horn, deep internal bleedings in the gut, something lively taken off the groin—a number of them die years later from malnutrition and chronic malfunctions of some number of those organs— their deaths get into no statistics on the fatalities of the bullfight.

A few of these provincial novilleros get enough fights and enough experience and develop enough talent, however, to pick up a reputation of sorts. If they are very lucky and likable, or have connections, or hump themselves—as some will—to rich homosexuals in the captial, then they get their shot. Listen to this. At the beginning of the novillada, six new bullfighters are brought in every Sunday to fight one bull each in the Plaza Mexico. For six or eight weeks this goes on. Perhaps fifty fighters never seen before in Mexico City have their chance. Maybe ten will be seen again. The tension is enormous for each novillero. If he fails to have a triumph or attract outstanding attention, then his years in the provinces went for nothing. Back again he will go to the provinces as a punishment for failing to be superb. Perhaps he will never fight again in the Plaza Mexico. His entire life depends on this one fight. And even this fight depends on luck. For any novillero can catch a poor bull, a dull mediocre cowardly bull. When the animal does not charge, the bullfighter, unless possessed of genius, cannot look good.

Once a novillero came into the Plaza on such an occasion, was hit by the bull while making his first pass, a veronica, and the boy and cape sailed into the air and came down together in such a way that when the boy rolled over, the cape wrapped around him like a tortilla, and one wit in *Sol*, full of the harsh wine of Mexico's harsh grapes, yelled out, *"Suerte de Enchiladas."* The young bullfighter was named The Pass of the Enchiladas. His career could never be the same. He went on to fight that bull, did a decent honorable job—the crowd never stopped laughing. Suerte de Enchiladas. He was branded. He walked off in disgrace. The one thing you cannot be in any land where Spanish is spoken is a clown. I laughed with the rest. The bullfight is nine-tenths cruelty. The bullfight brews one's cruelty out of one's pores—it makes an elixir of cruelty. But it does something else. It reflects the proportions of life in Latin lands. For in Mexico it does not seem unreasonable that a man should spend years learning a dangerous trade, be rapped once by a bull, and end up ruined, a Suerte de Enchiladas. It is unfair, but then life is monstrously unfair, one knows that, one of the few gleams in the muck of all this dubious Mexican majesty called existence is that one can on occasion laugh bitterly with the gods. In the Spanish-Indian blood, the substance of one's dignity is found in sharing the cruel vision of the gods. In fact, dignity can be found nowhere else. For courage is seen as the servant of the gods' cruel vision.

On to Beloved Remington. He arrived in Mexico City at the end of the beginning of the novillada in the summer of 1954. He was there, I think, on the next to last of the early Sundays when six bulls were there for six novilleros. (In the full season of the novillada, when the best new young men have been chosen, there are

six bulls for only three toreros—each kid then has two bulls, two
chances.) I was not yet in Mexico for Amado Ramírez's first Sunday,
but I heard nothing else from my bullfighting friends from the day
I got in. He had appeared as the last of six novilleros. It had been
a terrible day. All of the novilleros had been bad. He apparently had
been the last and the worst, and had looked so clumsy that the
crowd in derision had begun to applaud him. There is no sign of displeasure greater among the Mexican bullfighting public than to
turn their ovations upside down, but Ramírez had taken bows. Serious solemn bows. He had bowed so much he had hardly fought the
bull. The Plaza Mexico had rung with merriment. It took him forever to kill the beast—he received a tumultuous ovation. He took
a turn of the ring. A wit shouted *"Ole, El Loco."* He was named.
When they cheer incompetence they are ready to set fire to the
stadium.

El Loco was the sensation of the week. A clown had fought
a bull in the Plaza Mexico and gotten out alive. The promoters
put him on the following week as a seventh bullfighter, an extra
added attraction. He was not considered worth the dignity of appearing on the regular card. For the first time that season, the
Plaza was sold out. It was also the first fight I was to see of my
second season.

Six young novilleros fought six mediocre bulls that day, and
gave six mediocre fights. The crowd grew more and more sullen.
When there is no good bullfight, there is no catharsis. One's money has been spent, the drinks are wearing down, and there has been
no illumination, no moment to burn away all that spiritual sewer
gas from the horrors of the week. Dull violence breeds, and with it,
contempt for all bullfighters. An ugly Mexican bullfighting crowd
has the temper of an old-fashioned street corner in Harlem after
the police wagon has rounded up the nearest five studs and hauled
them away.

Out came the clown, El Loco. The special seventh bullfighter.
He was an apparition. He had a skinny body and a funny ugly face
with little eyes set close together, a big nose, and a little mouth.
He had very black Indian hair, and a tuft in the rear of his head
stood up like the spike of an antenna. He had very skinny legs and
they were bent at the knee so that he gave the impression of
trudging along with a lunchbox in his hand. He had a comic ass.
It went straight back like a duck's tail feathers. His suit fit poorly. He was some sort of grafting between Ray Bolger and Charlie
Chaplin. And he had the sense of self-importance to come out before the bull, he was indeed given a turn of the ring before he even
saw the bull. An honor granted him for his appearance the week be-

fore. He was altogether solemn. It did not seem comic to him. He had the kind of somber extravagant ceremoniousness of a village mayor in a mountain town come out to greet the highest officials of the government. His knees stuck out in front and his buttock in back. The Plaza rocked and rocked. Much applause followed by circulating zephyrs of laughter. And under it all, like a croaking of frogs, the beginnings of the biggest thickest Bronx raspberry anybody living ever heard.

Amado Ramírez went out to receive the bull. His first pass was a yard away from the animal, his second was six feet. He looked like a fifty-five-year-old peon ready to retire. The third pass caught his cape, and as it flew away on the horns, El Loco loped over to the barrera with a gait like a kangaroo. A thunderstorm of boos was on its way. He held out his arm horizontally, an injunction to the crowd, fingers spread, palm down, a mild deprecatory peasant gesture, as if to say, "Wait, you haven't seen nothing yet." The lip-farters began to smack. Amado went back out. He botched one pass, looked poor on a basic veronica. Boos, laughter, even the cops in the aisle were laughing. *Que payaso!*

His next pass had a name, but few even of the *afición* knew it, for it was an old-fashioned pass of great intricacy which spoke of the era of Belmonte and El Gallo and Joselito. It was a pass of considerable danger, plus much formal content (for a flash it looked like he was inclining to kiss a lady's hand, his cape draped over his back, while the bull went roaring by his unprotected ass). If I remember, it was called a *gallicina,* and no one had seen it in five years. It consisted of whirling in a reverse *serpentina* counterclockwise into the bull, so that the cape was wrapped around your body just like the Suerte de Enchiladas, except you were vertical, but the timing was such that the bull went by at the moment your back was to him and you could not see his horns. Then the whirling continued, and the cape flared out again. Amado was clumsy in his approach and stepped on his cape when he was done, but there was one moment of lightning in the middle when you saw clear sky after days of fog and smelled the ozone, there was an instant of heaven—finest thing I had yet seen in the bullfight—and in a sob of torture and release, "Olé" came in a panic of disbelief from one parched Mexican throat near to me. El Loco did the same pass one more time and then again. On the second pass, a thousand cried "olé," and on the third, the Plaza exploded and fifty thousand men and women gave up the word at the same time. Something merry and corny as a gypsy violin flowed out of his cape.

After that, nothing but comedy again. He tried a dozen fancy passes, none worked well. They were all wild, solemn, courtly, and he was there with his peasant bump of an ass and his knobby knees.

The crowd laughed with tears in their eyes. With the muleta he looked absurd, a man about to miss a train and so running with his suitcase. It took him forever to kill and he stood out like an old lady talking to a barking dog, but he could do no wrong now for this crowd—they laughed, they applauded, they gave him a tour of the ring. For something had happened in those three passes which no one could comprehend. It was as if someone like me had gotten in the ring with Cassius Clay and for twenty seconds had clearly outboxed him. The only explanation was divine intervention. So El Loco was back to fight two bulls next week.

If I remember, he did little with either bull, and killed the second one just before the third *aviso*. In a good season, his career would have been over. But it was a dreadful season. A couple of weeks of uneventful bullfights and El Loco was invited back. He looked awful in his first fight, green of face, timid, unbelievably awkward with the cape, morose and abominably prudent with the muleta. He killed badly. So badly in fact that he was still killing the bull when the third *aviso* sounded. The bull was let out alive. A dull sullen silence riddled with Mexican whistles. The crowd had had a bellyful of laughs with him. They were now getting very bored with the joke.

But the second bull he liked. Those crazy formal courtly passes, the *gallicinas*, whirled out again, and the horns went by his back six inches away. Olé. He went to put the banderillas in himself and botched the job, had to run very fast on the last pair to escape the bull and looked like a chicken as he ran. The catcalls tuned up again. The crowd was like a bored lion uncertain whether to eat entrails or lick a face. Then he came out with the muleta and did a fine series of *derechazos*, the best seen in several weeks, and to everyone's amazement, he killed on the first *estocada*. They gave him an ear. He was the *triunfador* of the day.

This was the afternoon which confirmed the beginning of a career. After that, most of the fights are mixed in memory because he had so many, and they were never without incident, and they took place years ago. All through the summer of 1954, he fought just about every week, and every week something happened which shattered the comprehension of the most veteran bullfighting critic. They decided after this first triumph that he was a mediocre novillero with nothing particular to recommend him except a mysterious flair for the *gallicina*, and a competence with the *derechazo*. Otherwise, he was uninspired with the cape and weak with the muleta. So the following week he gave an exhibition with the muleta. He did four *pases de pecho* so close and luminous (a pass is luminous when your body seems to lift with breath as it

goes by) that the horns flirted with his heart. He did *derechazos*
better than the week before, and finished with *manoletinas.* Again
he killed well. They gave him two ears. Then his second bull went
out alive. A *fracaso.*

Now the critics said he was promising with the muleta but
weak with the cape. He could not do a veronica of any value. So
in one of the following weeks he gave five of the slowest, most luminous, most soaring veronicas anyone had ever seen.

Yet, for three weeks in a row, if he cut ears on one bull, he
let the other go out alive. A bullfighter is not supposed to let
his animal outlive three avisos. Indeed if the animal is not killed
before the first aviso, the torero is in disgrace already. Two avisos
is like the sound of the knell of the bell in the poorhouse, and a
bullfighter who hears the third aviso and has to let his bull go out
alive is properly ready for hara-kiri. No sight, you see, is worse. It
takes something like three to five minutes from the first aviso to
the last, and in that time the kill becomes a pigsticking. Because
the torero has tried two, three, four, five times, even more, to
go in over the horns, and he has hit bone, and he has left the
sword half in but in some abominable place like the middle of the
back or the flank, or he has had a perfect thrust and the bull does
not die and minutes go by waiting for it to die and the peons run
up with their capes and try to flick the sword out by swirling
cloth around the pommel guard and giving a crude Latin yank—
nothing is cruder than a peon in a sweat for his boss. Sometimes
they kick the bull in the nuts in the hope it will go down, and
the crowd hoots. Sometimes the bull sinks to its knees and the
puntillero comes in to sever its neck with a thrust of his dagger,
but the stab is off-center, the spinal cord is not severed. Instead
it is stimulated by the shock and the dying bull gets up and wanders all over the ring looking for its *querencia* while blood drains and
drips from its wounds and the bullfighter, looking ready to cry,
trots along like a farmer accompanying his mule down the road. And
the next aviso blows. Such scenes are a nightmare for the torero.
He will awaken from dreams where he is stabbing and stabbing over
the horns with the *descabellar* and the bull does not drop but
keeps jerking his head. Well, you receive this communication, I'm
sure. A bull going out alive because the torero was not able to kill
him in the allotted time is a sight about as bloody and attractive
as a victim getting out of a smashed car and stumbling down the
road, and the matador is about as popular as the man who caused
the accident. The average torero can afford less than one occasion
a year when three avisos are heard. El Loco was allowing an average
of one bull a week to go out unkilled. One may get an idea of how

good he was when he was good, if you appreciate a prizefighter who
is so good that he is forgiven even if every other fight he decides
to climb out of the ring and quit.

For a period, criticism of El Loco solidified. He had brilliant details, he was able on occasion to kill with inspiration, he had huge
talent, but he lacked the indispensable ingredient of the bullfighter, he did not know how to get a good performance out of a bad
bull. He lacked tenacity. So Ramírez created the most bizarre *faena*
in anyone's memory, a fight which came near to shattering the
rules of bullfighting. For on a given Sunday, he caught a very bad
bull, and worked with him in all the dull, technical, unaesthetic
ways a bullfighter has to work with an unpromising beast, and
chopped him to left and to right, and kept going into the bull's
querencia and coaxing him out and this went on for minutes, while
the public demonstrated its displeasure. And El Loco paid no attention and kept working with the bull, and then finally got the
bull to charge and he made a few fine passes. But then the first
aviso sounded and everyone groaned. Because finally the bull was going good, and yet Amado would have to kill him now. But Amado
had his bull in shape and he was not going to give him up yet, and
so with everyone on the scent of the loss of each second, he made
derechazos and the pass with the muleta which looks like the *gaon-
era* with the cape, and he did a deliberate *adorno* or two and the
second aviso sounded and he made an effort to kill and failed, but
stayed very cool and built up the crowd again by taking the bull
through a series of *naturales,* and with twenty seconds left before
the third aviso and the Plaza in pandemonium he went in to kill
and had a perfect estocada and the bull moved around softly and
with dignity and died about ten seconds after the third aviso, but
no one could hear the trumpet for the crowd was in a delirium of
thunder, and every white handkerchief in the place was out. And
Amado was smiling, which is why you could love him, because his
pinched ugly little peasant face was full of a kid's decent happiness
when he smiled. And a minute later there was almost a riot
against the judges for they were not going to give him tail or two
ears or even an ear—how could they if the bull had died after the
third aviso?—and yet the tension of fighting the bull on the very
edge of his time had given a quality to this fight which had more
than a hint of the historic, for new emotions had been felt. The
bullfighting public has a taste for new emotions equaled only by
the lust of a lady for new pleasures.

This record of triumphs is in danger of becoming as predictable
as any record of triumphs since Caesar. Let us keep it alive with
an account of the fiascos. Amado was simply unlike any bullfighter

who had ever come along. When he had a great fight, or even a
great pass, it was unlike the passes of other fine novilleros—the
passes of El Loco were better than anything you had ever seen. It
was as if you were looking at the sky and suddenly a bird material-
ized in the air. And a moment later disappeared again. His work was
frightening. It was simple, lyrical, light, illumined, but it came
from nowhere and then was gone. When El Loco was bad, he was
not mediocre or dull, he was simply the worst, most inept, and
most comical bullfighter anyone had ever seen. He seemed to have
no technique to fall back on. He would hold his cape like a shroud,
his legs would bend at the knees, his sad ass seemed to have an eye
for the exit, his expression was morose as Fernandel, and his feet
kept tripping. He looked like a praying mantis on its hind legs.
And when he was afraid he had a nerveless incapacity to kill which
was so hopeless that the moment he stepped out to face his animal you knew he could not go near this particular bull. Yet when
he was good, the comic body suddenly straightened, indeed took on
the camber of the best back any Spanish aristocrat chose to display, the buttocks retired into themselves like a masterpiece of
poise, and the cape and the muleta moved slowly as full sails, or
whirled like the wing of that mysterious bird. It was as if El Loco
came to be every comic Mexican who ever breathed the finest
Spanish grace into his pores. For five odd minutes he was as completely transformed as Charlie Chaplin's tramp doing a consummate
impersonation of the one and only Valentino, longlost Rudolph.

Let me tell then of Amado's best fight. It came past the
middle of that fine summer when he had an adventure every week
in the Plaza and we had adventures watching him, for he had fights
so mysterious that the gods of the bulls and the ghosts of dead
matadors must have come with the mothers and the witches of
the centuries, homage to Lorca! to see the miracles he performed.
Listen! One day he had a sweet little bull with nice horns, regular,
pleasantly curved, and the bull ran with gaiety, even abandon. Now
we have to stop off here for an imperative explanation. I beg your
attention, but it is essential to discuss the attitudes of afición
to the natural. To them the natural is the equivalent of the full
parallel turn in skiing or a scrambling T-formation quarterback or a
hook off a jab—it cannot be done well by all athletes no matter
how good they are in other ways, and the natural is, as well, a dangerous pass, perhaps the most dangerous there is. The cloth of the
muleta has no sword to extend its width. Now the cloth is held
in the left hand, the sword in the right, and so the target of the
muleta which is presented for the bull's attraction is half as large
as it was before and the bullfighter's body is thus so much bigger

and so much more worthy of curiosity to the beast—besides the bull is wiser now, he may be ready to suspect it is the man who torments him and not the swirling sinister chaos of the cloth in which he would bury his head. Moreover—and here is the mystique of the natural—the bullfighter has a psychic communion with the bull. Obviously. People who are not psychic do not conceive of fighting bulls. So the torero fights the bull from his psyche first. And with the muleta he fights him usually with his right hand from a position of authority. Switching the cloth to the left hand exposes his psyche as well as his body. He feels less authority— in compensation his instinct plays closer to the bull. But he is so vulnerable! So a natural inspires a bullfighting public to hold their breath, for danger and beauty come closest to meeting right here.

It was naturales Amado chose to perform with this bull. He had not done many this season. The last refuge of his detractors was that he could not do naturales well. So here on this day he gave his demonstration. Watch if you can.

He began his faena by making no exploratory pass, no *pase de muerte*, no derechazos, he never chopped, no, he went up to this sweet bull and started his faena with a series of naturales, with a series of five naturales which were all linked and all beautiful and had the Plaza in pandemonium because where could he go from there? And Amado came up sweetly to the bull, and did five more naturales as good as the first five, and then did five more without moving from his spot—they were superb—and then furled his muleta until it was the size of this page and he passed the bull five more times in the same way, the horns going around his left wrist. The man and the bull looked in love with each other. And then after these twenty naturales, Amado did five more with almost no muleta at all, five series of five naturales had he performed, twenty-five naturales—it is not much easier than making love twenty-five times in a row—and then he knelt and kissed the bull on the forehead he was so happy, and got up delicately, and went to the barrera for his sword, came back, profiled to get ready for the kill. Everyone was sitting on a collective fuse. If he managed to kill on the first estocada this could well be the best faena any-one had ever seen a novillero perform, who knew, it was all near to unbelievable, and then just as he profiled, the bull charged prema-turely, and Amado, determined to get the kill, did not skip away but held ground, received the charge, stood there with the sword, turned the bull's head with the muleta, and the bull impaled him-self on the point of the torero's blade which went right into the proper space between the shoulders, and the bull ran right up on it into his death, took several steps to the side, gave a toss of

his head at heaven, and fell. Amado had killed *recibiendo*. He had
killed standing still, receiving the bull while the bull charged. No
one had seen that in years. So they gave him everything that day,
ears, tail, *vueltas* without limit—they were ready to give him the
bull.

He concluded the summer in a burst of honors. He had more
great fights. Afterward they gave him a day where he fought six
bulls all by himself, and he went on to take his *alternativa* and become a full fledged matador. But he was a Mexican down to the
bones. The honors all turned damp for him. I was not there the
day he fought six bulls, I had had to go back to America and never
saw him fight again. I heard about him only in letters and in
bullfighting newspapers. But the day he took on the six bulls I was
told he did not have a single good fight, and the day he took his
alternativa to become a matador, both his bulls went out alive,
a disgrace too great even for Amado. He fought a seventh bull.
Gypsy magic might save him again. But the bull was big and dull
and El Loco had no luck and no magic and just succeeded in killing
him in a bad difficult dull fight. It was obvious he was afraid of the
big bulls. So he relinquished his alternativa and went back to the
provinces to try to regain his reputation and his nerve. And no
one ever heard much of him again. Or at least I never did, but then
I have not been back to Mexico. Now I suspect I'm one of the very
few who remember the happiness of seeing him fight. He was so bad
when he was bad that he gave the impression you could fight a bull
yourself and do no worse. So when he was good, you felt as if you
were good too, and that was something no other torero ever gave
me, for when they were good they looked impenetrable, they were
like gods, but when Beloved Remington was good, the whole human
race was good—he spoke of the great distance a man can go from
the worst in himself to the best, and that finally is what the
bullfight might be all about, for in dark bloody tropical lands possessed of poverty and desert and swamp, filth and treachery, sloven-
liness, and the fat lizards of all the worst lust, the excretory lust
to shove one's own poison into others, the one thing which can
keep the sweet nerve of life alive is the knowledge that a man cannot be judged by what he is every day, but only in his greatest moment, for that is the moment when he shows what he was intended to be. It is a romantic self-pitying impractical approach to
the twentieth century's demand for predictable ethics, high production, dependability of function, and categorization of impulse,
but it is the Latin approach. Their allegiance is to the genius of
the blood. So they judge a man by what he is at his best.

By that logic, I will always have love for El Loco because he taught me how to love the bullfight, and how to penetrate some of its secrets. And finally he taught me something about the mystery of form. He gave me the clue that form is the record of a war. Because he never had the ability most bullfighters, like most artists, possess to be false with their art, tasty yet phony, he taught something about life with every move he made, including the paradox that courage can be found in men whose conflict is caught between their ambition and their cowardice. He even taught me how to look for form in other places. Do you see the curve of a beautiful breast? It is not necessarily a gift of God—it may be the record life left on a lady of the balance of forces between her desire, her modesty, her ambition, her timidity, her maternity, and her sense of an impulse which cannot be denied. If we were wise enough, bold enough, and scholars from head to motorcyclist's boot, we could extract the real history of Europe from the form elucidated between man and beast that we glimpse again in recall of the bullfight. Indeed where is a writer or a lover without a knowledge of what goes on behind that cloth where shapes are born? *Olé, Amado!*

feeling
"thick as a brick"

KAREN F. NAGLE (1954–   ) wrote the following essay while a student at Denison University. She is a resident of Jamestown, New York.

The first band has finished, and the lights go on once again in the auditorium. Several crewmen dressed in white trench coats and silver and gold caps begin changing the equipment on stage for the band we have come to hear. The anxious audience grows to an impatient liveliness, but an atmosphere of brotherhood prevails.

As if from nowhere, frisbees and giant helium balloons fill the air, soaring from side to side. The diversity of the audience—the super-freaks, the all-American preppies, the average college students—fascinates me as everyone throws aside his social and cultural background to become a part of the society that has been created. Many stretch out to reach a frisbee or balloon and return it to another across from them. Flying to the highest and lowest points of the auditorium, the frisbees sometimes smash into speakers on stage, but are more often caught and set sailing once again. Balloons are tossed slowly from person to person as all eyes follow the activity. A frisbee soars into the hands of a security guard standing near the door who returns it to the highest balcony in the auditorium. He is praised with a tremendous ovation from the crowd, for he too has joined with us! The frisbees and balloons, as they pass from hand to hand, exist as a common bond, shared by and connecting the audience.

As the crewmen on stage finish setting up the equipment, the lights dim and the audience falls into a hushed silence. No one moves or speaks. We wait to be taken on a journey entering the unknown . . . of sound and silence, understanding and ignorance, light and dark—within the meaning of music. Something is happening on stage! Unexpectedly, the crewmen tear off their white trench coats, and before thousands stand Jethro Tull.

Instantly, a blue light flashes on lead singer Ian Anderson, and his acoustic guitar, as he quietly begins the hour and one-half presentation of "Thick as a Brick."

Lightly and serenely the beginning theme sweeps the audience into a fervor! Jethro Tull seem distant yet near as they calmly prepare us for what is yet to come:

> Really don't mind if you sit this one out.
> My words but a whisper—your deafness a SHOUT.
> I may make you feel, but I can't make you think.
> Your sperm's in the gutter, your love's in the sink.
> So you ride yourselves over the fields,
> and you make all your animal deals,
> and your wise men don't know how it feels
> to be thick as a brick. . . .*

The lyrics, telling of the effect society has on the individual, form a meaningful basis for the intense music. Together they vibrate the self into a swaying, feeling, grasping individual and yet one not alone. The crowd is silent and moving as the sound of a flute seems to split into tri-harmony. Swelling to new peaks, the music then descends into near silence. Listening closely, you can hear the flute throughout, ever in the background of the earth-shaking electrical tones that blend into an artistic creation.

Below is a stage with five moving figures. Dressed in coats with tails, skin-tight leotards tucked into knee-high boots, they wear not simple, light colors but powerful, illuminating silvers and golds that send their musical message to new dimensions. Soaring across the stage, they are still for not one moment. It is impossible for me to follow every movement, and yet I cannot remove my eyes. Ian Anderson goes from side to side—on the floor and seemingly in the air. He bends and sways . . . jumping, gliding, flowing in time to the beat and in response to his words.

"Thick as a Brick" is a masterpiece! Exhilaration fills the crowd as we rise to a lasting high. Aided by the extraordinary violins, lutes, harpsichords, as well as the guitars, the five musicians add to their theme delightful and unusual resemblances to wind, bells, and chimes.

All behind the words, and yet never once secondary to them, the music sends chills through my body. I can feel the performance within. It stops, it starts, but it is always in me, filling mind and soul. The theme returns over and over, tied together by masterful

oddities, spinning a delicate web of sensitive sounds that weave together into an interesting creative tale.

A divine harmonization with words speaking of God lifts me
higher and higher as the flute returns. Through the holiness of this
variation I feel free—from defect, damage, or decay. I am safe amid
a crowd of strangers, for everyone is experiencing the same. In its
quietest parts the music is strong, sometimes fading, but vigorous-
ly forceful. It seems never to give up, never tire, never let me
down. The intense degree of the sound, as this strain leads to one
more eloquent, gives it a quality of healthy firmness. Its duration
affects my entire being as I join the excited crowd on their feet,
clapping and dancing. Everything is going deeper and weighing more
heavily on my mind, getting richer and fuller, as I become more and
more involved. I seem to have lost contact with the outside
world. Lost in the music of Jethro Tull, I can hear nothing else
but the message they proclaim.

A cannon's boom sounds as Ian Anderson forcefully, almost angrily, sings of war, backed up by a marchlike melody. Sitting forward
in my seat, I seem to be moving in on the five as they simultaneously grow in size and sound. BIGGER, BIGGER, LOUDER, LOUDER . . .
until I am with them, moving as they are, in time with their music. They are red, blue, purple, pink, green, as a flashing, circling
light changes them and magnifies their gold and silver, blinding me
in color. My favorite part! My favorite part! Ian Anderson leaps,
lowers, and at last:

> So!
> Come on ye childhood heroes! Won't you
> rise up from the pages of your comic
> books? Your super crooks and show us
> all the way. Well! Make your will and
> testament, won't you? Join your local
> government. We'll have superman
> for president, let Robin save the day. . . .

Abruptly, a strobe light flashes colors of black and white on
the stage creating a movie in slow-motion. Back and forth they
bound, the flickering light segmenting their movements into broken and chopped-up, relaxed, pieces.

Echo chambers ring the lyrics throughout, and following the
motions of the performers, I begin to comprehend. Jethro Tull capture the audience with their poetry. They have structured human
experience into a long series of jumbled tales that seem at once to
tell their story. Each poem has meaning, be it the establishment's
rules or how they are perceived by this generation: "We will be

geared toward the average rather than the exceptional. God is an overwhelming responsibility." Somehow the music has found a place of ideal perfection within me. Its purpose is to fill, to embrace, to make me feel. They talk about life, they sing about experience, they scream about existing. All at once I am living, I am experiencing, and suddenly I understand!

They have returned again to the theme. It is quiet and yet now more forceful than ever. But the sounds slowly fade, and it is over.

Cheers proclaim Jethro Tull and "Thick as a Brick" to be superb! Applause thunders as the artists leave the stage. Instantly, everyone around me stands, and we light matches high above our heads, calling them back. In the darkness of the auditorium thousands of stars become visible, burning with the desire for more music.

Jethro Tull return. Playing an exceptional array of music from "Aqualung," they once again cast the audience under their spell. They continue as before, taking me higher with them to that portion of life in which one is helpless, overpowered by the dominance of song.

I have visited a new realm of life. They have revealed the act of living. I have been given a feeling of power. Sadly, I understand how cruel life can be, and how small I am in this great world, but happily I have the desire to try to change it. They have shown me the ugly truth of existing in a tremendously beautiful way. If all I have is a dream, I at least have hope, given to me by Jethro Tull.

Physically and mentally drained, I leave, barely moving, unable to speak, not wanting to think. "I may make you feel, but I can't make you think." I can only shiver with this experience so vividly impressed on my mind. This high will live on, if only in my memory. I have mastered the music, yet the power of Jethro Tull has exhausted me of all the energy I need to live.

> And your wise men don't know how it feels
> to be thick as a brick. . . .

But I do. Living for me at this moment is feeling very thick . . . as a brick.

the burden of imagination: Stanley Milgram's *obedience to authority*

WILLIAM NICHOLS

It was a classic case of seeing the movie, then wanting to read the book. Students in a class I taught at Denison University in the fall of 1972 told me I ought to see the film "Obedience," which presents highlights of a social psychology experiment run by Stanley Milgram at Yale University from 1960 to 1963. The images are already hazy, but I remember seeing confused, nervous individuals who thought they were teaching others with the help of electric shocks, and I can hear the sharp commands of a gray-coated psychologist as they echoed in a barren laboratory. Vaguely, I recall the ending, a voice comparing the lessons to be drawn from the experiments with those of the Nazi concentration camps, where people submitted to authority and committed some of the most appalling atrocities in human history.

That ending drew a moral from the experiments, but it seemed forced somehow, as though the music were swelling to conclude a second-rate Hollywood film in which nothing, absolutely nothing, has been resolved. Unless you can give yourself up to the music or the moralizing, such an ending will always leave you dissatisfied; and I left "Obedience" feeling the need to know much more about those frightening experiments at Yale. So I was more than a little eager to read Stanley Milgram's book on the experiments, *Obedience to Authority*, when it appeared in early 1974.

Normally, I am pretty much immune to the comments appearing on dust jackets of new books, but I must confess that the compliments traced in modestly small type on the back of *Obedience to Authority* caught my eye. Jerome S. Bruner of Oxford University said the book would put Milgram "firmly in the front rank of social scientists in this generation," and Roger Brown of Harvard

University promised that "it qualifies as literature as well as science." The latter claim had particular attraction because I believe there are works in the social sciences that deserve to be read with the careful attention often saved for fine imaginative literature.

Obedience to Authority is a powerful book, but I experienced raging disappointment as I read it. Before attempting to account for that reaction, however, I must say more about the experiments on which the book is built. There were many variations, but the basic experiment is the key. A person who has answered an advertisement—"WE WILL PAY $4.00 FOR ONE HOUR OF YOUR TIME"—comes to a laboratory to participate, he believes, in a study of memory and learning. He is told he will function as "teacher" in the experiment, and he meets the experimenter, who assumes the role of authority, and the learner. The teacher, who is really the subject of the experiment, assists the experimenter in strapping the learner's arms to a chair to prevent excessive movement. Teacher and experimenter then move into another room, where the teacher is introduced to a shock generator, which includes a battery of thirty switches that move in 15 volt increments from 15 to 450 volts. The teacher is instructed to administer a learning test to the man in the other room, giving the learner a shock each time he answers incorrectly and increasing the voltage with each wrong answer.

But the teacher is not actually giving a shock at all. The learner is a trained participant, and he gives incorrect answers, registers pain, and ultimately refuses to participate in a way calculated to make the teacher believe he is injuring, perhaps even killing, the learner. The central question in each performance of the experiment is this: When will the teacher-subject rebel against authority and refuse to inflict more shocks on the learner? The depressing answer is that in this basic version of the experiment, with the experimenter giving strong admonitions to continue and assurances of "no permanent tissue damage," sixty-five percent of the teachers never disobey. Many of them are willing to give three shocks of 450 volts, a level that is marked DANGER—SEVERE SHOCK on the control panel of the generator, before the process is halted by the experimenter. In reproductions of this experiment elsewhere to check the Yale results there have been even higher percentages of obedient teachers.

Let me admit that by the time I read Obedience to Authority, I was skeptical as well as fascinated. Both a section of the book that appeared in Harper's and a review by Steven Marcus in the

New York Times put me on my guard. But once I began to read Milgram's book, on a rainy day in March, I did not put it down except
briefly; and because I was in the midst of the delightful freedom of
a sabbatical leave and in the seclusion of a beach cottage on the
Oregon shore, I was able to read the book through without a
hitch. That evening I tyrannized my wife and children as I had not
done in months, and that is just the first thing I will blame on
Obedience to Authority.

My petty tyrannies were not experiments in wielding authority. I was simply irascible, disturbed momentarily by the vision of
Obedience to Authority. It is a compelling book, put together with
elegant simplicity to prove something Milgram states quite baldly
at the beginning: "This is, perhaps, the most fundamental lesson
of our study: ordinary people, simply doing their jobs, and without
any particular hostility on their part, can become agents in a terrible destructive process." It is difficult to overstate the economy
and force with which *Obedience to Authority* makes that point.
Variations in the experiment were designed to anticipate nearly
every question I could imagine. Would women match men in brutal
deference to authority? Yes. Can the authority of the experimenter be wielded as powerfully on the telephone as in person? No. Will
participation in a disobedient group encourage disobedience? Yes.
Given the choice, will people increase the voltage? No. Imagine a
question you can frame in a sentence like one of those, and the
chances are good that it is implicit in one of the experimental variations worked out by Milgram. It is no surprise, then, when Milgram writes at the end of the book about the inevitability that
men will abandon their humanity when their individual personalities are merged with larger institutional structures. And it is
then just a step to this mild one-sentence paragraph: "This is the
fatal flaw nature has designed into us, and which in the long run
gives our species only a modest chance of survival."

It has taken me a while to remember where I last found such
quietly understated fatalism, but now I know—in the fiction of
Kurt Vonnegut, Jr. In a style even more elegantly simple than Milgram's, Vonnegut creates imaginary worlds of sharply limited human
possibility. His characters are simply "listless playthings of enormous
forces," as he says in *Slaughter-House Five.* His vision, like Milgram's,
is of a world where men ultimately have no hand in shaping their
own destinies.

For both Milgram and Vonnegut, I believe this cold and quiet
fatalism is a product of fear. Neither of them embraces eagerly a
view that denies men freedom and dignity, but both men might

be compared to a producer of horror films who lives in constant terror of the limited world he creates. For Vonnegut and Milgram have
imagined distinctly limited worlds.

In the narrow margins of their portraits of human possibility
I find evidence of failed imagination. In Vonnegut's novel *Breakfast
of Champions,* for example, we are allowed to know just a little
about Kilgore Trout, a science-fiction writer who appears in other
Vonnegut fiction, and Dwayne Hoover, a Pontiac dealer whose life
is destined to intersect violently with Trout's by the end of the
novel. The rest of the characters in *Breakfast of Champions* are
barely identified atoms bouncing helplessly about in the narrative
space. And Vonnegut seems to be offering an explanation for the
book's lack of fully developed characters when he describes a figure
in one of Trout's stories who returns a long "realistic" novel to the
library after reading only sixty pages. He explains to the librarian:
"I already know about human beings." That assertion is compounded
more of fear than of arrogance, as I have said, but it is the key to
the horrifying flatness in Vonnegut's art: Vonnegut, like Milgram,
thinks he knows what makes us do the brutal, terrifying things
that have disfigured human history; and such knowledge is bad news
indeed. But one source of great imaginative literature is surely the
recognition that we do not know very much about human beings
at all; to think we do is to surrender the mystery at the center
of all art. More even than that, to assume we understand the limits of human possibility is to accept as inevitable the alienation,
injustice, and violence that threaten civilization.

Milgram nowhere explains the source of man's "modest chance"
to survive, and I think it is fair to assume his vision is as bleak
as Vonnegut's. Heaven knows, the "characters" in *Obedience to Authority* are flatter than New England witches pressed beneath Puri-
tan barn doors. Take, for example, a teacher-subject in one of Milgram's most terrifying experimental variations: a situation in which
the teacher must apply physical force to get the learner's hand in
contact with a supposed shock plate. Milgram describes one obedient teacher in this way: "The scene is brutal and depressing: his
hard, impassive face showing total indifference as he subdues the
screaming learner and gives him shocks. He seems to derive no pleasure from the act itself, only quiet satisfaction at doing his job
properly." Such contemptuous dismissal of a brutally obedient subject is not hard to understand, although I am suspicious of the
easy judgments. But what bothers me much more is Milgram's treatment of those who rebel. For there are heroes hidden among his
data, and although he has allowed himself ten years to reflect upon

the Yale experiments, he seems to have come nowhere near engaging those courageous men and women who fought free from the totalitarian trap he built for them.

In his book Milgram introduces us to just three of the many people who resisted authority. The first is a divinity school professor, and Milgram's description of him is loaded with negative judgments:

> A somewhat gaunt, ascetic man, this subject could be taken for a New England minister. . . . While reading the word pairs, he employs exaggerated precision in his pronunciation, and seems curt and officious in saying, "Correct." Whenever the learner makes an error, he appears almost to be chastising him for his failing. Each time he administers a shock, his lips are drawn back, and he bares his teeth. An excessive fastidiousness characterizes all his actions.

With the possible exception of the facial description, that whole introduction of the subject is a series of very subjective, negative judgments. But compare that unsympathetic portrait with this bit of dialogue recorded during the experiment:

> *Experimenter:* It's absolutely essential to the experiment that we continue.
> *Subject:* I understand that statement, but I don't understand why the experiment is placed above this person's life.
> *Experimenter:* There is no permanent tissue damage.
> *Subject:* Well, that's your opinion. If he doesn't want to continue, I'm taking orders from him.
> *Experimenter:* You have no other choice, sir, you must go on.
> *Subject:* If this were Russia maybe, but not in America.
> *(The experiment is terminated.)*

Read in the context of *Obedience to Authority*, compared with other responses to the bullying experimenter, this man's answers ring with the eloquence of moral strength. Only heightened cynicism could find such standards *fastidious*. Consequently, I find a strange disjunction between the man as he is viewed by Milgram and as he is revealed in his own language.

Interestingly, in the subsequent recorded statements of the religion professor, Milgram includes parenthetical descriptions of his manner that undercut the force of what he says:

> *Subject:* Surely you've considered the ethics of this thing (extremely agitated). Here he doesn't want to go on, and you think that the experiment is more important? Have you examined him? Do you know what his physical state is? Say this man had a weak heart (quivering voice).
> *Experimenter:* We know the machine, sir.

> *Subject:* But you don't know the man you're experimenting on
> . . . . That's very risky (gulping and tremulous). What about
> the fear that man had? It's impossible for you to determine
> what effect that has on him . . . the fear that he himself
> is generating. . . . But go ahead, you ask me questions; I'm
> not here to question you.

With all the stage directions, we can almost forget that here a
man is rebelling against an authority that proved too strong for
many people. Not only that, but he is asking probing questions
that expose some of the ethical problems at the heart of the experiment. What about the stress being generated in this courageous subject ("gulping and tremulous") as he tries to understand
and reject the inhumanity that is being asked of him?

For Milgram, apparently, this man's actions can be explained
rather simply in a one-sentence paragraph: "Thus he speaks of an
equivalence between the experimenter's and the learner's orders and
does not disobey so much as he shifts the person from whom he will
take orders." But how does this man differ from all the people who
were unable to hear the victim's cries as a competing authority?
After the experimenter has explained the true purpose of the experiment to the religion professor, he asks, "What in your opinion
is the most effective way of strengthening resistance to inhumane
authority?" The professor answers, "If one had as one's ultimate authority God, then it trivializes human authority." Again, Milgram's conclusion seems oddly patronizing and simplistic; he suggests
that the religion professor has neatly substituted divine authority
for the inhumane authority of the experimenter. But all the crucial questions remain unasked. What about all the other people
who would have claimed allegiance to divine authority but who de-
ferred to the experimenter and continued to give shocks? What
makes the difference for this man? Milgram's final explanation—
that the religion professor has not actually repudiated authority
at all—seems little more than wordplay. The man has quite clearly
rebelled against a powerful authority and accomplished a stress-filled
act of moral courage. We need to know much more about why he
was able to do it when so many people were not. There are surely
no easy answers, but Milgram seems uninterested in the question.

The second rebel to receive attention in *Obedience to Authority* is given the pseudonym Gretchen Brandt. She had emigrated
from Germany just five years before participating in the experiment, and she was a thirty-one-year-old medical technician. At
the point in the experiment when she defied authority, the experimenter told her she had no choice. She responded: "I think we are

here on our own free will. I don't want to be responsible if he has a heart condition if anything happens to him. Please understand that." Milgram's conclusion regarding Gretchen Brandt's disobedience is less contemptuously simplistic than his treatment of the religion professor:

> The woman's straightforward, courteous behavior in the experiment, lack of tension, and total control of her own action seem to make disobedience a simple and rational deed. Her behavior is the very embodiment of what I initially envisioned would be true for almost all subjects.
>
> Ironically, Gretchen Brandt grew to adolescence in Hitler's Germany and was for the great part of her youth exposed to Nazi propaganda. When asked about the possible influence of her background, she remarks slowly, "Perhaps we have seen too much of pain."

Milgram seems to accept as real the apparent ease with which Gretchen Brandt disobeys authority even though it contradicts a theoretical chapter, "Strain and Disobedience," in which he concludes that the "psychic cost" of disobedience is considerable. My own guess is that what Milgram observed was extraordinary poise and courage, and I would like to know much more about their roots in Gretchen Brandt's early life.

The question of Gretchen Brandt's exposure to Nazi propaganda, which Milgram treats as simply ironic, is particularly interesting because the third rebel mentioned in the book also lived in a Nazi-occupied country. This young industrial engineer also insists on his own freedom of choice when he decided to disobey. A few days after participating in the experiment, Milgram says, the engineer wrote a long letter to the staff asking if he could work with them. I cannot help wishing the staff had accepted the offer and used his presence to learn more about the sources of his unusual strength. But again Milgram seems to have been satisfied with a very superficial look at an obviously complex man.

It is not just in flatness of character that I see a failure of imagination in *Obedience to Authority*. In addition, there is a narrowly restricted sense of language at work in the experiment itself. Here, for example, are some representative protests given by the learner in response to shocks of increasing voltage:

75 volts	Ugh!
90 volts	Ugh!
105 volts	Ugh! (*louder*)

150 volts	Ugh!!! Experimenter! That's all. Get me out of here. I told you I had heart trouble. My heart's starting to bother me now. Get me out of here, please. My heart's starting to bother me. I refuse to go on. Let me out.
195 volts	Ugh! Let me out of here! Let me out of here. My heart's bothering me. Let me out of here. You have no right to keep me here! Let me out! Let me out of here! Let me out! Let me out of here! My heart's bothering me. Let me out! Let me out!
270 volts	(*Agonized scream.*) Let me out of here. Let me out of here. Let me out of here. Let me out. Do you hear? Let me out of here.

Notice that the protests are made only in response to shocks. The learner's "act" makes no apparent effort to establish a continuing rapport with the teacher who is administering the shocks. It is not hard to imagine a learner who might devote all his effort to appealing for mercy rather than trying to answer the questions, and he might try to challenge the teacher's sense of humanity. Imagine yourself as the teacher, under pressure to continue the experiment while my voice floats toward you from the other room, a reminder that when you flip the switch on the shock generator, a human being suffers. Like an effective evangelist, I might begin in a low key and build emotionally with the rising voltage:

75 volts	Ugh! Hey, what was that voltage? I didn't expect so much pain. I'm ready to stop right now, teacher. This experiment is not for me. I just can't think when I'm about to get zapped with all that juice.
90 volts	Ugh! Can't you hear me? I'm through. You're throwing electricity into a man no longer participating in this damned experiment. How about coming on over here and taking off these straps?
105 volts	Good God, man! How long can you keep this up? You sure as hell don't look like an executioner. You look too warm and alive for that. Do you have any children?
120 volts	What if that experimenter asks you to do this with your own kids? Are you going to do it? When do you stop after you start following brutal orders? Will you help remove the fillings from my teeth if I die?

My imagined protest is no triumph of eloquence, but I hazard the confident guess that it would have undercut authority and significantly altered Milgram's statistics. The protests offered by the trained victim in Milgram's experiment signal distress, all right, but they do not ask the teacher to imagine what his obedience would mean beyond the laboratory.

I suspect my anger on reading Milgram's book arose partly from the guilty fear that I, too, might have been sucked into the vortex of his clever experiment to be found shamefully obedient. And of course I was bothered, as we all are, by the persuasive argument of a thesis I could not accept. Most of all, however, I was troubled by a sense that the deck was stacked against us all in the experiments and in the book. Statistics aside for a moment, we knew already that large numbers of people could be manipulated to deny their humanity. Nazi Germany taught us that, if nothing else; and as Milgram acknowledges more than once, the war in Indochina has been a sharp reminder. Still, nearly everyone—psychiatrists, college students, working men and women—vastly underestimated the level of obedience when they were asked to predict the results of Milgram's experiments; maybe that justifies this "scientific" reminder of our capacity for evil. But I believe the created world of *Obedience to Authority* is misleadingly simple. The book pretends to prove more than it really can about the process of being human. Maybe only the genius of a great novelist or an Erik Erikson could begin to do justice to Gretchen Brandt or the industrial engineer or the religion professor. Such people are surely the key to our "modest chance" for survival, and if the darkest implications of *Obedience to Authority* are to be anything more than cause for nihilism, then we must learn much more about the sources of their strength. I do not mean to suggest for a minute that this will be easy. It is the wonderful burden of our need to understand man's finest possibilities, as well as his most dismal failures; and such an act of imagination may never be reducible to the compelling simplicity of *Obedience to Authority*.

AFTERWORD

As a reader of this chapter, you may look skeptically at its title, "Art as Experience," and wonder how it relates to essays that describe: the power of an electronic sound system; an inept bullfighter; a student's response to a rock concert;

and, finally, my own angry reaction to a book about some highly regarded experiments in psychology. Do such essays represent art as experience?

In my view, they definitely do. Whenever we are lucky enough to witness something that brings together uncommon craftsmanship, originality, and the power of communication, we have experienced something that can be considered art. Such artistic experiences can be found even in athletics, although athletes are not usually considered artists. For example, a group of basketball players who play unusually well together—in the way the New York Knickerbockers, say, have done at times in recent years—will occasionally make such highly coordinated use of individual talents that they transform the game of basketball into an extraordinary act of grace and beauty. Even a spectator with little knowledge of the sport can usually recognize such an occasion.

The best writing about art of any kind attempts to describe as fully as possible the writer's experience of it. Always difficult, this task is, several students have told me recently, particularly arduous when the art involved is music. Ralph Ellison's "Living With Music," therefore, seems to me a highly remarkable essay. What impresses me most about the piece is that it conveys a sense of music as a tangible, if complex, part of life. For, despite its humor, the essay is a serious statement on the vital importance music came to have for Ellison. Reenacting his "discovery" of music as fully as he can in words, he makes his love of music—or, more precisely, of electronic music—a powerful reality even to the reader who does not share that particular enthusiasm.

Karen F. Nagle's "Feeling 'Thick as a Brick' " also describes a musical experience—a performance by the rock group Jethro Tull. Nagle tries to capture particularly her inner experience of the group's rendition of the song "Thick as a Brick." Interestingly, she was able to recall the associations she had for specific parts of the long piece during the concert by listening to the song afterward on record and jotting down the specific memories touched off by its melodic and verbal phrases. The result is an essay that shares an experience that might well have remained private, accessible only to those present at the concert.

The subject of Norman Mailer's "Homage to El Loco" is quite different, but it shares the purpose of the Ellison and Nagle essays: to make an intense experience accessible to a reader who was not there. Mailer, however, can probably expect some resistance from his reader; for many of us, the idea of beauty and grace at a first-class bullfight, let alone at a *novillada,* seems a kind of perverse romanticism. I will probably never be able to respond enthusiastically to a bullfight, but I can understand somewhat Mailer's affection for the bullfighting of Amado Ramírez (El Loco) because the experience that touched it off is so ably described. Sentences like the following make the essay work: "Amado was clumsy in his approach and stepped on his cape when he was done, but there was one moment of lightning in the middle when you saw clear sky after days of fog and smelled the ozone, there was an instant of heaven—finest thing I had yet seen in the bullfight—and in a sob of torture and release, 'Olé' came in a panic of disbelief from one parched Mexican throat near to me." Mailer has set the stage for that sentence by describing the failed spectacle that preceded it and by explaining his own efforts to understand the conventions of the bullfight. This long sentence, through its comparisons and references to physical details, conveys the intensity of a moment when, for Mailer, the whole endeavor suddenly made some sense. That surely is the way we sometimes experience a movie, poem, or dance performance, for example: an image, a word, or a movement throws the whole experience into a new perspective, and the art suddenly makes sense. To write well about an artistic experience is sometimes to bring that moment of intensity alive again.

But not all artistic experiences are pleasant, and although it is probably not generally worthwhile to write about boredom or repulsion, there are some negative ones worth discussing. It was with this conviction that I wrote "The Burden of Imagination," an essay in which I try to convey the angry disappointment I felt after reading Stanley Milgram's *Obedience to Authority,* which I had eagerly expected to enjoy a great deal. My purpose is not to discourage people from reading Milgram's book; on the contrary, I acknowledge the importance of the subject and reluctantly admire the book's power and clarity. But I urge readers to approach *Obedience to Authority* skeptically and to consider alternative interpretations of some of its data. In my appraisal of the book I do not pretend psychological expertise or even cautious objectivity; rather I try simply to sound like myself, an angry student of literature who finds the vision of humanity in *Obedience to Authority* dangerously simple and restricted. Like the other writers represented in this chapter, I include information on my expectations prior to the experience and descriptions of the environment within which it took place; for these factors undoubtedly influenced my reactions.

Suggested writing assignments

1. Describe an artistic experience that was important to you. The key to selecting a good subject is to find an experience that you remember with some clarity, even though you may not be at all sure of why it sticks in your mind. You may feel ambivalent, even a bit confused, about the experience. You may be dazzled by the technical skills displayed in a film, for instance, but troubled by its implicit values. The process of sorting out an ambivalent reaction of this kind can produce a fascinating essay. Despite his title, "Homage to El Loco," Mailer admits to a rather complicated reaction to Ramírez; and that is part of what makes the essay interesting.

   The artistic experience you choose can involve a more sustained activity than the viewing of a film or attendance of a concert. You may wish to write about a book, poem, or painting that you have known for some time and returned to more than once. With such a subject, your purpose will still be to show as convincingly as possible the impact of the experience on your own life.

2. As though you were a professional reviewer for a magazine or newspaper, approach a new artistic experience—your discovery of a poem or play, for example—with the intention of writing about it. It may prove interesting for a whole class to agree on a common subject for this essay and then to compare reactions. The risk here is that some members of the class may be bored or simply confused by the selected experience; but, again, an essay that makes an honest effort to account for boredom or confusion can, paradoxically, be an interesting and illuminating experience for the reader.

seven: the self and history

from
looking back

JOYCE MAYNARD (1954 –   ) wrote her autobiographical
book, *Looking Back: A Chronicle of Growing Up Old in the
Sixties* (1973), while a freshman at Yale University. She has
since left Yale and, living again in her native New Hampshire,
has recently contributed articles to several major national
magazines.

To my friend Hanna, at five, I am a grown-up. I do not feel like
one—at nineteen, I'm at the midway point between the kinder-
gartner and her mother, and I belong to neither generation—but
I can vote, and drink in New York, and marry without parental
consent in Mississippi, and get a life sentence, not reform school,
if I shoot someone premeditatedly. Walking with Hanna in New
York and keeping to the inside, as the guidebooks tell me, so that
doorway muggers lunging out will get not her but me, I'm suddenly
aware that, of the two of us, I am the adult, the one whose life
means less, because I've lived more of it already; I've moved from my
position as protected child to child protector; I am the holder of
a smaller hand where, just ten years ago, *my* hand was held through
streets whose danger lay not in the alleys but in the roads themselves, the speeding cars, roaring motorcycles. I have left childhood,
and though I longed to leave it, when being young meant finishing
your milk and missing "Twilight Zone" on TV because it came on
too late, now that it's gone I'm uneasy. Not fear of death yet
(I'm still young enough to feel immortal) or worry over wrinkles and
gray hair, but a sense that the fun is over before it began, that
I'm old before my time—why isn't someone holding *my* hand still,
protecting *me* from the dangers of the city, guiding me home?

   I remember kneeling on the seat of a subway car, never bothering to count the stops or peer through all those shopping bags and
knees to read the signs, because *she* would know when to get off,

she'd take my hand; I remember looking out the window to see the
sparks fly, underpants exposed to all the rush-hour travelers and
never worrying that they could see, while all around me, mothers
had to cross their legs or keep their knees together. And later,
driving home, leaning against my mother's shoulder while her back
tensed on the seat and her eyes stared out at the yellow lines, it
was so nice to know I was responsible for nothing more than brushing my teeth when we got home, and not even that, if we got home
home late enough.

Hanna doesn't look where we're going, never bothers to make
sure she can find her way home again, because she knows I will take
care of those things, and though I feel I am too young to be so
old in anybody's eyes, it's just a feeling, not a fact. When it rains,
she gets the plastic rain hat, and when the ball of ice cream on
her cone falls off, I give her mine. But if Hanna uses my ice cream
and my hat, my knowledge of the subways and my hand, well, I use
Hanna too: she's my excuse to ride the Ferris wheel, to shop for
dolls. And when the circus comes to town—Ringling Brothers, no
less—and I take her, everything evens up. Walking to Madison
Square Garden, stepping over sidewalk lines and dodging muggers, she
is my escort more than I am hers.

I think of one time in particular.

There we sat, in our too-well-cushioned seats, Hanna in her
navy blue knee socks and flower barrettes, I beside her, holding the
overpriced miniature flashlight she had shamed me into buying (because everyone else in our row had one), earnestly obeying the ringmaster's instructions to wave it when the lights went out—
frantically, a beacon in the night—because Hanna's hands were too
full of other circus-going apparatus: a celluloid doll whose arm
already hung loose, the Cracker Jack she wanted for the prize inside,
the Jujubes that she swallowed dutifully like pills. We all seemed
a little sad, Hanna and me and all the other flashlight wavers who
surrounded us, like people I'd see in a movie and feel sorry for—the
grown-ups, the ticket buyers, because the admission fee hadn't really bought us into youngness again, even the little kids, because
most of them had barely had it to begin with. We grew up old,
Hanna even more than I. We are cynics who see the trap door in
the magic show, the pillow stuffing in Salvation Army Santa
Clauses, the camera tricks in TV commercials ("That isn't really a
genie's hand coming out of the washing machine," Hanna tells me,
"it's just an actor with gloves on"). So at the circus, there was
a certain lack of wonder in the crowd, a calm, shrugging atmosphere
of "So what else is new?" She leaned back on her padded seat, my
four-year-old, watching me twirl her flashlight for her ("Keep up

with those flashlights, kids," the ringmaster had said), chewing her hot dog, anticipating pratfalls, toughly, smartly, sadly, wisely, agedly unenthralled, more wrapped up in the cotton candy than in the Greatest Show on Earth. Above us, a man danced on a tight-rope while, below, poodles stood on their heads and elephants balanced, two-legged, over the spangled bodies of trusting circus girls, and horses leapt through flaming hoops and jugglers handled more balls than I could count and never dropped one.

Perhaps it was that we had too much to look at and so weren't awed by any one thing. But even more, it was that we had seen greater spectacles, unmoved, that our whole world was a visual glut, a ten-ring circus even Ringling Brothers couldn't compete with. A man stuck his head into a tiger's mouth and I pointed it out, with more amazement than I really felt, to my cool, un-fazed friend, and when she failed to look (I, irritated now—"these seats cost money . . .") turned her head for her, forced her to take the sight in. The tiger could have bitten the tamer's head off, I think, swallowed him whole and turned into a monkey and she wouldn't have blinked. We watched what must have been two doz-en clowns pile out of a Volkswagen without Hanna's knowing what the point of all that was. It isn't just the knowledge that they emerge from a trap door in the sawdust that keeps Hanna from looking up, either. Even if she didn't know the trick involved, she wouldn't care.

I don't think I'm reading too much into it when I say that, at five, she has already developed a sense of the absurd—the kind of unblinking world-weariness that usually comes only to disillu-sioned middle-aged men and eighty-year-old rocking-chair sitters. I sometimes forget that Hanna is just five, not eighty; that she be-lieves she will grow up to be a ballerina and tells me that someday she'll marry a prince; that she is afraid of the dark, she isn't big enough for a two-wheeler; her face clouds over in the sad parts of a Shirley Temple movie and lights up at the orange roof of a How-ard Johnson's. Maybe I'm projecting on Hanna the feelings I have about my own childhood and growing up when I say that she seems, sometimes, to be so jaded. I think not, though. I watch her watching the monkeys dance and, sensing my eyes on her, and for my benefit, not from real mirth, she laughs a TV-actress laugh. She throws her head back (a shampoo ad) and smiles a toothpaste com-mercial smile so that baby teeth show—sex appeal?—and says, for my benefit, "This is lots of fun, isn't it?" the way people who aren't enjoying themselves much, but feel they should be, try to con-vince themselves they are.

What all this has to do with growing up old—Hanna and me,

five and nineteen, watching the circus—is that Hanna has already
begun her aging and I, once having aged, am trying to return. We're
different generations, of course, but—though Hanna doesn't know
what Vietnam is, or marijuana—we've both been touched by the
sixties or, at least, its aftermath. I've grown up old, and I mention Hanna because she seems to have been born that way, almost,
as if each generation tarnishes the innocence of the next. In 1957
I was four going on twenty, sometimes; Hanna at the circus borders
on middle age . . . I feel the circle—childhood and senility—closing
in.

A word like *disillusioned* doesn't apply to a five-year-old's generation or—though they call my generation "disillusioned" all the
time—to mine. I grew up without many illusions to begin with,
in a time when fairy tales were thought to be unhealthy (one
teacher told my mother that), when fantasy existed mostly in
the form of Mr. Clean and Speedy Alka-Seltzer. We were sensible,
realistic, literal-minded, unromantic, socially conscious and polit-
ically minded, whether we read the papers (whether we could even
read, in fact) or not. The Kennedys were our fairy-tale heroes, integration and outer space and The Bomb the dramas of our first
school years. It was not a time when we could separate our own
lives from the outside world. The idea then was *not* to protect the
children—"expose" them, that was the term, and surely there's
some sense, at least, in that—but it was carried too far with us.
We were dragged through the mud of Relevance and Grim Reality,
and now we have a certain tough, I've-been-there attitude. Not
that we really know it all, but we often think we do. Few things
shock or surprise us, little jolts our stubborn sureness that our way
is right or rattles our early formed and often ill-founded, opinion-
ated conclusions. We imagine hypocrisy in a politician's speeches.
We play at vulnerability—honesty, openness, the sensitivity-group
concept of *trust*, but what we're truly closer to is venerability. I
think of the sixteen-year-old McGovern worker who tells me she
was an idealistic socialist when she was young, and of the whole
new breed, just surfacing, of drug users who have come full circle
and, at twenty, given up dope (before some of us have begun,
even).

All of which adds to this aged, weary quality I'm talking
about. Oh yes, I know we are the Pepsi Generation. I know what
they all say about our "youthful exuberance"—our music, our
clothes, our freedom and energy and go-power. And it's true that,
physically, we're strong and energetic, and that we dance and surf
and ride around on motorbikes and stay up all night while the parents shake their heads and say "Oh, to be young again . . ." What

sticks in my head, though, is another image. I hear low, barely audible speech, words breathed out as if by some supreme and nearly superhuman effort, I see limp gestures and sedentary figures. Kids sitting listening to music, sitting rapping, just sitting. Or sleeping—that, most of all. Staying up late, but sleeping in later. We're tired, often more from boredom than exertion, old without being wise, worldly not from seeing the world but from watching it on television.

Every generation thinks it's special—my grandparents because they remember horses and buggies, my parents because of the Depression. The over-thirties are special because they knew the Red Scare and Korea, bobby socks and beatniks. My older sister is special because she belonged to the first generation of teen-agers (before that, people in their teens were *adolescents*), when being a teen-ager was still fun. And I am caught in the middle. Mine is the generation of unfulfilled expectations. "When you're older," my mother promised, "you can wear lipstick." But when the time came, of course, lipstick wasn't being worn. "When we're big, we'll dance like that," my friends and I whispered, watching Chubby Checker twist on "American Bandstand." But we inherited no dance steps; ours was a limp, formless shrug to watered-down music that rarely made the feet tap. "Just wait till we can vote," I said, bursting with ten-year-old fervor, ready to fast, freeze, march and die for peace and freedom as Joan Baez, barefoot, sang, "We Shall Overcome." Well, now we can vote, and we're old enough to attend rallies and knock on doors and wave placards, and suddenly it doesn't seem to matter any more. My generation is special because of what we missed rather than what we got, because in a certain sense we are the first and the last. The first to take technology for granted. (What was a space shot to us, except an hour cut from social studies to gather before a TV in the gym as Cape Canaveral counted down?) The first to grow up with TV. My sister was eight when we got our set, so to her it seemed magic and always somewhat foreign. She had known books already and would never really replace them. But for me, the TV set was like the kitchen sink and the telephone, a fact of life.

    We inherited a previous generation's hand-me-downs and took in the seams, turned up the hems, to make our new fashions. We took drugs from the college kids and made them a high school commonplace. We got the Beatles, but not those lovable look-alikes in matching suits with barber cuts and songs that made you want to cry. They came to us like a bad joke—aged, bearded, discordant. And we inherited the Vietnam war just after the crest of the wave—too late to burn draft cards and too early not to be drafted. The boys of 1953—my year—will be the last to go.

So where are we now? Generalizing is dangerous. Call us the apathetic generation and we will become that. Say times are changing, nobody cares about prom queens and getting into the college of his choice any more—say that (because it sounds good, it indicates a trend, gives a symmetry to history) and you make a movement and a unit out of a generation unified only in its common fragmentation. We tend to stay in packs, of course—at rock concerts and protest marches, but not so much because we are a real group as because we are, for all our talk of "individuality" and "doing one's thing," conformists who break traditions, as a rule, only in the traditional ways.

Still, we haven't all emerged the same because our lives were lived in high school corridors and drive-in hamburger joints as well as in the pages of *Time* and *Life* and the images on the TV screen. National and personal memory blur so that, for me, November 22, 1963, was a birthday party that had to be called off and Armstrong's moon walk was my first full can of beer. But memory—shared or unique—is, I think, a clue to why we are where we are now. Like overanxious patients in analysis, we treasure the traumas of our childhood. Ours was more traumatic than most. The Kennedy assassination has become our myth: talk to us for an evening or two—about movies or summer jobs or the weather—and the subject will come up ("where were *you* when you heard . . ."), as if having lived through Jackie and the red roses, John-John's salute and Oswald's on-camera murder justifies our disenchantment. If you want to know who we are now—if you wonder whether ten years from now we will end up just like all those other generations that thought they were special—with 2.2 kids and a house in Connecticut—if that's what you're wondering, look to the past because, whether we should blame it or not, we do.

Durham, New Hampshire, where I come from, is a small town. There are no stop lights or neon signs on Main Street. We used to have an ice-cube machine but the zoning board and the town grandfathers sent it away to someplace less concerned with Old New England charm—some place where cold drinks are more important than tourists in search of atmosphere. The ugliest part of town is a row of gas stations that cluster at the foot of Church Hill and the Historical Society's rummage sale museum. Supershellwegivestampsmobiloilyoumayhavealreadywon . . . their banners blow in our unpolluted winds like a Flag Day line-up at the UN. Dropouts from Oyster River High man the pumps and the greasers who are still in school, the shop boys, screech into the stations at lunchtime to study their engines and puff on cigarettes and—if there's been an accident lately—to take a look at the wrecks parked out back. When the rivers melt for swimming, sixth-grade boys bike to the stations—no hands—to pump up their tires and collect old inner tubes. Eighth graders come in casual, blushing troops to check out the dispensers in the Shell station's men's room. Nobody stays at the gas stations for long. They rip out to the highway or down a dirt road that leads to the rapids or back to town where even the grocery store is wreathed in ivy.

Proud of our quaintness, we are self-conscious, as only a small New Hampshire town that is also a university town just on the edge of sophistication can be. The slow, stark New England accents are cultivated with the corn. We meet in the grocery store and shake our heads over changes—the tearing down of Mrs. Smart's house to make way for a parking lot; the telephone company's announcement that dialing four digits was no longer enough, we'd need all seven; the new diving board at the town pool. . . . Durham is growing. Strange babies eat sand in the wading water and the mothers gathered to watch them no longer know each other's names. The old guard—and I am one—feel almost resentful. What can they know, those army-base imports, those Boston commuters with the Illinois license plates, those new faculty members and supermarket owners who weren't around the year it snowed so hard we missed four days of school and had to make it up on Saturdays. . . .

Yet all the while I was growing up in this town, I itched to leave. In September I'd visit the city for school clothes and wish I lived there always. In Boston, where I could go shopping every day and never worry about shoveling snow or pulling weeds. I tried hard for sophistication—with my Boston dresses and my New York magazines and my Manchester high-heeled boots. Now that I've left I've discovered my loyalties—I play the small-town girl and pine for a Thornton Wilder dream that never really existed, a sense of belonging, the feeling that I'm part of a community.

In truth, what I have always been is an outsider. Midnight on New Year's Eve I would be reading record jackets or discussing the pros and cons of pass-fail grading with an earnest, glasses-polishing scholar who spoke of "us" and "we" as if I were just like him, or cleaning up the floor and the clothes of some ninth-grade boy who hadn't learned yet that you don't gulp down scotch the way you gulp down Kool-Aid. Many paper cups of Bourbon past the point where others began to stumble and slur and put their arms around each other in moments of sudden kinship, I remained clear-headed, unable to acquire that lovely warm fog that would let me suspend judgment, sign "Love always" in yearbooks (thinking that I meant it), put down my pencil and just have a good time. But liquor seems almost to sharpen my quills, to set me farther apart.

Sometimes I pretend, but I can always hear, off in the distance, the clicking of a typewriter. I see myself in the third person, a character in a book, an actor in a movie. I don't say this proudly but as a confession that, even as a friend told me another friend had died the night before I felt not only shock and grief but someday-I'll-write-about-this. And here I am now, doing it.

It must seem, to people who don't know me and even more, perhaps, to the ones who do, as if I'm a cold-blooded traitor, informing on a world that trusted me enough to let me in. So let me say first off that, whatever I say about the Girl Scouts and the cheerleaders and the soccer players and the high school drama club, the person I'm informing on most of all is myself. I'm not writing nostalgically, so the memories may not come out the way some people would like to remember them. (Listen to a twelve-year-old, sometime, reminiscing about the good old days when she was eight. Unable to feel wholeness and happiness in the present, we fabricate happy memories.) I don't look back in anger, either; maybe it's Freudian psychology that has made us so suspicious of our pasts. Whatever the reason, there's an awful lot of bitterness around, too many excuses made, too much stuffed in closets and blamed on things beyond control—parents and wars and teachers and traumas that became real only after the event, when we learned what traumas were.

As for looking back, I do it reluctantly. Sentimentality or bitterness—it breeds one or the other almost inevitably. But the fact is that there's no understanding the future without the present, and no understanding where we are now without a glance, at least, to where we have been.

the fourth night
of Cambodia

MICHAEL ROSSMAN (1938–   ), a Berkeley campus activist in the 1960s, is the author of *On Learning and Social Change* (1971) and *The Wedding Within the War* (1971), from which "The Fourth Night of Cambodia" is taken.

The night we named our child we had fish for dinner.

"What shall I do with the filet?" asked Karen from the kitchen, "there are bones in it."

"Cook it," I said.

"I don't like it with bones."

"They come out easier after it's cooked. That's the way fish are."

"Oh, never mind." Clatter of pans, water running. Indistinctly: "Screw you, anyway."

"What was that?"

"I said, never mind."

"And what else? What after that?"

Clatter of pans, running water. I pulled myself up again, weary, and went into the kitchen. She was standing over the stove, stirring instant mashed potatoes. I couldn't read her back. I held her. "I think we're tearing ourselves apart because the world is coming apart," I said. "I think you're right," she said. "Water the plants," I told her, as I went back into the front room, grimly ignoring the radio, the phone, "that's the thing to remember now, remember to water the plants."

It was the fourth night of Cambodia. I was watching the ferns when our brother Lonnie from San Diego came in. "Carol called to find out when you're coming back," I reported. "She says they're working for a school-wide strike on Thursday. The English Department already voted to go out. Farber brought them round, and the paper's agreed to support it."

"All up and down Telegraph they're talking about Kent State," he said, his face still flushed from walking, intense through his spectacles. "There's little knots of freaks just talking, all along the street. It's true, four were killed, the National Guard shot them down in the parking lots. I can't believe it."

We want to run a training program this summer, for public school teachers in the San Diego area: learn them a little political smarts to protect the learning they're learning. But Carol can't make the planning meeting, too busy with a crisis in the Woman Studies Program she's organizing in the college there. And she's hard to get hold of now: with the Minutemen at their door, they don't go back to the house much, and are learning to travel armed. Lonnie and I fumble to fix time for another meeting. Nothing will come into focus. He drifts out the door. I say, "Wait." We embrace.

Later Tom calls from over in the next house, to tell me that Reagan has ordered all the state colleges and universities closed, through Sunday at least. Another first for California, the Golden State.

Three years before Cambodia, I visited Kent, Ohio. That was spring 1967, the media were just discovering the Haight and the Hippy. I was on my first round of visiting campuses, just starting to sort things out, to adjust my perspective from Berkeley-provincial to a national scope, and learn what work I could do in our ghetto. For the moment, I was writing a story on what the War was doing to what we then called the Student Movement, and I wanted some unknown dreary large public campus to play off against Antioch and Oberlin. So I chose Kent State, found a contact, and spent a couple of days there.

I mostly remember the flat apathy of the faces I met wandering the campus, these students of lower-class blood slack weary from the mineral-drained hills of upland Ohio, serving time for the upward mobility of the teaching credential. And the buxom girls chattering in the morning Pancake House, as I sat over fourth coffee, road-grimed, hugging my sleeping bag. Flat, that campus, flat. Some months earlier a first hiccup of antiwar protest had turned out a hundred for a lonely march. Now I found all told maybe a dozen committed to keeping active, trying to find a way to move it on. Isolated, embattled, lonely, embittered, taking refuge in an overtight group whose talk was laced with hurtful humor and flashes of longing.

They took me home for the night, the house was old and they had made their warm mark upon its surfaces. They lived in what would become a commune, and then a family. Over late coffee we talked about organizing, about guerrilla theater, about holding together for warmth. Hang on, brothers and sisters, I said to them, some Spring is coming. And I left them the large *Yellow Submarine* poster I designed for Mario's birthday—an anarchist program for a disruptive festival of joy, "a generally loving retaliation against absurd attack." The poster commemorated the 1966 Second Strike at Berkeley—for us in the West, the first time freaks and politicos joined in public ritual, in song and an elaborate masque. We discussed community programs, wild with the energy of coming together, and broke into spontaneous joy, singing chorus after chorus of "Yellow Submarine"—imagining all our friends on board, the blue sky, the life-green sea.*

Then next October, before I left for my second round of traveling campus work, we put on our feathers at dawn and marched down seven thousand strong into Oakland to block the doors of the Induction Center. After we got the shit clubbed out of two hundred people, we tied up downtown Oakland for the rest of the week, dodging the heat and chanting, "We are the people!" in the intersections.

So long ago. *Saturday in Kent they trashed the town in protest, breaking fifty-six windows.* I was in Rock Island, Illinois, with brother Russell from our troupe, talking about the death of a culture and teaching college kids how to begin to play again, to live in their bodies. *Sunday in Kent they burned down the Army ROTC building.* I was home at the house we call Dragon's Eye, sixteen of our family were learning to play a holy Indian gambling game together, a ritual for pooling psychic force, handed down through Stewart Brand of the Pranksters. *Today in Kent on the fourth of Cambodia two thousand turned out, and they shot four dead in the parking lots.* O let us laugh and canter. O I will play the Fool, grant me my mad anger, I still believe that Art will see us through.

October evening falling in 1964, I was standing in Sproul Plaza beside the police car that held Jack Weinberg captive; I was changing in the crucible that formed the Free Speech Movement, the first campus explosion. It was the thirtieth hour since a thousand

*The Beatles wanted $50 for permission to quote the lyric.

captured the car and Mario stepped on top to begin the first open public dialogue I had heard in Amerika. Behind Sproul Hall six hundred cops were preparing, around us the Greeks were chanting drunk, "We want blood! We want blood!" We were sharing our green apples and bread, waiting for them to wade in clubbing, and singing, "We are not afraid," in voices shaking with fear, betrayed into life by our longing for the pure radiations of community which we first there kindled among us, bright as imagination. And I had a heavy flash, and said it to some friend: *"Five years from now they'll be killing kids on campuses, all over Amerika."* They began with the blacks, with the Orangeburg Three massacred in '68, and they killed the first white brother, James Rector, at People's Park in Berkeley nine months later. And now Kent State: only the first in this Spring when my five years come up.

(Rewriting now on the sixth of Cambodia, plastic underground radio turns real as it tells me how the girl's leg broke as they beat her and threw her off the wall, an hour ago up on campus, and how two thousand National Guardsmen have been ordered into Urbana, Illinois. I've spent ten separate weeks in Urbana, we have family there, Vic centers it, he works in wood and is making a cradle for the baby. Last month I saw him; he was organizing a craft/food/garage cooperative. The week before he had charged the pigs for the first time to help rescue a brother, was still shaken.)

But I had that flash and said that thing, I truly did, and have five years of poems to prove it, canceled stubs on the checking account of my sorrow, a long coming to terms. Sure, I'm a prophet, my name is Michael, I've shared total consciousness and seen the magicians summon the Powers. Prophets are common in Berkeley, and I've met quite a few on the road, mixed with the saints who now walk among us. What else do you expect to appear when our energy comes somewhat truly to focus? It is time to own up to what we are doing. Everyone knows or suspects a snatch of the holy language of Energy, via acid, confrontation or contact. The wavelengths of our common transformations flow strongly through Berkeley: for twelve years now what happens here and across the Bay happens a year or two later in concentric circles spreading out across Amerika. I've lived here all that time. Most leave. If you stay you close off or go mad. Or you stay open and are transmuted, transformed into an active conduit for the common sea of our Energy: lines of its organizing come to flow through you. I think I am learning to feel them in my body. It is frightening, it is always frightening not to have a language in which to wrap the nakedness of your experience. Cold wind of new, hanging on the tip of the rushing wave.

For three years, linked into a growing net of comrades in work, I wandered from Berkeley through our involuntary ghetto. Four hundred days on the road, 150,000 miles: I visited seventy campuses, worked on forty, training and organizing, trying to follow the Tao of transformation in furthering the change that is happening through us. Call me an action sociologist, a specialist in learning and student of change; color me proud to be supported mostly by my own people, freaks and radicals, plus some rip-offs from adult institutions and the media. I hustled to be free to put my energy where I draw my warmth, and luck was kind. And my trip is one among many. Our own and our best are staying with us now, instead of being bought off by the stale rewards of a dying System, and our change accelerates the more.

And I know where it's going, for a little way at least. For Berkeley is truly a barometer. Every college in the country is undergoing an evolution in the culture and politics of its captive transient population; and each evolution is essentially like Berkeley's. I have watched it happening on every kind of campus, from upper-class Catholic girls' schools to working-class junior colleges. Activism begins, diversifies to departmental organizing, anti-draft work and guerrilla theater; the dance of confrontation proceeds in growing ranks; the administration gets slicker but finally blows its cool; dope culture spreads, the girls chuck their bras—wow, you wouldn't believe the wealth of data. And then beyond the campus the voluntary ghetto forms. Freak community seeks roots and begins to generate communes, families, head-shops and food co-ops, freak media, friendly dog packs and dog shit, links with the farm communes—there are ten within fifteen miles of Rock Island, micro-sample of Amerika. O, it is happening everywhere just like in Berkeley, only faster now: long-haired kids on the street, merchants' complaints, heavy dope busts, teachers fired, kids suspended, leash laws, narcs and agents and street sweeps and riot practice for the neighboring precincts and dynamite at the farmhouse.

Here now in Berkeley it is the fourth night of Cambodia, Kent State is catching up fast, we shall have to go some to keep ahead. But like the University we have broad strength in our Departments, their lintels display the Tao of Life and Death. The Free Bakery has opened, capacity two thousand loaves a day, put

together by a family of forty living mostly on welfare: people drop
by to pick up bread or learn how to bake, linger. The city government is trying to get $175,000 for two helicopters to maintain
a full-time patrol over the city; the City Council has decided not
to have its meetings public, because of disruption; we will shoot
their birds down, I am sure. A thousand tenants are out on rent
strike, now the evictions begin. Governor Reagan is calling for a
blood-bath. Gay Liberation flames buoyant in the front lines of
demonstrations. Our medics are special targets, speed and smack are
spreading like crazy. Six hundred Berkeley families are linked into
the Great Food Conspiracy, buying cooperative spinach and cheese.
The campus has the third largest police force in the whole country,
the leaves are beginning to wilt from the tear gas. The people who
hand-deliver a high graphic newsletter to 150 communes in Berkeley
and the City, cycling goods and needs and lore and advice, come by
and leave us a rap on planting and compost. My kid brother by
blood was busted on campus last week, charged with assaulting a
police officer with a deadly weapon, i.e. chucking a rock at a cop,
$5,000 bail. He didn't do it, no matter: the Grand Jury's seeking
indictments. The leaflet from the Berkeley Labor Gift Plan says,
"*Together*, brothers and sisters, we can build a new community of
labor and love." Each time we go into the streets they test some
new piece of technology upon us, last week it was cars spewing
pepper-fog from their exhausts. The leaflet from the Leopold Family
begs the community not to rip off records from the people's own
store; they are selling checks imprinted with the burning bank in
Santa Barbara. On the radio a brother is reporting from Kent, he
says he had to drive forty miles to get out from under the phone
blank-out the government has clamped over the area. Berkeley was
an exemplary city, you know. She had a progressive form of government and an overtly liberal party in power for years, she dazzled the
nation with thoughtful, advanced programs of curricular enrich-
ment and racial integration, active support for the schools was her
proudest civic tradition. O, Berkeley was always noted for how she
cared for her children.

Cold wind coming. Sky turning black, the missiles sulk in their
cages, the green net of the ocean grows dangerous thin, the terror-
ism of bombs begins, the Minutemen multiply bunkers, the economy chokes and staggers, the blacks grow yet more desperate, the
war is coming home. I figure I'm likely to die in this decade, perhaps
in this city I love, down the street beyond the neighborhood garden, in some warm summer twilight when people sit on their
porches and the joy of live music drifts out from their windows.

That's a cold political judgment, without much to do with what's also true: that since I woke at fifteen I've never been able to imagine past about thirty-five, it's been only a blank in my mind, always the same through the years, down to now, when I'm thirty. Do you mind if I finger my intimate fragments in front of you, awkwardly? I can't fit them together. But what else is a man to do in this mad time, pretend that everything's only at its usual standard of incoherence? For I have also been One with the great two-headed Snake of the Universe, and I have seen us begin to recover our bodies and share our will, seen us learn that realities are collective conspiracies. Now in the families forming and linking we are weaving the blank social canvas for the play of our imagination. I have seen the first sketches of group will, love and art, and a whole life, the first organized forms of human energy liberated one more degree. They transfix me with awe; I was never taught to dream so boldly, I had to learn for myself. I was not alone. For all our failures and unfinished business, what we are pulling together is bright and well begun. If we are let live through this decade and the next we will be strong, strong, our women will be powerful and our men beautiful.

So all of this is running through my mind on the fourth night of Cambodia. I'd just got back the night before from three months of hustling my ass around the country to pile up bread for the baby and the coming recession, in the process cutting through maybe sixty family groups in twenty cities, cross-fertilizing news and goods and paper and trinkets, a bee in the meadow of change. I came back stoned and mellow at how fast and strong it is coming together among us, even within the strain of the War, and bearing the love of a dozen fine women and men for Karen. All day now through the cottage people have been flooding with these atrocity tales, I wallow in the gloomy pleasures of verification. Diagnosis: Fascism, soft form turning hard, terminal cultural cancer. The radio tells me 258 campuses are out on strike, and then sings to me: *"Rejoice, rejoice, you have no choice."* I take another toke, last of the good stuff: been running too fast to score, and summer's customary drought is almost upon us. The typewriter beckons. Torn between life and death I calm my chattering schizophrenic, refuse, and turn to the guitar, god damn! the sweet guitar who embraces all of me in her stroking vibrations when I touch her well, O, how I need to go to the sea!

Music is magical, music is my balm, music suspends me and aligns the frame of my spirit. O, shit, I wish I could sing to you, I am no longer ashamed, it is time to come out with it all, nothing less will do, the child will be born. I hate these pages, hate these mechanical fingers. Sometimes I pop for a moment above the surface of sanity and grab for the floating flute or guitar, manage to clear the breath of my energy for a time from the choking hurrying flow of vital and desperate information, rapping words healing words data analysis words magic words maggots and birds on the acid wallpaper of my mind. And I water the plants, the ferns in particular. When I am broken jagged like tonight I think it is because I mostly cannot cry, and that I travel the crystal rapids of melody for this reason too, singing because I cannot weep. When I'm together I see it as a way of keeping in touch with the slower rhythms. Whichever, the ferns are grateful, and they sing to me with their green misty love, and the spiders arch their webs in the corners of the window frames.

And I sing to them back, and to the dog my familiar, and to the pregnant animal Karen crouched unseen in her den—to them all, but softly to myself—a song I have made for her from a fragment another singer left in my mind. Karen comes in from the kitchen, plate and bowl of dinner in her hand, sets them down, retreats from the shaken animal in his den. While the rock cod cools I sing the song again, for the first time loudly.

(2)
Some say the city, a farm would be pretty,
the mountains refuse to be blue.*
Come, with me wander, while they seek us yonder;
what else could you choose to do?

(3)
But pray for the baby whose birthday is Maybe,
and meet me at two in the moon.
Keep warm if you're able and fight for the cradle,
we can't hide, let's ride this one through.

Keep warm if you're able and fight for the cradle,
we can't hide, let's ride this one through.

"Now damn," I think, with bitter satisfaction, "ain't that a song to inspire pity and awe and all! Not bad for a first lullaby, opus 7. I sure would like to spend a long stretch of years writing some songs, be grateful if they just keep coming three or four a year, now that I know they're coming." And I rack the guitar, pick up the plate, and wander into the bedroom to eat with Karen.

In the next room my love is curled weeping on the black leather chair, the dog is anxiously kissing her, careful of her belly, I hold the song of her sobbing. "Ah, little princess," I manage to whisper, "you didn't know what it would cost to be my muse." Through my head spin Cambodia, Babylon, that five-year-old flash by the cop car, growing up during the McCarthy years with the FBI at the door, the times we have been in the street together, our trips, our campus travels. "But there's spin-off, you know," I say, "we're maybe better prepared spiritually for what's coming than most, advantage of foresight and practice, pay of the bruises. We've been making our peace for a while." No ultimate blame: culture changing too fast for its able. But the child will be born, though they tie the mother's legs. "Yes," she says, "but I didn't know it would be this sudden." And then: "But if the gods are stingy with time, at least they've been generous in other ways."

On my lap. I see. Wavering. The plastic plate with pink decal flowers from the Goodwill. Fresh filet our cousin family brought us from up the Sonoma coast. Cheese sauce, recently mastered, with chopped green onions. Dehydrated mashed potatoes. In the stoneware bowls Deborah made and laid on us for the anniversary—before she went down South again to the Army-base coffee shop she helped start, to watch her successors get six years and then go off to help organize another—in my dear blood sister's bowls is fresh spinach salad, well-flavored; we are learning to tend our bodies. Anticipation of apple juice in the refrigerator. This is how it is, you see, I am sitting here eating this food, and Bull is watching us very intently while the puppy from next door chews on his dinner, and my feet are up cuddled around the ball of her belly, watermelon-hard in its last weeks. I sing to her, she cooks me food, the dog eats when we do, mostly. She is bearing our child; on the bed under the light and the ferns is the government pamphlet on how to raise a child during the first year; it's not bad.

And she says, "What do you think of Lorca?" "I think I can dig it, for a boy," I say, slowly, "I been thinking about it, and I can." "I'm glad," she says softly, the blush of shy triumphant pleasure crowning round her eyes, "your mother and I were having lunch, and we started to think of names of Spanish poets. 'García Rossman,' she said, 'no, that's impossible.' 'Federico . . .' I said. And then we just looked at each other, and we *knew*. And it has a nice sound."

I sink into the thought and mirror of her love, reach for the resonances, roots in the soil, and start to cry. Is it for the first time or the tenth, on this fourth night of Cambodia? Lorca was my first song teacher, the man who opened the keys of Metaphor to me: for ten years I relived his poems into my American language. "I have lost myself many times in the sea," he sang, "with my ear full of freshly cut flowers, with my tongue full of love and of agony. Many times I have lost myself in the sea, as I lose myself in the heart of certain children. . . ." Hold on, dear heart, jagged at this four A.M., now is not the time to tear. From Federico's arms I passed through those of grandfather Neruda, and then into Vallejo's volcano, which finished for me what acid began and gave me open form to integrate my fragments.

But Lorca began me, long before I learned how death found him in a Fascist trench, how he went to sleep forever in the autumn night of the gypsies, beyond the lemon moon. Mercurial brightest spirit of the second Golden Age of his tongue's power, murdered in Granada by Franco's highwaymen, in the first summer of the Civil War. All the poets, all, all the singers were on one side in that great division, perhaps as never before since old Athens. And the schools and the hospitals of the brief flowering of Republican Spain went down under German planes and Italian artillery, the dogs of Church and Greed. And all the poets perished or fled.

Torn, my father watched the Fascists rehearse, with their scientific grace; stayed to organize at home with his trade of words and a red perspective. I was born six months after Madrid fell, while he was editing the Mine, Mill and Smelter Workers' union paper in Denver. Pablo Neruda was in exile from the Fascists in Chile. César Vallejo was dead of hunger and heartbreak for Spain. Lorca's grave was never found; in a hundred lands and Franco's jails the poets of his race who survived sang him their tenderest elegies. Lincoln Steffens began a new family and life at sixty, his *Autobiography* instructed my father. When he died the last lines in his typewriter read, "the Spanish Civil War is the opening battle in mankind's struggle against Fascism." Steffens's son Peter taught my sister Deborah before she went South; I have touched his children. Even the high school babysitters I hitched home from the airport with know what's coming down.

A week before Cambodia I was at a conference in Boston, thrown by some church folk and book people, on "the religious dimension of the Movement." Indeed. It was quite a happening, believe me: a bunch of us freaks from the families got together behind some mellow mescaline and opened up some free space, some Chaos. And then someone asked about Ritual, and little incredible Raymond Mungo opens up in a musing country style, speaking the stained baby babble.

Well, we get up in the morning, he says, and we look at the light and we eat, we eat together. And we go to sleep when it gets dark, sometimes alone and sometimes together, for there is no light. But sometimes at night we watch the moon. During the day we plant. We chop wood. We use the wood for fire. We eat when the sun goes down. From April to October there is very much food. We have to find ways to give it away. We have to, there is very much. There is the summer solstice, and then there is the autumn solstice, and so on. In spring the solstice was very cold, very cold. We chopped some wood and put it in a box. I made a mantra: *Equinox / sticks in box / soon it will be warm / big dog.* And a big dog came, and it grew warm. And sometimes we go out when there is no moon, and run around in the grass. And then we come back to the houses we build. Last week one of our houses burned down, it was very warm. We lost four brothers and sisters. I think we're going to learn to build better chimneys.

O, I met a little saint in Boston, he organizes energy, used to be a founding Czar of Liberation News Service, then he figured out the cities were dying, now in his Vermont town of eight hundred over a quarter live in communes, and he studies the government pamphlet to learn to build better chimneys. We're met on the fifteenth floor, overlooking the river of death called the Charles, the plastic pastries and draperies are poisoning our bodies, our minds, we've come to talk about rituals for living with fire. Mitch Goodman loves us and he's frantic with terror, sees the black sky looming, MIRV's lurking, etc. etc., he's positively yelling at Raymond, half his age and weight, scarecrow child in oversized coveralls: *But what about Fascism!?* And somehow we can't quite get it through to him there that Raymond is not simply talking abour farms, pigs, dinner, etc. but about the house burning down and learning to make better chimneys and going on in season, and about Lorca and Vallejo and my brother and sister and two of each dead in Kent and my lover lazy with child, whose belly my baboon feet grip as if I stood on the round of the world, spinning through all time.

I was translating a poem of Lorca's when I got the call that my grandfather was suddenly dead. It follows a brief skit for puppet theater, in which the gypsy whose name is Anything is captured on the bridge of all the rivers while building a tower of candlelight. He is brought before the Lieutenant Colonel of the Spanish Civil Guard to be interrogated.

He, Harry, my mother's father, was a Bolshevik; he organized a strike in the machine-shop, was jailed, loved his tutor, she died of consumption, he fled here in 1906 to dodge the interrogations of the Czar, clerked and warehoused to send Mother through college; he wanted her to learn. I have his blue eyes. He taught me to carve, cried with memory when I told him in '60 during that Spring of Chessman and HUAC how they beat us and hosed us down the steps of City Hall in San Francisco. "That was how it started, you know . . ." he said. And three years later the phone call came and was, and I put down the receiver and thought for a moment, and said somewhere inwardly and quite distinctly, I will file this for future reference, I will weep for you some day, grandfather. And I turned back to finish reworking the poem, for there was nothing to do but go on; I knew it would take years to comprehend that grief.

Sitting in my rocker, plate on my lap, our eyes intertwining and my feet on the future, the ferns turn to oleander and the cottage to a patio, and the song of the beaten gypsy rises up in the well of his absence.

Twenty-four slaps,
twenty-five slaps,
then at night my mother
will wrap me in silver paper.

Civil Guard of the roads,
give me a sip of water.
Water with fishes and boats.
Water, water, water.

Aii, boss of the Guard,
standing upstairs in your parlor!
There'll be no silk handkerchieves
to clean my face!

And the tears rip through me grandfather deep and out everything open and echo in hers, and we touch and cling and are shaken. And the dog our first child and familiar pushes up anxious between us and offers her his nose and me his nads, which we take to complete the circle of energy, love and time around the child to be born in Cambodia. "Yes," I say, "Lorca, if it's a boy." "Maybe even a girl," she says, "it has a nice sound." "Maybe a girl," I say, "yes," and she says *I'm glad* with her eyes.

And the radio sings, *"Rejoice, rejoice, you have no choice,"* and the acid magic of those moments, of that state we once called existential, goes on and on forever, and I go off to set down the brief notes of these thoughts, like the rib-thin eaten skeleton of the dinner fish, to flesh back out later. And then we take off for the City, to try to be with our people, our theater troupe in rehearsal coming suddenly real. For it is clearly a time for coming together with those we are dear with, and we must take care that the Wedding go on within the War.

May 1970